Feathered Canyons

Finding Treasures in the Golden State

**Jeannette Hanby
illustrated by David Bygott**

Also by Jeannette Hanby and David Bygott

Beyond The Oasis
Spirited Oasis
Lions Share
Kangas: 101 Uses
Ngorongoro Conservation Area: Guidebook
Kilimanjaro National Park: Guidebook
Gombe Stream National Park: Guidebook
Bwindi and Mgahinga National Parks: Guidebook

Also by David Bygott

David Bygott's Gnu Book: A Light-hearted Look at the Gnu, or Wildebeest
David Bygott's Birds of East Africa: An Unreliable Field Guide

Feathered Canyons

Finding Treasures in the Golden State

Kibuyu Press
3005 North Gaia Place,
Tucson, AZ 85745
USA

www.kibuyupress.com

Copyright © 2022 by Jeannette Hanby & David Bygott
First Edition - 2022

Cover and interior design by David Bygott

All rights reserved

No part of this publication may be reproduced in any form, or by any means, electronic or mechanical, including photocopying, recording, or any information browsing, storage, or retrieval system, without permission in writing from Kibuyu Press.

Three excerpts used as epigraphs at the heads of Chapters 3, 5 and 16:
By Henry Miller, from *Big Sur And The Oranges Of Hieronymus Bosch,*
copyright ©1957 by New Directions Publishing Corp. Reprinted by permission of New Directions Publishing Corp.

Poem at head of Chapter 17 used with author Joe Cottonwood's permission

Image credits:
Cheri Anderson: photos p. 240.
David Bygott: photos pp. 98, 135, 143, 144, 161, 228 and all drawings and maps.
p.57 is after a photo by Brooke Elgie; p.76 is based on a 1912 photo by E.H.Kemp.
Jeannette Hanby Archive: photos pp. 60, 78, 90, 110, 127, 136, 170, 172, 179, 180, 186, 192, 217, 220
Fassett Family Archive: photo p. 28

This book uses the fonts Golden Metafor, Avenir Next Condensed and Arno Pro

ISBN
978-1-7364953-5-3 (Hardcover)
978-1-7364953-6-0 (Paperback)
978-1-7364953-7-7 (Kindle)
978-1-7364953-8-4 (ePub)

1. BIOGRAPHY & AUTOBIOGRAPHY / *Adventurers & Explorers*
2. FAMILY & RELATIONSHIPS / *Friendship*

To all the unsung heroes of our lives

Table of Contents

Maps	X
Prologue	1
Chapter 1 Los Angeles	6
Chapter 2 On the Road	12
Chapter 3 Big Sur	18
Chapter 4 Nepenthe	26
Chapter 5 Hot Springs, Sex and Seekers	32
Chapter 6 Hargis	38
Chapter 7 Moving Along	46
Chapter 8 Friendships	54
Chapter 9 Merrimac Stage	62
Chapter 10 Bald Rock Canyon	68
Chapter 11 Ringtails	78
Chapter 12 Big Pool and Old Miners	88
Chapter 13 Transitions	96
Chapter 14 Proposals	102

Chapter 15 Mexico	**110**
Chapter 16 Hawks and Happiness	**120**
Chapter 17 Feathered Canyons	**128**
Chapter 18 Gardeners of Eden	**136**
Chapter 19 In the Canyon	**144**
Chapter 20 Turning Point	**154**
Chapter 21 Going for Gold	**162**
Chapter 22 Bare Ass Bar	**170**
Chapter 23 Dredging Up	**180**
Chapter 24 Winding Down	**192**
Chapter 25 Hurt Hawks	**202**
Chapter 26 Bald Rock Adventure	**212**
Chapter 27 Bows and Flows	**222**
Epilogue	**226**
Acknowledgements	**231**
References	**232**
Life lessons	**235**

MAPS

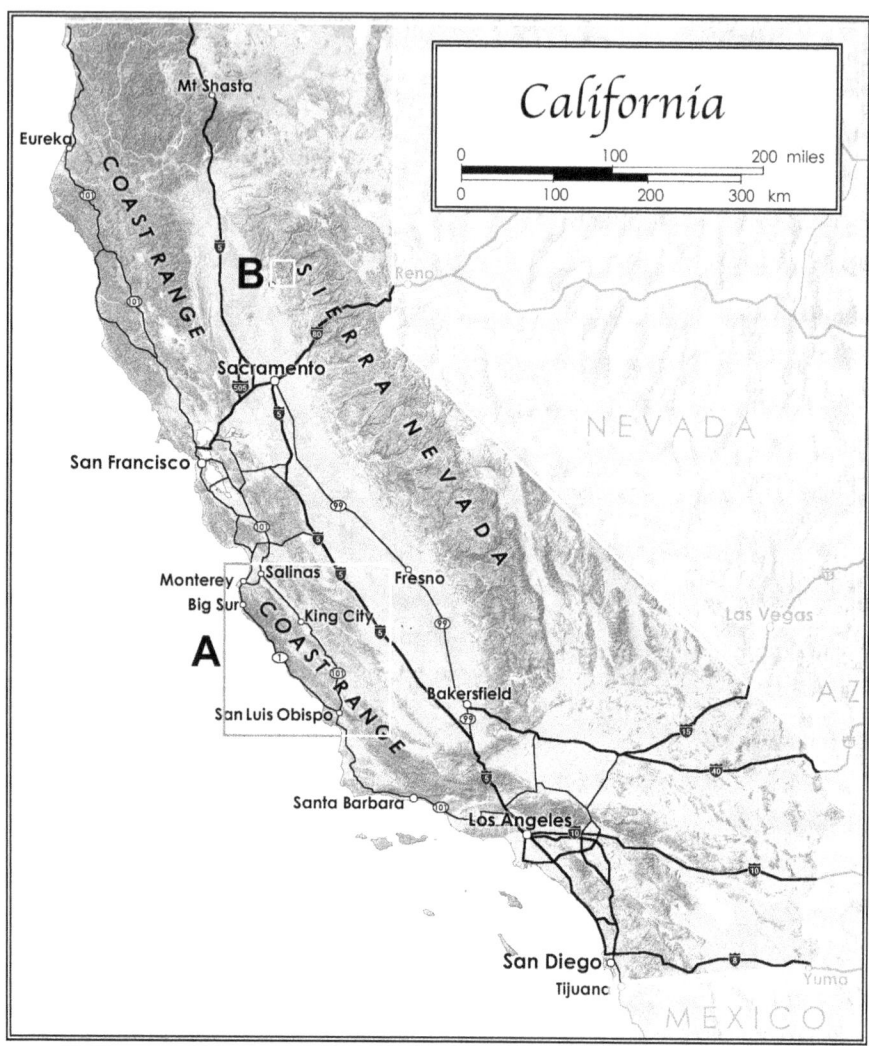

Map 1: The state of California
Box A represents the area shown in Map 2.
Box B represents the Oroville area shown in Map 3.

XI

Map 2: The Big Sur Coast

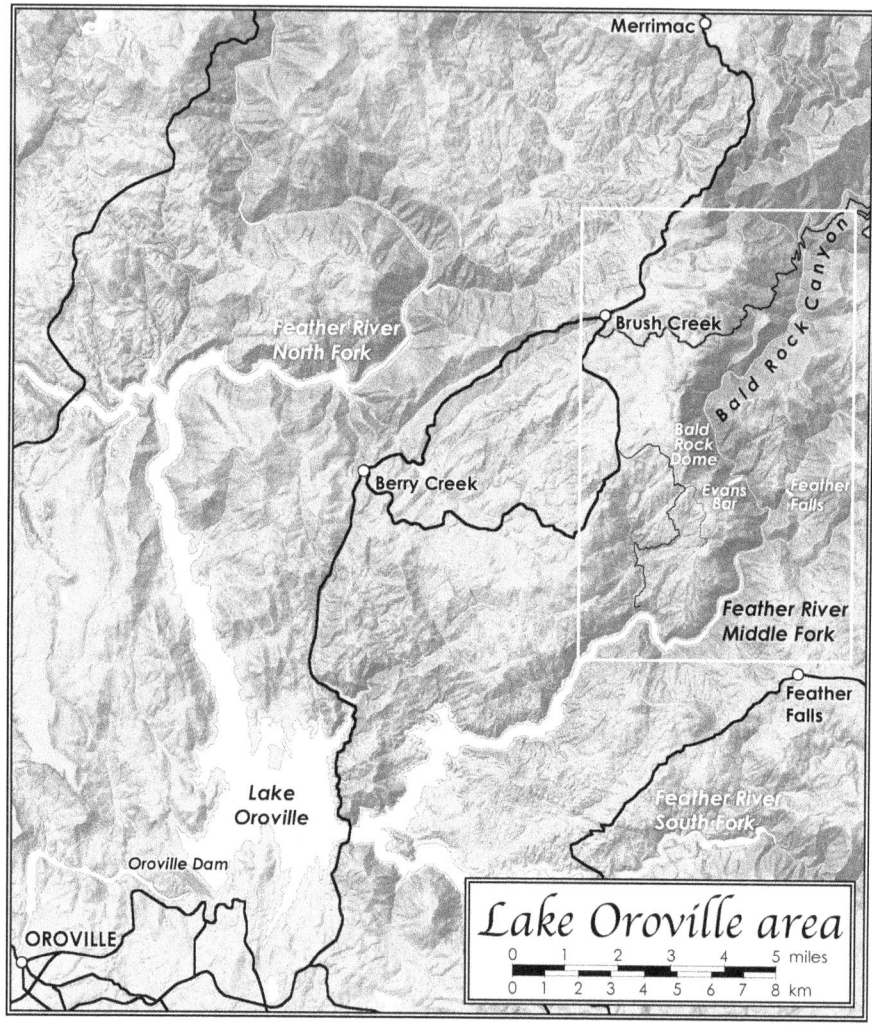

Map 3: Lake Oroville area today
During the period of this book, the dam was being constructed and the lake had not yet filled.
The box at right shows the Bald Rock area. See larger map on page 212.

Prologue

> We are talking about the 1960s, a decade that gets so much attention you begin to think it must have hired a press agent.
>
> —Walter Truett Anderson, *The Upstart Spring*

I brushed a biting fly off my naked butt, leaving a black smear of soot. Sweat pooled beneath my breasts and rolled down my back. Picking up the kettle, I poured water over my head, soaking my braids. They dripped water on my shoulders as though crying about the intense heat.

Turning my head, I saw Susie, also naked, holding her baby Delisa while trying to chop carrots. I stirred the browning venison in the big cast iron pot, added some twigs to the fire and went to confer. We sat together in the shade of the buckeye tree to plan the evening meal.

Abruptly, Susie asked me, "Why did you decide to join this crew? Was it Bill, this canyon, or the excitement of mining for gold?" I sat, my braids dripping, and tried to think.

How could I answer? It was all of that and more. The story of how I became involved with the mining team is the subject of this book. You'll meet Susie in the middle of it, but I start chapter one at the beginning. I tell my story for those caught in the limbo of facing choices for a future. My life in the mid-1960's illustrates how one young woman wobbled her way into a life of adventure and happiness.

In 1962, three years before I met Susie, I was a recent graduate of the University of California Berkeley. Confused about my future, I made a major decision. I decided to return home to live with my family, tucked away in a citrus grove in Southern California. That decision led to me getting a job while I tried to puzzle out what next.

I was cutting my mother's hair in 1963 when the radio announced President Kennedy's assassination. The event shook me as it did the nation. Kennedy's murder brought me to another decision. It made me realize that anything could happen at any time. If I were to experience more of life, I'd better get moving. I wanted to do more than drive ugly freeways to work in a stressful setting. I wanted to get out of the consumer culture, to travel, and experience more of the world.

I decided to expose myself to the winds of fate. I'd travel. I quit my job and bought a ticket to Mexico City. Fate foiled my attempt at that first foray abroad. Instead, I found myself swept into the realms of Hippies and Dreamers in Big Sur and a wild canyon in the Sierra Nevada mountains.

Taking chances, making plans, and being ready to abandon them are what this book is about. No matter who you are, as you mature, you will be forced to make or accept decisions. Choosing paths in life is seldom easy, but there are some lessons to lead one to a more positive outlook.

My maturing years were in the mid-1960s, often called tumultuous times. Young people like me in California were tumbling about, pebbles and grains of sand. I was one of those grains caught in the cross currents of the decade. That was when I met Susie, who called herself a "hippie chick."

Susie and I were only four years apart in age, but far apart in how we saw ourselves. I didn't think of myself as a free-living hippie. I was born the year Pearl Harbor was bombed. My siblings and I were restrained and protected. We inherited a deep sense of caution as well as a puritanical work ethic. Susie was born at the end of World War II, more optimistic, freer from constraints. We exemplified the end of the Silent Generation and the beginning of the Baby Boomers.

When mixing with the Baby Boomers, we war-years children became acquainted with affluence, indulgence, and protest. Most of us at the time had no clear plan, but the rising economic tide buoyed us. We stepped out into the whirling world to see what fate had in store or hunkered down to follow traditional paths.

I didn't know which way to turn, feeling like a tightrope walker above a roiling river, using conservative values as my balancing pole. I had no idea what to do with my life, but I thought that throwing myself into the adventures might strengthen and guide me. To my delight, I found many signposts and paths during four crucial years.

This is the story of those years.

CHAPTER 1

Los Angeles

Early Spring 1964

In the mid-1960s there was a general feeling in circulation that something exciting and important was happening and that it was happening in California.
—Walter Truett Anderson, *The Upstart Spring*

My friend Perky was late, very late. This was the day we were to set out for Mexico. Where was she? I sat outside on the steps of my parents' home in the southern California heat, waiting, wondering, worrying.

I didn't have Perky's phone number to check where she was. She and I had seen each other almost every day at work; we didn't need phone calls. During breaks and after-hours, we'd laid our plans. She would pick me up then drive to San Diego to take the plane to Mexico City. This was to be my first exciting adventure out of the USA into a foreign land!

I'd quit my job so Perky could keep hers. We both worked at McLaren Hall, a home for abused and abandoned children run by the Los Angeles County Corrections Agency. The Hall was a cultural experience, as well as a wage earner. Growing up in a white, middle-class neighborhood in the fifties didn't prepare me for racial diversity. I'd made the decision to take the job at the Hall partly to expose myself to the mix of peoples living in the Los Angeles basin.

I found multi-colored friends there, one being African American Perky. She was an alert, insightful person who could joke about being black but could also tell me how hurt she was by the words and actions of snobs and racists. Because of Perky, I chose to become a member of a book group at the Hall. We read books on utopias and discussed them from our different points of view. We were middle-class or poor, white, colored, with even an openly homosexual fellow who wore eyeshadow, disconcerting at the time. Perky was my guide in this milieu, the pivot person to help me understand the confusing society of dystopian Los Angeles.

Perky and I spent many enjoyable sessions imagining the places we wanted to visit. We decided to pin ourselves down with a trip to Mexico together. When we asked for the time off the director of the Hall told us, "No, we can't let you both go for a vacation at the same time." Perky needed the job; I needed the adventure. I decided to quit.

The job had paid well, and I'd saved money by paying only a low rent to live with my folks. I had enough to travel plus a reserve that might last me a few months of exploring. With my final paycheck, I went to my savings bank and exchanged part of the money for the few silver dollars the banks still allowed. With the rest I bought traveling clothes, a suitcase, and a wad of pesos.

As I sat on the steps waiting for Perky, I simmered in heat and impatience. I fretted so hard I felt as though my brain was blistering. Finally, drenched in sweat and aggravation, I gave up sitting, pacing the driveway, and going in and out of the house. The day had evaporated. We'd missed the plane.

I went inside and phoned the Hall. I asked the secretary if anyone had Perky's number or a number for a friend or family member. I tried every number they gave me, but no one answered. I left messages imploring anyone to call me back. Where was Perky?

The phone rang. Miranda, one of Perky's roommates, told me, "Perky's in the hospital." I groaned, took a deep breath, and waited for more. "She had an appendicitis attack on the freeway coming to get you. She drove off the road and smashed into a road sign. An ambulance came and took her to an emergency room in south L.A. She's still there. She's OK."

I was both relieved and disappointed. Perky was alive, but our trip was dead. Perky would need time to recover; months would pass before we could organize our journey again. Meanwhile, I had no job. Even though I suspected the Hall would take me back, I didn't want to return. I still needed an adventure.

My first mini-adventure was to visit Perky in the hospital. I lived on the eastern side of Los Angeles in the San Gabriel Valley. Perky lived somewhere on the south side of Los Angeles, a part of the smoggy, sprawling metropolis I detested. Many of our children at the Hall were from South L.A. Immigrants from all over, and lots of African Americans lived there because of their extended families, as well as racially unjust housing regulations. I'd only been there once. A Hall worker I was dating took me there to see a marvel, the Watts Towers.

The experience remains vivid because my boyfriend's car broke down when we arrived at the Towers. He fussed with the car while I wandered around the spectacular, ornate spires. An Italian had built them using rebar, concrete, and pieces of old plates, tiles, glass, bottles, mirrors, and seashells. To me, the towers seemed to writhe with the broken bright spirits of the surrounding city.

While I mused about my Watts Towers visit, I missed my turn off the crowded freeway. I spent many frustrating minutes asking directions until I found the right hospital. As I parked and locked up, I wondered if my car's wheels would be

CHAPTER 1: LOS ANGELES

Watts Towers

gone when I returned. Maybe the whole car would be stolen. That didn't worry me much. My car, a battered white Renault with a cherry red top, wasn't worth a donkey's snort and needed constant repairs.

Hospitals scared me and this one's entrance was small and unwelcoming. The smile of the receptionist eased my urge to flee. She gave me directions. Other staff helped me navigate. Everyone seemed kind and competent, but my discomfort increased as I passed through the disinfectant-smelling and noisy halls. Finally, I found Perky, propped up in bed next to a window with an outstanding view of an ugly parking lot.

She looked less perky than her name. Her usually glossy chocolate skin had a powdery, gray sheen; her normally neat Afro hair was frizzy, making her look young and vulnerable. She lifted her head to look at me with sad, brown eyes. I hugged her. We commiserated. I told her I'd managed to get our tickets changed. Luckily, they were good for a year. We planned anew. She said miserably, "Even if we get there next year, what are you going to do between now and then?"

I shrugged, "I don't know. But I think I'll travel up the California coast, exploring. During my vacation last year, I drove from the Mexican border to the Oregon border. I tried to follow the coast and take time in intriguing places—the best being Big Sur."

Perky opened her eyes and nodded. "Big Sur. Yes, you did mention it. Tell me more."

I sat on her bed and tried to describe Big Sur. "Well, imagine standing on a cliff overlooking the sparkling Pacific Ocean. Behind you are golden grass-covered hills creased with canyons full of redwood trees. The scenery is stunning."

"Yep, I can see it," mumbled Perky. I was afraid she was falling asleep.

Placing my hand on hers to keep her in touch, I continued. "I camped in state parks and on beaches. While in Big Sur, I splurged on a meal at the Nepenthe restaurant. It's built on a cliffside, hanging hundreds of feet above the Pacific Ocean, so dramatic!"

Perky said something like "Wow," encouraging me to continue. I explained how I sat on Nepenthe's terrace, trying to figure out how I could contrive to spend more time in Big Sur. The friendly bartender told me that the owners were planning to build a gift shop next to their fancy restaurant. They'd already given the shop a name: "The Phoenix."

I paused, looking off into the parking lot where some boys poked knives at a car's tires. I felt the familiar urge to get away from the unrelenting ugliness of Los Angeles. The word Phoenix conjured an image of a bird rising out of the heat shimmer, ascending into a Big Sur sky, me in its talons.

Perky patted my hand, so I leaned closer. She whispered, "The Phoenix?"

"Yes," I sighed. "I got up my courage and talked to Lolly and Bill Fassett, the Nepenthe owners. Imagine my surprise when Lolly said yes, there was a possibility I could work in the shop. But that would be when they opened, maybe in a year. That was a year ago."

I looked at Perky, her eyes were closed. She murmured, "Go, Jeannette. Go soon."

And so, I went.

CHAPTER 1: LOS ANGELES

Phoenix sculpture by Edmund Kara at Nepenthe

Zebras and Hearst Castle

CHAPTER 2

On the Road

Spring 1964

Afoot and light-hearted I take to the open road,
Healthy, free, the world before me,
The long brown path before me leading wherever I choose.

—Walt Whitman, *Song of the Open Road*

I drove slowly because the road demanded care. This was Highway One, following the coast, the most scenic road in California. The dangerous road wriggled along hillsides and cliffs, snaking around curves with blind spots. My old Renault had the power surge of a tortoise, so I couldn't pass any of the cars ahead.

Roadside turnouts beckoned me to stop. I pulled over to wait while the smelly line of cars, trucks, and camper vans passed me by. Resting my eyes on the sweep of ocean, I considered what I'd left behind and what lay ahead. I'd left before dawn, heading west, crossing through the unloved sprawl of Los Angeles. By sunup, I became trapped among vehicles packed like stalled schools of fish in a clogged stream. Rush hour had begun.

I floundered my way through the traffic and headed north. I found an eddy current off the freeway as I neared the Spanish-style city of Santa Barbara. With relief, I stopped for coffee and an ice cream cone. I thought about where I was going, full of apprehension and questions.

Here I was, free of a job, entanglements with boyfriends, and obligations. I wasn't fleeing from the law, a broken romance or marriage, a sad home life, or any of the lecherous men who'd pursued me in Los Angeles. Even so, I wasn't contented with my freedom.

Carrying on north, I put aside my worries to appreciate the increasingly pretty scenery. I stopped at San Simeon where the tan California hills swept down to the sparkling blue Pacific Ocean. I stepped out of the car to stare at "The Enchanted Hill" with its castle built by tycoon William Randolph Hearst in the 1920s. I gazed

Sealions and rocks

at the zebras grazing in a pasture. Their striped hides stood out among other wild animals that Hearst had imported to grace his extensive grounds.

The coastal section of Highway One began there at Hearst Castle. Leaving that bastion of modern civilization behind, I continued, driving slowly. The two-lane road with its sheer cliffs dotted with pampas grass was beautiful but daunting. My hands numbed as I gripped my steering wheel and shifted gears. There was no power steering or automatic transmission back then.

Crazy drivers in sports cars caromed along the narrow cuts through wooded canyons and across rocky ridges. Mainstream tourists dawdled along and pulled over unexpectedly. Families in recreational vehicles toiled slowly, seemingly oblivious to the frustrated drivers behind them. I lurched right and left as I moved from lane to lane, my teeth clenched. I got off the road to let people pass. My shoulders felt like I was wearing a harness, my back hurt, and my eyes grew weary.

When I passed the village of Lucia, I stopped at another viewpoint. Guzzling some orange juice, I tried to think about where I was going on my crazy venture. Big Sur valley was still at least an hour's drive ahead and Nepenthe a bit closer. I'd go even more slowly on the last leg of my journey.

As the traffic whooshed past, sweeping road dust and strands of hair into my face, I gazed seaward. A trail tempted me downslope through the sagebrush, leading me to a precipice. I looked over the cliff and got a shock. A sandy beach curved far below me. I scooted backward into a thick bit of brush and caught my breath. I craned to take a good look.

CHAPTER 2: ON THE ROAD

What were those clumps of slippery animals flopping around down there? The seashore seemed dotted with sea lions! Or were they seals? Why had I not noticed them at previous stops? I didn't know a seal from a sea lion. As I looked up at the sky, then over at some trees, I realized I didn't know with any certainty a hawk from an eagle, or a pine from a fir.

My parents weren't very keen on natural history. We four children grew up in a middle-class suburb in the San Gabriel Valley. Domesticated plants and animals were part of our predictable world. I became acquainted with wilder nature on visits to my uncle's ranch in the San Vicente Valley near San Diego. The ranch was my favorite place, in a hidden valley with a few houses and dirt roads, surrounded by a fortress of rocky hills.

My uncle taught me to ride and fall off his parade and rodeo horses. At the ranch, I could saddle up and trot across pastures and along willow-lined creeks that exuded a spicy, secret smell. Even at the ranch, I mostly accepted the animals and plants without asking questions. I had no instruction from people or books, but I did learn an important lesson about myself. I could be almost ecstatically happy riding alone on a horse in the countryside.

Now here I stood on a cliff on the California coast, wondering why I'd never learned more about the natural world. After 16 years of formal education, how much useful knowledge did I have? In college, I'd majored in psychology, focusing on physiology. I thought knowing how the body and mind work would help me understand myself and humans in general. I learned about conditioning, hormones, genetics, the nervous system, epigenetic landscapes, and the most useful—cognitive dissonance. I also learned that I didn't know much and would have to spend the rest of my life learning.

After graduation, I deliberately tried to broaden myself. I chose to enrol in a marine invertebrate biology course during my post-graduate summer. Note the word "invertebrate." I learned about little coastal critters without backbones, but not about the big marine mammals. To pass the course, our professor made us memorize 100 scientific names. That taught me to appreciate Greek and Latin names such as that of the pink-toned barnacle, *Megabalanus tintinnabulum*, and the common sand crab, *Emerita analoga*.

In addition to learning names, the course reinforced another important lesson: humility. It helped me extricate myself from a long-held assumption. I was brought up to believe that humans are the pinnacle of creation. We were chosen by God to be lords of the Earth. A look at the star-studded night with a

Barnacle, Megabalanus tintinnabulum

little understanding of the cosmos was my first lesson in humility. My second lesson was understanding evolution. We humans are not the center of the universe. Only our human egos could convince us we are of more value than all other creatures.

Learning to be wary of making judgements made me examine my own values. Throughout my childhood, I'd mostly seen other middle-class people of European or Hispanic backgrounds with Christian values. In college, I became much more aware of the variety of people and faiths surrounding me. The sixties exposed me to new music, racism, sexism, sit-ins, and political rallies. After graduation I needed to get immersed in a larger pool of people with different points of view. After my summer course, I returned to Southern California to live with my parents. I wanted to have a job that would expose me to my modern society.

My cultural education started when I got the job of a probation worker at McLaren Hall. This was a holding facility for children in Los Angeles County. In the 1960s, the Hall was dedicated to helping Los Angeles with some of its social problems. Its staff tried to deal with children abandoned in cardboard boxes on freeways and parking lots, traumatized sons beaten by fathers, boys who'd slashed siblings, girls who carved themselves with knives, young thieves who ran blackmail and extortion schemes.

McLaren Hall was where these young people ended up temporarily. While probation workers, courts, and cops wrangled with parents, a small, dedicated number of us tried to keep the young bodies busy. We tried to prevent theft, fighting, mauling, self-mutilation, suicide, and murder. The job was challenging.

At the Hall, I worked with boys from five to 18 years old. I won the job despite my stature and gender. Before taking the job, I was subjected to many comments designed to discourage and degrade me: *You're too short, a walkover! Work on the boys' wing? They'll run circles around you. You're a female. The boys won't respect you. You must be crazy!*

I didn't give up. The Hall was so desperate for workers they took me on the day of my interview. I watched a kid almost die after he ate a banana for lunch. Good introduction to learning about allergies and facing an emergency. After a few days I was very glad my supervisor agreed to let me on the boys' wing. Perky worked on the girls' wing. I knew her job was far harder because I had to substitute there occasionally. The girls were meaner than boys and sneakier. Instead of hitting and wrestling, they bit and pinched. Girls also lied more, stole, mocked, and were generally moody and difficult. I much preferred working with the rowdy, straightforward boys.

The job forced me to develop relationships with officials, staff, colleagues, and lawyers, as well as the children we tried to tame. I learned how to cope with the disdain of higher-ups (mostly men), disconcerting events, shocking behaviors, deep distress, and disorder. I still cringe to remember a five-year-old girl who had been raped, who leaked blood across the foyer as the officer carried her in. And a teenaged girl with slashes all over her arms and neck, moaning, "I want to die, let me die!"

Working at the Hall was profoundly disturbing. I found it difficult to talk to other people about the place. One outlet for my emotions and thoughts became letter writing. I wrote long letters to my friend Nathan. He and I had become close during my Berkeley days, living through personal traumas, exploring sex and drugs, and earning money by grading statistics papers together.

Besides being super smart, Nathan was a traveler, an explorer of physical as well as mental spaces. He'd been to Central America, Europe, and Indonesia. His many stories inspired my wanderlust. Nathan also explored mind-altering drugs everywhere he went. He enticed me into eating and smoking marijuana, as well as trying LSD, peyote, and mescaline. That was before those mind-altering substances became illegal. Nathan knew all about Timothy Leary and how to lay his hands on "experimental" drugs.

I learned that these drugs weren't on my lust-for-life list. Smoking made me cough and sneeze and I didn't like my mind whirling out of control. I still have moments when I can see colorful mescaline mandalas, like a kaleidoscope behind my eyes. But without any potions, I can feel overwhelmingly happy just lying on my back on the ground, arms outstretched under a starry summer sky.

During my drug-defining days, I vicariously absorbed experiences from Nathan, and we supported each other during difficult times. When my roommate's huge boyfriend tried to rape me, I jumped out of the bedroom window and ran to Nathan and hid with him. My relationship with Nathan taught me that sharing emotional crises creates strong bonds. He became what I called a "trauma friend." After college, we moved apart in distance but kept close by writing letters and sharing time when we could.

Years later, Nathan sent me a stack of my letters. They provide me with a rich deposit to mine about my life in the 1960s. For instance, when I quit my job at the Hall, I wrote, "I'm more than ready to swim up from the polluted waters of southern California. I want to surface and breathe in the clean world of coastal California. Instead of going to Mexico as I'd hoped, I'll explore a new place—Big Sur. Maybe I'll have exciting adventures to share with you."

And here I was, living that adventure.

Sand crab, Emerita analoga

"I tossed it into the ocean."

CHAPTER 3

Big Sur
Spring and Summer 1964

It was here in Big Sur that I first learned to say "amen."
—Henry Miller, *Big Sur and The Oranges of Hieronymus Bosch*

As I stared out at the vast ocean from my precipice, my body relaxed. I stopped trembling and looked up at the unnamed species of seagulls flying above and down at the seals/sealions below. OK, I thought, here I am. I consciously tried putting my upbringing and deficiencies aside. That meant smiling at myself, shrugging my shoulders, and turning my attention to what was around me.

A pure joy bubbled up inside me. I spun around to gaze inland over grass covered slopes creased by mysterious canyons sweeping up to forested ridge tops. Turning seaward again, I blinked at the sparkle and glare of the ocean. I inhaled the salty, stinging smell of sea and the pungent scent of sage. The incredible beauty bolstered my spirits. Hallelujah, I cried out, and smiled an "amen."

All the sensory stimulation was exhilarating. It seemed a good time to free myself of another weighty remnant of my past. I wanted to make a symbolic gesture, so drove on to an observation point with access to the shore. Scrambling and sliding to the edge of some rocks, I stood and let the waves spray me with saltwater. Duly baptized, I twisted off the fake wedding ring I'd worn since my last year in college. It had helped shield me from questions about my unexpected pregnancy. I tossed that symbol of a traumatic time into the ocean.

The token was a small gift to the bigness of Big Sur. I wanted to go unburdened to meet whatever was ahead. Washed in feelings of freedom, the dust of apprehension and doubt left me. A quote from Jack Kerouac's book, *On the Road*, sums up my feeling at the time: "Nothing behind me, everything ahead of me, as is ever so on the road."

Back on my way, I negotiated another cliff along the curving highway. On the seaward side splashes of gold, blue, pinky-purple, orange, and bright yellow attracted my eye. I pulled off to get a closer look at the flowers. Poppies, lupines, and nasturtiums bloomed on the steep, sunny ocean slopes. They danced gaily in the sea breeze while the magenta flowers of ice-weed plant glowed more stolidly. I squished through their mats of fleshy stems to get another view of the surf and shore far below.

On the way back to my car, I picked white daisies to tuck into my braids. Then I remembered that a flower in the hair was currently a mark of a "hippie." I resented that. Since my childhood, my mother had planted flowering shrubs for her three girls. We regularly wore gardenias, camellias, and geraniums in our hair.

I took the daisies out with a frown. I didn't want to arrive at Nepenthe looking like a hippie. They were often stereotyped as sloppy, high on drugs, irresponsible. I knew first appearances mattered and I wanted my possible employers to see me as a respectable, dependable girl. Smoothing the skirt of my dress, I slipped into the car. But if I was to reach Nepenthe looking composed and cheerful, I knew I needed to smooth my spirit too.

As I neared the heart of Big Sur, I readied myself for social encounters. Meeting new people always required mental armor and preparation. As a youngster, I'd felt awkward and timid around others. At the same time, I wanted to be included in events and games, so had to learn how to be friendly. Alas, that wasn't my natural bent. I pushed myself to enter the "fun" and often felt exhausted later. Then in high school, the social pressure to be noticed and liked made me even more desperate to fit in. I read books on how to be popular. Quiet, shy people didn't have many friends, so I worked on acquiring social skills.

I followed the rules: dated boys, attended dances, forced myself to go to football games. I even became a cheerleader—not a pompom girl, but one of those who leaped about leading cheers with a megaphone. Being in a small, select group out in front of spectators made me very visible. But it felt better than being insignificant while sitting with the crowd in the grandstand. I could fit in by standing out!

In my last year of high school, a thoughtful teacher took me aside and said, "You are the most extroverted introvert I've ever known. You'll have to find a balance in your life." That took me a while to process. Many years later, I think I understand what he saw—a girl trying hard to be outgoing but inside wanting out of the competition. I compromised by pushing my cheerful self to the front and letting my inner self lurk in the shadows. I learned to have a sociable smile full of teeth.

Getting to Big Sur alone was fine for my inside self. Arriving at my destination, I had to reinstate the Friendly Face of my outside self. By the time I reached the famed Nepenthe, I only wanted to hide somewhere. I needed to get myself under control.

Pulling off the road, I sat for a while talking to myself to lessen my apprehension. Soon I would have to meet people and be judged. I spoke aloud, "Now, calm down, practice smiling. Relax. Get out of the car. Stretch. Come on, gal, don't take this so seriously. Lighten up." I smiled, remembering my father's voice. He often told me not to be so serious.

Standing outside the car, I breathed in the mingled sage and sea smell of Big Sur and immediately felt better. I looked around and noticed two huge, bareheaded men working down the road. They were hoisting planks into place on a structure. I guessed it was to be the Phoenix gift shop. That would be the shop where I hoped to have a job. But it was very obviously not ready.

As I stood staring, one of the muscled men called, "Hello, there!" He walked right up to me, winked, and asked, "Young lady, are you looking to help us out here?"

I laughed, and met Frank, one of the two Trotter brothers. Frank told me where to find the Nepenthe owners in their house alongside the terraced restaurant. I drove on to the parking area and immediately saw Bill Fassett striding down to the worksite. I'd only met him briefly on my previous visit and had no hope he'd remember me. Putting on my best smile, dimpled, and full of teeth, I greeted him.

"Hello, I'm Jeannette. We met about a year ago. Please, could you tell me where I can find Lolly?"

He peered at me, obviously without recognition, and said, "She's up in the bar. Or she was, a few minutes ago."

He strode on down to where Frank and Walt Trotter were tossing lumber around. I stood for a while looking at Nepenthe, taking in the large veranda, dance floor, and fire pit with terraced benches overlooking the view. People sat in the silky sunlight, eating and drinking.

The entrance to the restaurant was dark in the late afternoon light. I was reluctant to go inside. It felt good to stand entranced by the view, alone, not having to meet anyone. My body started moving against my will, perhaps wanting to get this introductory stuff over. A swarthy, mustached man with a wonderfully hawk-like nose was polishing the bar. He nodded at me, and said, "Hi, can I help you?"

Keeping my best smile on my face, I said hello and asked, "Is Lolly around?"

"She's up in the big room," he said with a gesture of head and hand towards the back of the restaurant.

I went up some steps and saw Lolly, as large and imposing as when we first met. Lolly nodded when I introduced myself, then told me, "I'm real busy right now. Go get yourself settled at the campground. Rory's arranged with Berley about a trailer there for you to rent. Come back later, and we'll talk."

I was somewhat startled to be recognized. I'd only met the Fassetts once. I did write a couple of letters to keep them aware that I was still available for a possible job in the shop, but they'd never answered. I'd also written to Rory, a man I met at Nepenthe on my

Lolly Fassett

visit. He'd been doing some carpentry and we'd flirted a bit. Rory wrote back only once to encourage me to come to Big Sur.

After the wreck of Perky and our plans for Mexico, I'd written Rory about the possibility I might return to Big Sur to see about the job. I'd not said anything specific because my sudden change of plans left my arrival unsure. So, I was quite surprised that Rory and Lolly had conferred about my coming. Even more amazing was that they'd even organized tentative accommodation. Were they psychic?

Being so quickly disposed of by Lolly, I felt relieved of the burden of talking about the job, or its absence. I'd been let loose for some time on my own. Gratefully, I left Nepenthe to find where I was going to live.

From the restaurant, I left the sea cliffs and drove north, descending into the Big Sur valley. It was only a few miles away, but it took me half an hour to drive there. After a few houses and shops, the valley opened to pastures and patches of redwoods. I found the Big Sur campground situated in a shady grove. A feeling of entering a mystic place accompanied me into the forest. All my life, I've preferred open spaces—deserts, grasslands, coasts—to forests and canyons. But as I drove over the soft carpet of redwood needles covering the nearly invisible road, I was content to be among sheltering trees.

Now I had to find Berley, the campground manager. The man matched his name, burly and broad-shouldered, framed in a workman's suit. He showed me the trailer I was to call home, a metal shell with a cooking area, table, and bed. It even had a shower and toilet. It was not my dream home, but, heck, it was a place I could afford on my meager savings until I earned enough to move. And earning remained my central question. While the gift shop was being built, what earnings could I get?

I learned the answer when I went back to Nepenthe to talk to Lolly Fassett. She sat me down in the spacious upstairs room bordered on one side by a shelf of mattresses overlooking the Nepenthe terrace. The broad bed looked so very tempting to my tired self.

Lolly gazed at me with a wry smile. "Yes, you obviously noticed the shop isn't finished yet. The building is taking longer than expected."

She paused to deal with a child who brought her a bowl of something that smelled delicious. I realized I was hungry. Turning back to me, she said, "Since you're already here, you'll have to be willing to do other jobs," she paused, lifting an eyebrow, "if you stay."

Hmm, I thought, if I stay? She asked me what skills I might have, in addition to having managed to graduate from college. Student skills weren't going to be much use to me, but I felt I had some "natural smarts" to offer. Luckily, practice and those books I'd read prepared me to have some positive things to say about myself.

"Well... I can act in a friendly, polite manner. I can work hard, keep my mouth shut, size up a situation, and make the best of bad ones."

Lolly laughed and commented, "You just might be able to fit in here."

We also made a useful mutual discovery—I could sew. My first job was to sew some of Lolly's voluminous blouses, virtual tent-like tunics, or smocks. She was a big person with a big voice to match her size, ordering this and that to be done, very clearly in charge. She had five children, plus a host of friends, also with children. And she had dealings with all sorts of merchants to keep the restaurant going. I found it hard to keep track of all these people. Lolly was an imposing, demanding, and effective person. I admired her for her magical abilities to run things. And when she was in an affable mood, smiling with her dimples showing, I liked her a lot.

Lolly and Bill Fassett had invented Nepenthe. In 1947 they bought a cabin owned by writer Orson Welles and his actress wife, Rita Hayworth. The log cabin had been built in 1925 by the father of Frank and Walt Trotter. The Fassetts created a unique restaurant on the site that soon boasted a widespread reputation for its view, architecture, bohemian ambience, and the simple and dependable menu. They'd chosen the name Nepenthe carefully; it fitted the place perfectly. Nepenthe comes from Ancient Greek, a medicine for sorrow, literally an anti-depressant, a "drug of forgetfulness." You could forget a lot of bad stuff at Nepenthe while you sat on the terrace in the twilight, sipping a concoction.

While the shop was being built, the Fassetts let me earn some money from sewing jobs, babysitting, and part-time waitressing. I worked for tips, not wages. One of the yummiest parts of this smorgasbord of jobs was to eat at Nepenthe. Also food related was my job to take food and drink down to the workers at the gift shop site.

I liked all the construction crew, especially the Trotter brothers. They constantly laughed and joked, performing stunts like hoisting my little car off the ground, throwing each other planks, lifting me and my tray into the air, and chugalugging fluids nonstop without choking. They made me feel part of the gang.

Trying to fit into the Nepenthe restaurant scene was more difficult. I felt like a hermit crab looking for a shell to hide in, scuttling through an ongoing beach party where shorebirds ignored or pecked at me. I felt exposed and peripheral, with no real role or job, not an actual Big Sur resident, and not a tourist.

Constantly meeting strangers and residents was stressful. I lifted my eyebrows and smiled greetings so often that I got headaches. Once while I sat eating with some of the staff and the Fassett children in Lolly's big kitchen, the busboy looked at me with a lopsided grin. He said, "Well, when you first came here all wreathed in smiles, I thought you were a real phony. But these kids laugh and play with you; they seem to like you. So, I have to conclude you might be OK after all."

The comment not only embarrassed me, but it also made me realize how hard I'd been working to fit in. And I couldn't stop trying, with both clients and Nepenthe staff. I found most of the guests responsive to my service; they usually gave me good tips as well as flattery. But the rich snobs, or grumpy parents with fussy children who worked me hard, leaving no tips, irritated me. Verbal abuse, cleaning up spilled milkshakes or wine, waiting patiently while people treated me like a slave was great for character building, but I didn't thrive on it.

Jeannette as Nepenthe waitress

Eventually, the waitresses caused me the most trouble due to my lack of awareness that they were a threat. I tried so hard to be an outstanding waitress that they complained to the Fassetts that I wasn't necessary, got in their way, and should do something else. Yes, they had noticed I was taking away some of their glory and tips. I could have tried to efface and ingratiate myself but I hadn't yet learned those social lessons. As it was, I was glad to get moved sideways into a job as a bargirl. Like a crab finding the right sort of shell, being a barmaid suited me. I liked being busy, and I liked the surge in income from the bar tips.

The downside of the job was having to work evenings and nighttime. From an early age, I'd realized I was not much good after about 9 p.m. If reading or doing homework, I'd fall asleep at the table. At concerts, on dates, at dances or parties, I'd go into a stupor as the evening wore on. To be a good barmaid, I learned to take midday siestas to have the energy to keep those welcoming smiles on my face and the drinks tray in my hand.

The various Nepenthe bartenders were fun to work with. George was my favorite. He looked very Italian with his striped t-shirts and big nose. His waxed mustache added a touch of the pirate to his persona. George invented many different drinks and sometimes allowed me to prepare common drinks like Nepenthe C&C (warmed cognac and chartreuse) and ordinary B&B (Benedictine and brandy).

I particularly enjoyed the bar job because I could be outdoors on the terrace in sunshine, star- and moonlight. The undulating blue ocean in the background and music in the foreground made for an entrancing, romantic work setting. Favorite tunes played endlessly. I must have listened to "The Girl from Ipanema" several hundred times. I admit I came to like it. The music blended so beautifully with Nepenthe's ambiance. The soft Brazilian voices settled gently on the ears, and Stan Getz's mellow sax could melt one's mind. The song still evokes the feel of the Nepenthe terrace every time I hear it.

Music at Nepenthe included folkdances, Latin American, Jamaican, and Cuban tunes, tangos, and rumbas. The swinging music inspired dancing at Nepenthe. I'd often join in the round and line dances. Grabbing hands and swirling around with laughing people made me happy. I was included, out there in front, pretending and often sincerely filled with joy. I wasn't alone, or a spectator, and didn't feel as self-conscious.

George Lopes, the barman

One evening after work, I sat listening once more to "The Girl from Ipanema" on the terrace. I chose a spot on a far bench with my feet over the railing, relaxing after some lively dancing. An old moon shone near the horizon, its face close to the ocean, as though putting itself onto a watery bed for the night. People were drinking at their little tables all around me, some playing chess or dominoes. A note of loneliness crept into my soul.

I did attract some company sometimes. Rory, in particular, might come sit with me. He was a quiet man. Keeping a conversation going with him was hard work. We'd sit and watch the view in less-than-comfortable silence. I wondered if I'd ever get to know him or any of the Nepenthe and Big Sur people in any depth.

I wrote to my friend Nathan: "Here I am in one of the most beautiful places on the planet feeling alone and a bit lost. Deep inside, I feel a spirit balloon wanting to be let free into the sky but held to earth by a flimsy string called a job and a body. My balloon needs another link. I need a friend here."

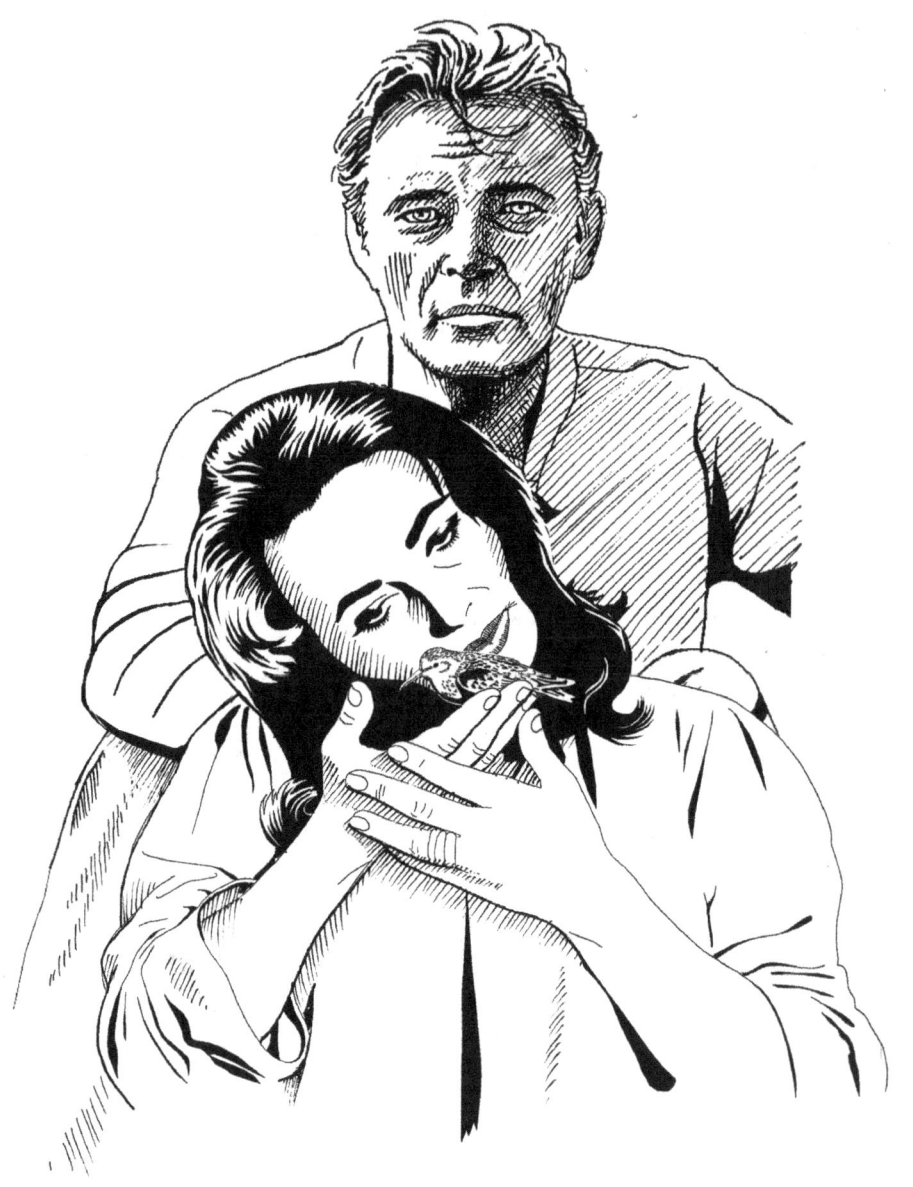

Burton & Taylor

CHAPTER 4

Nepenthe

Spring and Summer 1964

Though some are dirty
They are much cleaner than the Establishment.
And many are as fragrant as their flowers.
What is best about them is their music, though few know how to play.
Yet here in Big Sur, the evenings are
Nostalgic and medieval
As suddenly, round a bend in the road
Come the sounds of flutes and recorders,
As the girls leave their house cleaning jobs
And play their way homeward
To their shaggy and rebellious loves.

—Eric Barker, "Girl Hippies" from *Under Orion*

Nepenthe kept me in a whirl. My job forced me to be superficially sociable with little time to develop supportive friendships. While spinning around, working, trying to please everyone, I did manage to pay attention to specific events. The most notable event at the time was the filming of the movie *The Sandpiper*, a Hollywood production of Metro Goldwyn Mayer (MGM).

Elizabeth Taylor and Richard Burton were the big-name stars. The storyline had Taylor as a bohemian artist raising her son alone on the Big Sur coast. Her son was semi-delinquent, forced to go to an Episcopal school. Enter Burton, the married headmaster. Of course, the free-spirit mom and the stiff headmaster fall into a love affair.

The proceedings fascinated me. MGM built an entire wooden house which was Liz Taylor's "shack" in the movie. It hung over a cliff with the marvelous coastal landscape all around. Sadly, the movie men removed the house after finishing the film.

The film crew often came to Nepenthe. We workers watched the famous couple with a mix of awe and irritation. We were bossed around like ping-pong balls. Other actors, photographers, sound people, and support staff came for dinners and drinks. A lot of anti-depressant Nepenthe fluids went down the actors' and directors' throats.

Nepenthe was a theatre itself. As a bargirl, I was a minor but active participant. One day the Sandpiper filmmakers came to Nepenthe to take pictures for the preview of the movie. Some of us hanging around or working were conscripted to join in a dance. Presumably, our dance on the terrace was to show us as free-living hippies in the imaginary bohemian world. One of the Fassett gals grabbed my hand and pulled me into the circle. While whizzing around, I wondered if my pretense as a happy-go-lucky bohemian would fit into the film. I didn't think about that again for nearly fifty years.

Nepenthe dancers. Jeannette is the second dancer from right

Nepenthe in the 1960s was a hot spot, a social nexus. You could expect encounters between all sorts of people. Celebrities regularly came to the restaurant. I didn't know names or faces of most of the famous, such as Steve McQueen, the King of Cool, when he came to Nepenthe, but I did recognize Kim Novak and the MGM stars. The gossip about intrigues between actors, writers, sculptors, musicians, and poets fascinated me. All this was part of Nepenthe's distracting charm and fascinating lessons in human social behavior.

The Nepenthe scene challenged my abilities to absorb and sort out people. Besides the famous, the transient tourists, and my fellow workers, there were drifters, mostly hippies. I still thought hippies could be identified because of their unkempt clothes, long hair, and lazy, vague, manner. But I was amused when I realized one of the best ways to spot hippies was their common question, "What's your sign?" To me it was a meaningless question, like asking your shoe size or head shape to guess your intelligence.

In college psychology classes we ran experiments in which astrological signs were randomized, then assigned arbitrarily. We learned that people would believe any of the blurbs about any of the signs. Asking one's birth month might be useful as an icebreaker, but it was useless for insights or predictions about someone. People were more complex and interesting than being stamped as Aquarius or Virgo.

Many of the Nepenthe people were worth a closer look. The most interesting was Lolly Fassett, with her many skills and imposing presence. She was a marvel, and so was George, the hawk-nosed bartender in his striped shirts. Another was a Russian man named Chaco. He dressed in white sailor-type clothes and wore a beret. Chaco was especially kind to me and gave me a big glossy picture of himself. I never knew what he'd been hired to do at the restaurant, but he worked well as a living adornment.

In addition to the Nepenthe crowd, I gradually became aware of others living in Big Sur. The community had a core of long-term residents, what I thought of as ordinary people. I came to know people like Rory, the Trotters, and others. Some were retired but most had small businesses like Berley, the owner of the campsite where I lived. There were part-time residents, too; most of those were rich. They could afford to own houses without any effort to fit in or participate in the core community.

Take the Sandpiper movie producer Marty Ransohoff as a prime example. A wealthy Hollywood figure, he came to Big Sur with the movie crew. He liked the place and built an impressive house on a ridge overlooking the ocean. He, like other rich transients, seldom stayed in his Big Sur house, so had caretakers. I got to know one, a hippie named Hawk. He looked after Ransohoff's house. Lucky for me, Hawk invited some of us locals for a night visit to the house.

That visit earned a genuine WOW! I went with four others at sunset. We drove down an unpaved entryway and parked near the big redwood house. The structure stood out from the Big Sur chaparral, a bold object in the wind-shaped landscape. The whole edifice glowed as the sun shone a golden glint on the windows then slipped into the ocean. We went inside. I was immediately struck by the openness: uncluttered space, just a few appliances, smooth wooden floors, wooden stairs, and polished surfaces. The house was slumbering, breathing slowly, an abandoned nest ready for occupancy.

Upstairs was ready for the birds to alight and mate. In the dim light, I scanned around the huge loft covered in all kinds of furs. I took my time fondling the furs one by one, amazed by their textures and hues. I couldn't distinguish mink from ermine, beaver, sable, or chinchilla. My ignorance made me feel naïve and childlike. Finding a dark corner, I took off my clothes and rolled around on the furs while wondering at the expense and purpose of it all.

The Ransohoff house embodied a life of wealth, power, and sensuousness that I could stroke in the furs. Probably not a life for me, I thought. I didn't have any ambition to get rich nor an appetite for such extravagance. I couldn't quite imagine being a sexy concubine for a wealthy man. Such thoughts led me to ask myself, what did I want? Immediate answer: a life less pretentious, more sustainable, more attainable.

I pondered the question as I went outside on the deck to watch the afterglow on the ocean. I leaned over the railing to inhale the scent of salty sea and spicy chaparral. The rising moon behind me tangled the mass of plants on the slope below into light and dark patterns. I felt an urge to get to know the fragrant scraggly sage, the pearly, pendant-flowering manzanita. The natural world was tangible, knowable, and non-threatening. I realized I wanted to make the effort to learn and dare to ask more questions about nature. Meanwhile I could observe human nature.

Parties on the beaches were an excellent venue for watching. I went alone or with a gang of what I thought of as rubes (me) and hippies (others). I could be part of it all while hiding in the dark. Sitting on the sand and listening to music—the ubiquitous guitars and bongo drums—was like being in a real-life movie. The beach fires were hypnotic. Watching the silhouettes of people dancing, drugging, drinking, singing, and lovemaking created a lasting mental movie in my memory.

Gatherings on ocean shores, ridges, redwood canyons, and all kinds of houses were places to watch and learn. Immersed in this social swirl, I tried my best to smile, dance with grace, and avoid the naked sexiness of it all. The sexual advances from men who sought me out at these places made me uncomfortable. I felt like a bitch in heat, with males sniffing after me. I kept my distance, still struggling with sexual attitudes inherited from my parents' generation.

My sisters and I were born during the war and grew up in the post-war years. We girls were controlled and inhibited by our cultural and family expectations. We had little access to sex education and none to birth control methods. We were supposed to say No, firmly, to sexual advances. And I did. I got lots of practice saying no. Looking back over the years, I think that constant refusal to get sexually aroused may have seriously impaired my sexual life.

In college I gave my virgin self to my first real love. But lovemaking with quick withdrawal wasn't very satisfying. I tried other men, other satisfactions. During the early sixties, the fear of pregnancy was first on my mind. Condoms were not freely available, and men disliked using them. I bought myself a diaphragm when I thought I had a steady man in my last year at university. Alas, neither the diaphragm nor my lover was a success. Later, I chose the pill and eventually an IUD to prevent pregnancy. I tried to avoid men sexually but found the pressure from my body's desires combined with theirs hard to deal with.

By the time I reached Big Sur, I was still trying to sort out man-woman relationships as "free love" came into vogue. Sex was taken out of marriage and waved around like a pheromone-soaked flag. Often it seemed easier to go to bed with a man than keep him at bay. Aware of all this, I shouldn't have been so astonished when a date called me a prick tease and demanded I suck him off if I wouldn't "fuck."

CHAPTER 4: NEPENTHE

We who entered the sixties with the morals of the fifties were naïve and constrained. Nepenthe and Big Sur forced me to take note of sex in all its forms. Sex swam in the social whirlpool, stroking itself, luring. I needed a man I could link to. Or I needed to loosen up. Maybe I needed to try harder to get out of the whirlpool?

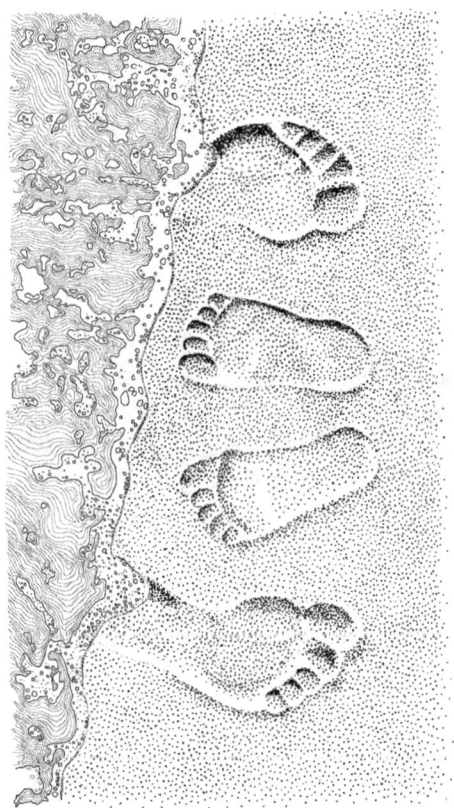

Note:
I didn't see the movie "*The Sandpiper*" until about 45 years after production. I didn't think much of it, appreciating only the Big Sur scenery. Five years after seeing the movie, when I started writing this memoir, I bought the book *My Nepenthe* by Romney Steele. Reaching the chapter on *The Sandpiper*, I had a surprise. There I was, in an old black and white photo of dancers on the Nepenthe terrace!

I was unmistakable as the shortest person, in a short dress, a flower in my dark hair. And of course, I had on my best smile. I investigated online for the original film trailer and found the dance scene on Nepenthe's 60th-anniversary video on YouTube. The color video is worth watching for the views of Nepenthe alone. And there we are, as Dorcas Fassett introduces the dancing, at 2.3 minutes into the clip.

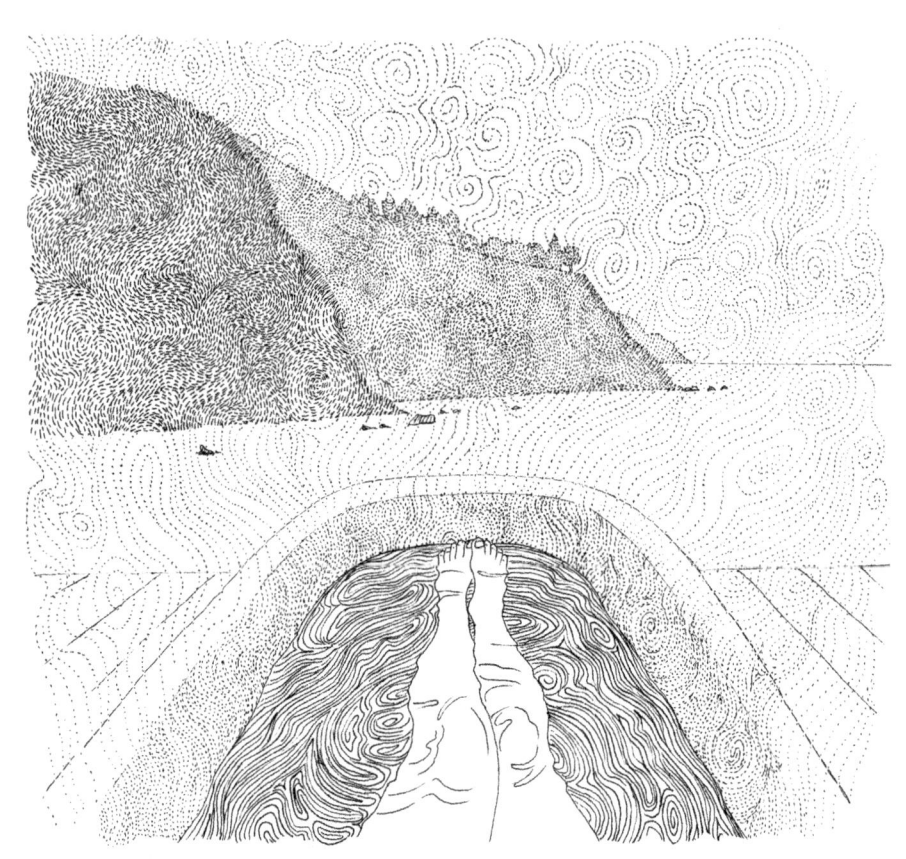
"The joy of wallowing in the warm water!"

CHAPTER 5

Hot Springs, Sex, and Seekers

Spring and Summer 1964

> The English man of letters has his club to repair to, the millionaire his yacht, the muezzin his minaret. As for me, there are the hot sulphur baths at Slade's Springs.
>
> — Henry Miller, *Big Sur and The Oranges of Hieronymus Bosch*

The mid-sixties were an exciting time, but I seemed to be swimming against the tides. The outgoing current swept away old notions; the incoming tide brought sex, drugs, and alternative lifestyles. I stayed afloat as best I could. Whenever possible, I swam out of the flow to flop into calmer pools to rest and ponder.

My favorite quieting pools are hot springs. As a child, I loved the feel and smell of warm, soothing waters. My mother sometimes took us children in winter to stay at Desert Hot Springs, a small town near the more famous and expensive Palm Springs. We delighted in leaping from cool pools to hot pools, floating in the water, and looking up at the stars.

On vacation from my first real job after college, I roamed the California coast looking for hot springs. I wanted to find places where I could immerse myself in a natural pool open to the sky. California had many of those unique places. And Big Sur had one of the best. Where else can you soak while listening to the surf boom at the base of the cliffs, watching hawks fly above, sea otters and whales below?

When I first visited Slade's Springs, also called Big Sur Hot Springs, it was not my idealized wild bathing spot. It had weathered wood shelters and rather scuzzy, old-fashioned bathtubs with rusty faucets. The paths were small and unlighted. But oh, the joy of wallowing in the warm water! In the baths, my mind mellowed as I stretched my body and view to the horizon.

The springs had a long history. The Esselen Indians used the area for generations until they were decimated by disease and the survivors herded to missions. In came the Spanish and Mexicans, followed by Big Sur pioneers such as the Pfeiffers and Posts. The 20th century brought tourists and writers, such as Henry Miller and Jack Kerouac, who made the whole area famous. All sorts of people came to bathe in the hot water and bask in the beauty of the surroundings.

Then in the 1960s came the soul searchers. When I returned in 1964, Big Sur Hot Springs had morphed into The Esalen Institute. The place had changed from a bathing spot to a center for "spiritual development" and "personal growth." People came for courses and retreats. After I started work at Nepenthe I wanted to go for a hot springs soak but wasn't sure if non-residents were allowed.

Fortunately, I met Tom, who had a job at the Institute. He worked as the in-house massage and bath captain. Tom and other workers sometimes came to Nepenthe for drinks, hang about, and listen to music. He and I struck up a loose friendship. I encouraged him because he was funny. For instance, he told me: "A Zen student named Alan Watts came for a seminar at Esalen. He transformed the place. Now you don't just soak in water over the ocean; you soak in spiritual vibes." Tom left amusing notes around the baths, on pieces of colored paper. On his door, he hung a sign, "Home of the Swim Reaper." A note stuck on the doors to the baths read, "Time in the tub 20 minutes or dress." A poster on a wall said "Soak Art" together with a wet handprint. Others proclaimed, "No life swapping here"; "No worries, all things must Bath."

Tom left punning notes on my car and my trailer as well as at the baths, quips such as: "Reverse EVIL to LIVE." Many I had to puzzle out, such as "CCCC the day," One note had "You are the ..." then a big written GRAVITY with the V circled; I finally realized it meant to say I was the center of gravity. Others I remember are, "Lie low sweet merry mint," "You're my hair apparent," "You are B-U-T full." My favorite was "Lift-life-live-lie" written in a tangle of cut-out letters he hung from a redwood branch by my trailer.

Tom often invited me to the springs and gave me a job to do there. He asked me to paint a ring of Chinese symbols on the door to his massage room. My pay was a full massage. He pummelled me on a deck over the ocean. I felt grateful for his friendship without sexual overtones. Visiting him at Esalen also let me feel some of the currents going through California culture.

For example, one afternoon, I joined him during a gathering at the Institute. Heading to the communal baths, I stopped at the edge of the open space. A group was sitting in a semicircle on the grass, listening to a sage named Fritz Perls. I'd learned about his Gestalt therapy ideas in my psychology classes in college. And yes, Perls sat casting pearls of wisdom to his audience. He spoke authoritatively, like a self-styled saint with an odd demonic rapture about him.

I stared at Perls, intrigued by his evident confidence and self-regard. He must have noticed my attention or my skeptical look as I stood, full of curiosity about the man. I felt frightened when his eyes settled on me with intensity. He paused in what he was saying, lifted his head and waved an arm in my direction. He intoned,

CHAPTER 5: HOT SPRINGS, SEX AND SEEKERS

"You there, on the edge of the circle, you are ready for Enlightenment."

I didn't know if he was joking, serious, or just wanted to distract his audience. Somewhat alarmed at being directly spoken to, I slunk away. The encounter bothered me. Enlightenment? Was that wisdom? I needed many more years to ponder what enlightenment meant.

Although I seemed to be able to negotiate some male friendships such as the one with Tom, sex was always in the background. It seemed to be common currency in Big Sur. I tried hard to steer away from entanglements, but I was in mating mode hormonally, and Big Sur was a sexy place. Perhaps that is why I became more intimately involved with Rory who made it clear he was available.

Rory was soft-spoken and kind, a tight-skinned, worn-out sort of man with a leathery hue in eyes and hair. I was grateful he'd helped find me a place to live at the campground before I arrived in Big Sur. When he came to check on how I was getting on, he was polite and always offered to help. He was a do-anything kind of guy: carpenter, plumber, electrician, and builder. I started seeing him more regularly. He and I shared meals sometimes in the down-home restaurant in the redwood valley near the campgrounds. He didn't drink alcohol, a trait I liked.

Rory was a staunch member of the Baha'i Faith. I'd never heard of Baha'i even though I'd gone to many different churches during my teenaged religious questioning phase. The Baha'i message was unity, the equality of all peoples, and the importance of education. It sounded good to me, but I do not follow creeds. I like the traditions of some religions but not the mumbo jumbo, and magical, irrational thinking. I thought of myself as a skeptic striving to keep the unattainable "open mind."

Rory was a useful companion, fixing things in my trailer and showing me around Big Sur. His company helped keep other men away. However, he expected me to be his woman, and that included being his sex partner. Sex with Rory was unimaginative and downright dull at times. I asked myself why I was having unenjoyable sex with a man I wasn't committed to. I felt ashamed, realizing that I was using sex as payment for having the security of Rory's company.

Rory lasted until a previous lover caught up with me. My brother had introduced me to "The Dude," as he called him, at a beach party in San Diego. I called him Adonis because of his beautiful body. He was super sexy, and that, plus his connections to the surfer crowd, resulted in my spending several weekends with him. He taught me a bit about surfing and encouraged me to become a scuba diver.

I became one of the early licensed scuba divers in California after taking a challenging diving course offered by Los Angeles County. I made my own wetsuit, cutting and gluing the neoprene material. Afterwards, I took any opportunity to be underwater in seaweed forests among bright fishes in the Pacific Ocean. Diving experience would be a big help later in my 1960s sojourn.

Adonis and I had a brief affair, but I didn't pursue the relationship. When I quit work in L.A. and moved to Big Sur, I didn't tell him. He found out where I lived from my brother. Adonis drove up in his expensive sports car to the door of my trailer in the redwoods one late afternoon. Luckily, I was home, so came out to greet him. "Hello!" he called and pulled me off the steps. He swung me around in a joyful hug, saying, "I've come to sweep you off your feet!" Indeed.

Off we went to a fancy restaurant in Monterey. During dinner, he told me, "I've gotten a real good job now, earning lots of money. I want more than a fling. Let's get married!" I sat speechless. He hadn't yet absorbed the idea that I wasn't his girlfriend eager for more romance. I lifted my head to look at him in the face saying, "No, sorry. I'm not ready for marriage. Also, I'm involved with another man."

Adonis was in a grumpy mood on the way back down the coast. I clutched the sides of my seat as he roared too fast on the winding road. Screeching around a curve south of Carmel, we almost drove into an overturned car, its wheels still spinning. He swerved around the vehicle and stopped just beyond the wreck.

The wrecked car had skidded on the curve, hit a railing and turned upside down, sliding sideways, almost blocking the road. The motor was still running, the smell of fuel in the air. I peered into the car. The driver, possibly drunk or dead, was inert. Without thinking, I put my arm inside the passenger's window to turn off the engine. As I touched the keys, a hand grabbed my wrist and I let out a yell.

The woman trapped in the twisted metal started screaming. In shock myself, I tried to calm her by patting her shoulder and muttering, "It's ok, hold on, help will come." Other people assembled around the car. Adonis found someone to phone the police and an ambulance. People crowded around, trying to help the screaming woman. Her cries hurt me, a kind of agony, knowing I could do little to help.

We were on Highway One, only two lanes and the only road up and down the coast. Cars started pulling up behind and ahead. Horns honked, people pushed and shoved. We heard sirens and stepped aside as flashing lights approached. I looked at Adonis; he looked at me. We got in his car and drove south.

I never knew the outcome, but the accident thoroughly rattled me. Still does. I never wanted to see Adonis again. I wanted him and the memory of the night out of my mind. When we arrived at the trailer, I told him to go away. He'd expected to spend the night with me, but I was adamant he had to leave. I shoved him out the door.

He came back in with protests, "Why can't I stay? I love you. I want to marry you. Comfort you. Let me stay." The more he pleaded, the more alarmed I got.

Then Rory drove in. He saw us struggling at the doorway, came over, and pulled Adonis down the stairs of my trailer. Rory pushed Adonis, saying, "The lady is telling you to leave. Leave now!"

He commanded it in a low nerveless voice that frightened me. Adonis swung a fist at Rory, but the wiry man turned aside and gave his opponent a hard slap and push that toppled him. I tried to stop the fight and was yelling at them both when Adonis suddenly turned, jumped into his car, slammed the door, and roared off.

Fight at the trailer

I tried to breathe some calm into myself as Rory took my arm and led me into the trailer. We spent the night together, a night I remember little about except for the fear Adonis would return. I also had an irrational fear someone would ask me to return to the scene of the wreck. Jolting fears of death jumped daily into my brain and nightmares galloped through my sleep. Somehow the relationship with Rory, my savior, didn't survive the trauma. We seldom saw each other after that night, never mentioned it, and were never again intimate.

Avoiding all advances from men, I tried to relax into the routine of work at Nepenthe, trips to the hot springs, and social gatherings. Gradually I felt more in control of myself. Then, into this slipstream of my life, came a special man who changed everything.

Bill Hargis

CHAPTER 6

Hargis

Summer 1964

There he was—smart, rugged, and slim.
I found myself in an awkward situation,
My mind told me to love him,
But my body declined the invitation.

—Genetta, "Love Him"

I finished my shift, turned in my tray and towel at the bar, and headed outside. I hid in the shadows at the far end of Nepenthe's terrace to listen to the night and the zillionth rendition of "Girl from Ipanema." A low voice from nearby startled me. "Hi there, Short Stuff, wanna play dominoes?"

I'd noticed the enigmatic man before. He usually sat alone on the terrace with a glass of wine, smoking, while casting glances around like he was fly-fishing for trout. Clothed in a loose-fitting work shirt and chinos, he fitted in with the locals. They obviously knew him. He greeted them in a low, gruff voice, with a poker face while his eyes danced about. He was obviously amused by the Nepenthe scene. I took the domino bait and went to join him.

"Bill Hargis," he said, reaching over the table to offer his hand. "Jeannette," I muttered in response. While Bill put out the dominoes, I sneaked a look at him. His dark hair, streaked with gray, accented his weather-beaten face. This fellow, I thought, has been outdoors a lot. He resembled Humphrey Bogart and acted a bit like him, too, with a diffident, no-nonsense demeanor. I found his sly, know-it-all expression a bit off-putting, but his hazel eyes were clear, and his voice was seductive. He certainly intrigued me.

Before he could ask me about myself, I asked him about himself, a defensive social ploy I'd learned years earlier. I dove in with the insipid question, "What do you do here?"

Bill looked around the terrace as though trying to decide if I meant Nepenthe or more generally. He answered, "Right now, I'm here in Big Sur installing water systems. I do a variety of jobs in Salinas and the Central Valley, too."

"Do you live in Big Sur?" I asked.

"No, I have a base in the Salinas Valley and King City, too. I usually stay with friends when I'm working here." Bill placed some more dominoes and added, "And I have a cabin at my mining claim down the coast by Lucia. My masterpiece though, is a cabin up on the coast ridge."

So many places to live or keep up? I wondered how often he went to each of them. My mind wandered away as I tried to picture all that driving on highways, backroads, and over the mountains that divided Big Sur from the central California valleys. What sort of car survived those roads? I turned my attention back to Bill.

He looked at me from under his bushy eyebrows, paused a few seconds to ensure I was listening and said, "I also work up in the Sierra Nevada Mountains. I do some placer gold mining. Up there I live in a cabin." I raised my eyebrows, impressed at the range of abodes. He nodded, his lips raised in a smirk of a smile, and added, "Yes, I drive around this state all the time. And I love every bit of it."

Bill knew California a lot better than I did. We started discussing what we both loved about the state, particularly the coast and mountains. He knew a lot about the Big Sur and Monterey Bay area. Growing up in the region, he'd absorbed its history and told me about the early Indians, settlers, farmers, and fishermen.

Then he turned the conversation to current developments in the area, all of which irritated him. He began a rant about defending the remaining wild spaces from the invasion of "all those irresponsible hikers, insensitive tourists, callous big shots, ignorant miners, and irritating numbskulls!"

I tried to hide a smile at this extravagance of invective, but Bill caught me and snorted. He shook his head, and proclaimed, "Those are bad enough, but add on the bureaucrats who do next to nothing to protect wilderness areas. They are thieves and cowards with no moral fiber!"

"So where are the people with 'moral fiber'?" I asked, noticing I was losing the domino game. Bill picked up the question, his brain fingered it. He leaned over the table and told me what he admired: the honesty and work ethic of rural people, people who had to struggle to make a living, those who work hard, explore, discover, and build. He ended with, "People with grit! People like the Trotters, people not wasting their time pushing paper and their egos around." Bill obviously considered himself a member of the Moral Fiber Club.

After our domino game, Bill and I spent an evening playing bridge with some of the Nepenthe staff. The next time, we played hearts with Lolly's children. Most people at Nepenthe treated Bill with cool respect. That made me puzzled about the warm joking relationship he had with Lolly Fassett. She told me that his full name was really William Hawley Hargis, Jr. and he came from a well-off family in the Salinas valley. She treated Bill like a wily, untrustworthy family member. I suspected there were past events that might never be revealed.

CHAPTER 6: HARGIS

One evening Bill and I sat alone on the terrace and talked about Big Sur. Like me, Bill didn't care for Progress. To him that meant more shopping centers, tract homes, highways into the byways. He also complained about monoculture farming, charismatic religions, talk shows, old folks' homes, TV, especially soap operas. He ended his long list of dislikes with a puzzling statement: "And songs that fade out at the end really irritate me. They leave me hanging, needing a proper finish."

I wondered if Bill's conclusion was merely cranky, or if it meant he was uncomfortable when things didn't end the way he expected. Maybe he wanted his jobs, relationships, and life to end emphatically, not vaguely. That made me a bit wary about what he expected of me and our developing relationship. I asked him, "Tell me, just what you do like, besides your jobs and wilderness?"

He liked certain books. He read widely, preferring history and biographies. His favorite writer was John Steinbeck, not unexpected when I learned that he'd known Steinbeck personally as a boy. Bill told me, "Steinbeck is a real writer. He knows real people and can bring them to life. None of his characters are phony." While Steinbeck was one of Bill's heroes, he disliked local author Henry Miller. "That man writes over-rated books and paints awful pictures. But at least Miller appreciates the beauty of Big Sur and the hot springs. I see him there in the baths sometimes, pale and flabby, usually talking about himself."

The name Bill seemed a name too bland for such an opinionated man. I often thought of him as Hargis, a man who spoke his mind. That mind was not only eclectic but conservative and old-fashioned. When I teased or questioned him about his views, he retaliated by pestering me to reveal my own. He asked about what I knew and felt about events or local people. He'd give his low laugh or put on a wry expression when I admitted my ignorance. He pretended to be shocked to discover I didn't know that the California sea otters were back in numbers and thriving or that the pampas grass was an exotic weed invading Big Sur.

I was both embarrassed and pleased by Hargis' attention and questions. He was a cube of colors with sides that didn't always match up, but the contrasts piqued my interest. I found him fascinating. I knew he was interested in me too, because he went out of his way to "drop by" Nepenthe to see me. He'd arrive on the terrace or park his beat-up VW Beetle next to my Renault and wait for me after work.

I welcomed his company and the chance to absorb some of what he knew. On one walk, he tore a twig from a big tree, scrunched the leaves, and thrust them at me, saying, "Do you know this tree? Take a good sniff!" I inhaled. My sinuses exploded, my eyes watered, and I had to catch my breath. Bill laughed and said, "California bay

Bay leaves

leaves, you should know them." Indeed, I did come to know them and sometimes pulled a milder form of the same trick on unsuspecting visitors.

Mostly I saw Bill at Nepenthe, but one evening he joined me at the little restaurant in the valley not far from my campground. A homey sort of place, it was cheap and clean with friendly, down-to-earth staff. Cooking inside my trailer was about as enjoyable as trying to start a fire outside in the rain. Eating at Nepenthe was easier, but meant either supping with the staff or having to wrangle a meal by myself. I liked the neutral café in the valley. Obviously, Bill did too because he entered, greeted everyone, and came to sit at my table, uninvited. I just sat and looked at him until he opened the conversation.

"You've been working at Nepenthe for a while now. Do you like it?" His bushy eyebrows went up in a way that was both enquiring and mocking.

"Well, yes and no," I said, shaking my head, confused. Unable to produce a witticism, clever comment, or insight, I just spilled words. "I like the ambiance and the view and most of the people, too. The food is good. The work isn't difficult and often fun." I paused to think about what was wrong with this pretty picture. "The real problem is it's so temporary. There's no real future there for me. And I'm not earning much."

"Do you think you'll earn more when you start work at the new shop?"

"I doubt I'll earn more than what I get now. And in many ways, I'll be less free with the shop job."

"Freedom is worth a lot, for sure. To me, it's worth more than cash," he said, placing his hands on the table. He added, "Freedom is especially valuable here in Big Sur, where there are priceless rewards all around."

"Oh, I agree," I enthused, feeling immature and silly.

"Oh yes," he said brightly, imitating my enthusiasm. "But you really haven't seen much, have you?"

"Hmm, well…" I squirmed, trying to assess just how much I'd seen.

Bill rumbled a laugh at my evident perplexity. He asked, "Have you been up Partington Ridge? Have you hiked to the top of the mountain right behind here?" He waved his arm in the direction of Mount Manuel and almost hit the skinny busboy who was bringing us glasses of water.

"Have you been to Pick's or Willow Creek? Have you met the Posts? Do you know Eric Barker or Emile Norman or other Big Sur sculptors, poets, and artists? Have you met the Verens? They are some of the REAL people in Big Sur."

I kept shaking my head, not knowing any of the people he'd mentioned. He took pity on me, half smiled, and said, "Well, seeing as how you've missed much of the best of Big Sur, how about going along when I tackle a job for a lady who owns a house near the waterfall?"

"What waterfall?" I naïvely asked, falling into Bill's trap. He shook his head in mock dismay. "It's about the most awe-inspiring sight on the coast, where a stream falls off a cliff into the ocean at a lovely beach."

CHAPTER 6: HARGIS

Julia Pfeiffer Burns State Park

I sat frowning at myself, how had I missed that?

"The woman I'm doing the job for only comes seasonally. She's willed the property to the state for a park. The authorities will demolish the house. You should see it. It's one of the prettiest places on the coast."

He then repeated a phrase I would hear many times, "I know you'll love it."

And I did. The view was unforgettable. A thin plume of water dropped off a cliff decorated with pines and shrubs. The sea gathered up the falling water at a graceful curve of sand where it met the cliffs. The incredible beauty of the cove filled me with awe.

The sight expanded my growing love of Big Sur. It was like finding extra space in the lungs to breathe more deeply. Bill made a point of assuring I breathed beauty whenever we were together. He introduced me to local fauna and flora, handing me fragrant flowers and clumps of leaves pulled off shrubs. I began to discern the components of what everyone called chaparral. His comments on the coastal pines and oaks, the different sages, and wildflowers helped me pay closer attention to nature. I couldn't absorb it all, but I knew this was the kind of enlightenment I was ready for.

Bill took me to other special places in his cramped, bashed-up Volkswagen. He'd named it The Hesperus, as in "the wreck of…". The literary Hesperus was a boat that sank. Hargis' Hesperus had obviously had a crash and roll in the past but survived to become Bill's hardworking companion. He used it like a Jeep or Land Rover, bouncing over roads needing four-wheel drive and high clearance. Hesperus lacked both.

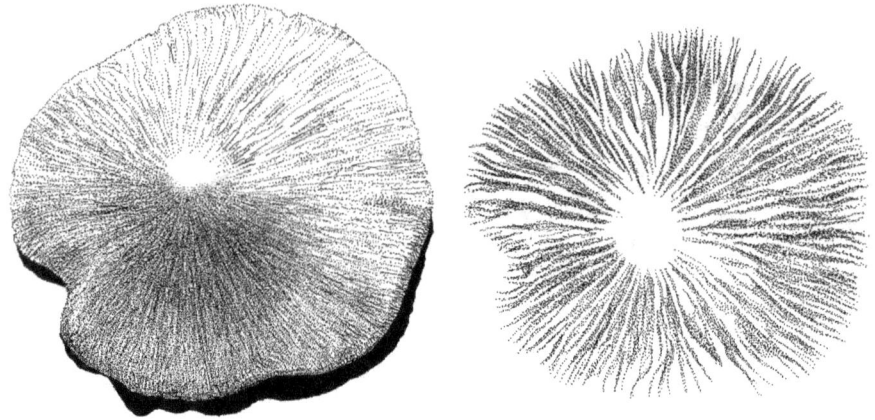

Mushroom spore print

One rainy day, Bill asked me, "What do you know about mushrooms?"

"Nothing," I admitted.

Bill showed me how to identify mushroom species by checking colors, shapes, gills, and pores, and how to do spore prints. I learned the difference between shaggy manes and puffballs, boletus and shelf mushrooms. We explored along Big Sur back roads and into the coastal canyons to pick chanterelles and oyster mushrooms. Tromping through secret pastures in the Salinas Valley, we searched for pink-gilled meadow mushrooms.

Learning about mushrooms, both edible and deadly, gave me a lifetime hobby. Recognizing a few dangerous mushrooms seemed relatively easy, such as when finding the bright red cap with white spots of a deadly amanita. I learned the hard way to recognize another kind of poison. That was the skin irritant that came from the leafless twigs and vines we crawled under when hunting chanterelles.

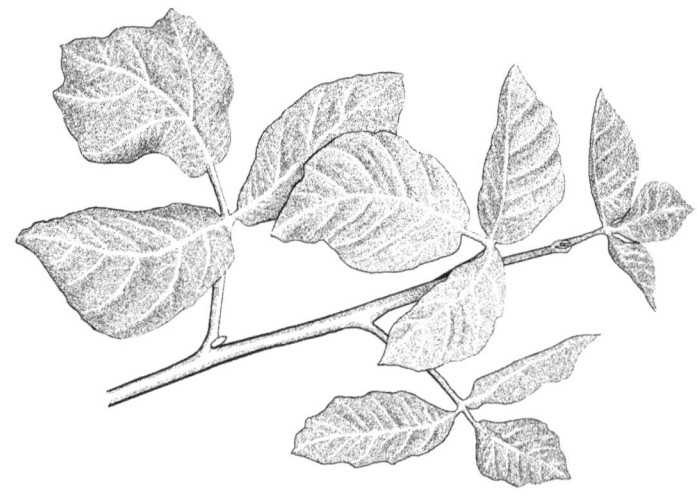

Poison Oak

Poison oak—*Rhus diversiloba*—grew everywhere and I grew allergic to it. In mushroom season it lost most of its identifying leaves, but their stems could still smear oily resin. My coworkers at Nepenthe had some good laughs at my expense when I came in with a puffy, red, and swollen face. I soon learned to wash my body and my clothes thoroughly after every mushroom expedition.

My daytime explorations with Bill came to a stop when Lolly told me the shop was ready. The Phoenix looked wonderful, fitting into the landscape as though it had grown up right there, which of course, it had. I moved from barmaid to shop attendant and started helping the manager arrange merchandise.

The Fassetts had hired a highly-strung man to manage the new store. He fidgeted constantly and was quite the finicky boss. He'd order me to move this basket or shelf of stuff here and there as he changed his mind. He delegated to me the most boring of sorting, recording, and cleaning tasks. He chastised me if I let visitors leave the shop without buying anything. Bossman liked to sneak off in the afternoon. He'd leave me holding the bags and keys. I quickly found that being a shopgirl wasn't much fun.

About the time I started at the Phoenix gift shop, I moved out of my trailer at the campground. I'd taken to hitchhiking from the campground to Nepenthe because my car often refused to take me to work. One day a gentleman with a round face and a sweet smile offered me a lift. He introduced himself as Boris Veren. Another day, he brought his bright-eyed wife, Filippa, to say hello at the Phoenix shop. They were two of Hargis' "real people." I was glad to meet them both. Bill was pleased too. One day he decided to take me to his mining claim further south along the coast at Willow Creek. "I need to check on the cabin. It's in a really beautiful location. You'll love it. And we can stop by to see Boris and Filippa on our way."

We found the couple beside the main highway up the road a bit by their swimming pool. Bill had built and installed solar panels to heat it. Boris used the pool for physical therapy for his legs, damaged by polio as a child. The Verens invited us for supper on our way back from Willow Creek. We agreed with enthusiasm. After a fine meal, at the end of the evening, Filippa offered me space to stay in her studio. I happily accepted.

Driving back to my trailer, Bill exclaimed, "Wonderful! Now you can leave this less-than-salubrious campground and live with my special people! You'll love them." Unfortunately, after only a few weeks it was obvious that Filippa didn't like a young woman living with them. I left the Veren's home in haste and found a temporary base with the Post family. Their place was close enough to Nepenthe that I could walk to work.

Bill was disappointed I'd left the Verens. He had suggestions for other places to live but I wanted to find my next spot myself. I needed to reaffirm my independence. We were spending so much time together that others saw us as a couple. People assumed we were having sex. I loved being with Bill but wasn't sure I wanted to get sexually involved. However, I knew would soon have to decide.

Driving the Coast Ridge road in Hesperus

CHAPTER 7

Moving Along

Summer 1964

Wild ridges and canyons in stormy weather
Rain falling as we snuggle together.
Trees tower, the incredible superfluous joy
Flees as banal concerns come to destroy
Those days of exaltation, replaced by new places
With destinies lost in oceans of new faces.

—Genetta, "Renegade Love"

Bill asked me if I'd like to go up the coast ridge. He wanted me to see the cabin he'd built on Santa Lucia peak. "You'll love it, but," he said raising an eyebrow, "you'll have to take at least a full day off work to see it properly."

By now, I knew that a raised eyebrow and a "proper visit" meant agreeing to go at the Hargis pace, an open-ended tear in the fabric of time. He prodded my desire to explore by adding, "On the way, I want to take you to one of my favorite spots, Pick's Valley. So beautiful. A little creek and waterfall, wild country, big pines. You'll love it."

Of course, I'd love it. I summoned the courage to ask for time off. Lolly grumbled. I asked to leave early one afternoon and take but one full day off. With a frown, Lolly finally agreed. Bossman didn't only frown, he scowled. "You should have come to me first. You probably knew I would've refused."

I knew I'd have to pay for my time away but had no idea what those life-changing hours with William Hawley Hargis Jr. would cost me. Bill picked me up in his trashy Volkswagen. I grimaced, trying to find a spot for my sleeping bag and kit among the spare parts and junk in the back seat. Bill proudly pointed out the paper bags of food he'd bought for our outing. I looked but didn't see a backpack that we could carry the food in. I kept quiet, trusting that Mr. Outdoorsman would supply something.

We turned off Highway One to drive up a dirt road. Hesperus growled its way up the golden grass slopes until we met the ridge road. I was amazed at the number of gates we had to pass through. Bill had a huge ring of keys and knew all the codes to the locks. Driving along the ridge road was spectacular. The poet Robinson Jeffers' phrase, "divinely superfluous beauty" described our surroundings. At each stop to open a gate or fence, I paused to scan the views over the broad blue ocean and raise my eyes to distant forested mountains. And the sky, decorated with clouds and hawks (or were they eagles?) flying high. Exhilarating.

After a long dusty drive, we reached a high point. True to form, Bill parked and gave me a lesson. "Look out there to the west. Can you see that the trees are a different color and shape?"

Coulter (L) & Jeffrey (R) pine cones

Before I could reply, he launched into a comparison of Coulter pines, with the biggest cones on the planet, and the introduced Jeffrey pines, whose smaller cones are less spiny. I nodded, nonplussed at this impromptu lecture. Mostly I felt grateful for Bill's lessons, but they also made me feel inadequate, reminding me of my ignorance and leaky memory. I reckoned he didn't have many new people he could impress with his knowledge about the natural world. And here I was, a willing and eager student. As he rambled on about the distribution of needles of the pines, I interrupted him, asking, "Are we going to go see those trees or hike?"

He paused, frowned, and said, "Hmmm, well, we don't have time to go all the way to the cabin. Let's park a bit further on and gear up. We need to get to the valley before dark." He looked up at the sky and intoned in a fake weatherman's voice, "The clouds are building up. There's a 96.3% chance it will rain on us."

The rain started while we were hiking over the ridge. I'd brought a rain jacket. Bill wrapped some sort of waterproof tarp over his shoulders, a duffle, and the bags of groceries. A stream started flowing down the trail. Soon we couldn't find our way. We searched for a niche between big rocks while the sky grew darker. Bill and I contrived a makeshift shelter of brush and boughs woven over and into a rocky overhang, surprisingly good protection.

We wriggled under the shelter to sleep in our bags, but they were soon sopping wet underneath. Morning hid its face in thick clouds that squeezed out splatters of rain. Bill said, "The trail will be hard to find now, and the ridge road will be muddy and slippery. We should stay put here until the rain stops."

I watched appreciatively as Bill made a small fire among the rocks, producing enough warmth to dry us and our bags a bit. Stranded in the space and time, I thought I'd try to learn a bit more about this man. I brought up what I knew would be a touchy subject, his war years.

Bill had been a Navy fighter pilot in World War II. I got that bit of information not from him but from people at Nepenthe. As expected, he was reluctant to talk about those days. All I could get out of him was that he was a part of Air Group Four, one of the Red Rippers. Much later I discovered the Red Rippers were a well-known bunch of fighter pilots, and Bill had been a Top Gun. He'd won many medals he kept hidden in a box at his mother's house.

Hargis the Navy fighter pilot

Aa an obvious tactic to avoid talking about the war years, Bill swung the conversation to me. He asked lots of questions as we spent the day by the fire, talking and snuggling. Bill kissed me, hugged me tight, and said, "You are the first woman I've felt close to for many years. And you're the first person in decades who might match me in my love of the wilderness. Here you are, looking cheerful in the rain! You love the outdoors. You have the same heartfelt involvement I feel."

He went on to tell me about myself, praising my intelligence and practical ways. His words alarmed me as much as warmed me. I knew he didn't have any realistic idea of my ignorance, stubbornness, and impatience. Even so, his lovely false impressions were seductive. I could feel his emotional tendrils wrapping around me, making me feel valued and special.

On that second night in our rustic shelter, we made love, sort of. I wasn't sexually aroused by kissing and fondling, so I was only a bit disappointed when he came too soon. He explained he had seldom had sex with a woman since his first love, decades before. She'd chosen to marry a wealthier, more established man. I accepted his apology and hoped our sex life might improve with time. The thought of spending time with Bill made me realize I wanted to be with this man. Sex was still an ambiguous glue in any relationship, but I was willing to let it adhere and endear me to Bill, if possible.

While Bill and I were bonding in the Santa Lucia Mountains, my puritanical companion, Mr. Work Ethic came for a visit. My conscience reminded me I'd be very late to get back to Nepenthe. I knew I was in for trouble. Arriving late at the shop the next day, the shop manager blitzed me with his intense displeasure.

"I've had to work your shift," he grumbled as he came from behind the counter to glare at me, hands-on-hips. "I haven't been able to get away. You've made me miss my appointments in Monterey."

I lowered my head to receive his abuse, gritting my teeth. Pointing his hand with its sparkling, ringed fingers at me, he said, "I should have you fired!"

That didn't intimidate me much. I hated the job. I disliked trying to sell silly mementos, key rings, overpriced clothing, and even the worthwhile local artwork. I wasn't a good salesperson, unable to promote Things. Also, I earned less as a shopgirl than I did being an unpaid bargirl. Even so, I shut my mouth, groveled, worked extra hours for free, and persevered.

Bossman had an excuse to get rid of me soon after my trip with Bill to Pick's Creek. Boris came to see me at the Phoenix gift shop. He asked me to meet for supper in the café in Big Sur village. He wanted to find out why I so suddenly left their house. I begged Bossman's permission to leave early on the day of my rendezvous. He reluctantly agreed in exchange for covering for him on other days, for his "appointments" in Monterey.

Of course, Bossman didn't return in time. I fussed and fidgeted like I did when waiting for Perky while she crashed her car on the L.A. freeway. When I was close to despair, I decided not to wait any longer. Boris was more important than my boss. I locked up the gift shop and went directly to the café. Boris was understanding and we made another date to meet. I returned to the gift shop.

Predictably, while I was gone, Lolly came down to see how the customers were doing. She was astonished to find the shop closed. Who was to blame? I started to explain when the manager returned. Lolly stomped out, not pleased with him either. Bossman fired me on the spot.

Being fired was like being released from a taut bungee cord; I felt both freed and stung. I walked back to the Posts' compound. They commiserated with me, but I knew that I'd have to find another job and place to live. The Posts' place was crowded, too busy, and I no longer needed to be close to Nepenthe and the Phoenix shop. They suggested I look at a house for rent nearby on "Three Acres."

The small house sat hunched among lichen-laced oak trees along the coast highway. It looked a bit forlorn in the shady, damp spot, but soon became home. My home. I could relax and have visitors too, something I'd been missing. My brother came. Even my friend Nathan came to stay. He teased me about living the "hippie" scene, even though he seemed more a hippie-gypsy type than I ever could be.

Nathan had moved on from his beatnik lifestyle in San Francisco. He'd become the World Traveler. He lived in Amsterdam for many months and loved it. He brought me photos and postcards from other places in Europe and Asia. His vivid stories watered the travel-lust seeds planted in my spirit soil.

Having occasional visitors was comforting but I still needed a job. By now, summertime had squatted on Big Sur. A fog creature lounged over the ocean, crept up the valleys, and laid down on the slopes. The fog damped down sounds and caused traffic jams on the highway. To look for work, I joined lines of tourist cars crawling through the Big Sur valley. The managers at the café in the village were delighted to give me a job.

The two happy-go-lucky gay guys grinned a welcome, twirled me around, and gave me a frilly apron. "Oh, yes, you'll be a great waitress," they told me. I loved working there: the joking owners; the fat, jolly Mexican cook; the skinny, sallow busboy whose long dark blue apron made him look scary; and the strung-out, dyed blonde waitress. We made an eclectic and fun team.

Lucky for me, my new situation let me spend happy hours outdoors. Since I worked in the afternoons and evenings, I could walk and explore during morning hours. My favorite walk was along an unpaved road leading onto nearby Rancho Rico. I followed switchbacks through dense stands of oak trees to the open ridges that divided the Big Sur valley from the ocean.

I didn't have binoculars so didn't get to know the birds very well. But one vivid woodpecker with red in its feathers seemed to greet me whenever I passed certain chapparal clumps. Hargis told me it was a Northern Flicker. I didn't ask but guessed the name came from the flash of red flame as it flew. I came to love flickers and picked up any feathers they left behind.

On one of the highest ridges of Rancho Rico lived the ranch managers. The couple had the use of a big farmhouse with windows looking out on the Ventana Peaks of the Santa Lucia Mountains. They let me buy cheap trays of reject eggs from the farm: cracked, double-yolked, or with blood spots inside. I ate a lot of eggs.

Northern Flicker

Rancho Rico was splendid, with very few houses and massive amounts of open space. The managers allowed me to explore on my own. Walking in the dappled light among the shady oaks on the valley side made me sing with joy. The smells of sage, warm grass, and salty sea on the ridge top intoxicated me. I spent hours walking, humming, soaking in the "incredible beauty of joy," as Robinson Jeffers put it.

Reaching the rocky private beach on the coastal side of the ranch gave me a special thrill. After a very long descent, I stood on a clifftop before plunging down the trail to where a small spring leaked out, surrounded by bright yellow monkeyflowers. A splash on my face and arms cooled me; then I'd drift along the beach to collect shells and wade in the cold Pacific Ocean water. I cut long tubes from the fronds of the shore-stranded seaweed and left them to dry. When they were crisp, I'd snip off the ends. When I blew over the opening, the horns made deep, otherworldly sounds, like whales underwater.

I learned a fundamental life lesson from these outings: I wasn't going to become an artist. In high school, I took classes in art and was inspired by a fellow named Bob Mackie. He was a year and eons ahead of me. He did fabulous things with paint, sets for plays, and costumes. Emulating him, I'd tried making collages, some sculptures, and paintings. In Big Sur I realized that trying to be like someone exceptional was a mistake. But it also made it clear to me that my efforts were not satisfying to me, let alone worthy to show others. So, I hid or threw most everything away. I kept a few things, such as seashells, special stones, and a gourd full of flicker feathers. They reminded me to be content with the natural beauty all around me.

Once I came to terms with my flawed creativity, I enjoyed my walks more. Even so, the questions of what I was going to do in life remained open and worrying. I made sporadic efforts to think about choices. I read books, like *Escape From Freedom* by Eric Fromm. The paradox of feeling freer by tying oneself down made me think of options, such as becoming a writer, a marine biologist, a tailor, or even a candle maker. I wondered if leading a peripatetic life with Bill would satisfy me. His lifestyle, free to pursue what he found interesting and challenging, fascinated me. Would I be able to stride along as he did, with no clear vision of the future?

Mulling over thoughts about life one day, I sat alone on Rancho Rico's sandy beach, blowing a kelp horn. The haunted sound matched my mood. I heard something else: voices. A group of people came down the cliff road. They were all strangers to me, but obviously, not to the beach—they walked like they owned the place. And they did. I stood and prepared to apologize for being there. A lovely, willowy woman came right up to me and said, "You must be Jeannette, the one who lives at Three Acres and buys all our useless eggs!" I had to laugh, saying, "You're too right."

"I'm Claire," she said with a big smile, "one of the huge family that owns this place. But don't feel frightened, none of the Chappellet family bite."

I was immediately impressed by Claire's grace and good humor. What an attractive person: tall, poised, gentle, and with a lovely smile! I automatically followed

CHAPTER 7: MOVING ALONG

"I sat alone on Rancho Rico's sandy beach, blowing a kelp horn."

her along as she cruised the shore looking for shells, whalebones, driftwood, and other treasures. We chatted about this and that while the others swam and foraged. They kindly invited me to join them for their picnic. The natural good manners and conversation of these people intimidated me. I envied their ingrained social skills.

Claire turned to me with a smile. "I'm so excited. I'm starting to build my house. I've chosen the site, up there, on the ridge top. It'll have multiple levels and decks. I've arranged to use the redwood timbers from the old Russian River bridge." She paused, looking up the ridge at her site. "I'll build in the Big Sur style, in keeping with the dramatic setting. The house will even have a studio where I can do my artwork!"

She added, "You must come to see what we're doing when you can."

We'd finished lunch, and I withdrew with gratitude and a genuine smile. The encounter made me glow inside. As I walked along the long road back to my house, I knew I'd take any opportunity to get to know Claire better. She lived a life I could never have and offered me the opportunity to view that life vicariously. As for me, I still wanted to explore, have adventures and challenges. Maybe I'd find some of Fritz Perls' enlightenment. In the meantime, my worldview had been stretched and remained as open as the ocean.

Dave walks the railing of Bixby Bridge

CHAPTER 8

Friendships
Autumn 1964

I don't want a courtship.
I don't want a guilt trip.
We don't need a steamship,
airstrip or spaceship.
We already share our Earthship
So let's just dance and sideslip
Into a fine firm friendship.

—Genetta, "Friendship"

While I was adapting to my new home and job, I saw Bill less often. Based at his father's shop in King City, he was busy working on jobs and making equipment for his gold mining project on the Feather River. On his brief visits to Big Sur, he flooded me with adoring words, telling me how much he loved and needed me. We had uncomfortable, too brief sex, leaving me feeling frustrated and ashamed. I wanted more time with him, as a companion, a friend, not just a fly-by lover.

I needed, even longed to find friends. With or without Bill, I resolved to make efforts to be more sociable. Although meeting people made me uncomfortable, social events also added balance to my life. I still had a deep need to feel included, part of a group. I began attending community gatherings at the grange in "downtown" Big Sur village. I joined the Big Sur square dance group, sewing bright colored dresses with full skirts and sashes. Work at the café also offered chances to meet new people, like Dave.

Dave came into the café one afternoon and ordered coffee. When I returned with the mug, I found him sitting at his table holding a large chart with symbols in front of his handsome face. Curious, I asked him what he was doing. "Eye exercises," he said. He raised his head, focused on me, then started twirling his eyes around in his head. That struck me as outrageously funny, and I laughed 'til my sides hurt. He joined in until all the people in the café looked at us, smiling or laughing too.

"Hello," he said with a chuckle, "I'm Dave Korshell." Soon we were talking about Big Sur and its beauties. After that amusing encounter, I saw Dave frequently at the café. Like me, he came from Southern California. Unlike me, he had no fixed abode and was camping in the state park. From time to time, he invited me to meals and to go along on hikes. We did one memorable hike along the Big Sur River. Going back to my car, Dave stopped to stare at Bixby Bridge, the picturesque 260-foot-span that led Highway One along the coast and over the river. He told me, "I am going to walk across the bridge, on the railing."

"Don't!" I cried out. I remembered his eye exercises, immediately worried about his sense of balance. The slim raised edge of the bridge—less than a foot wide—prevented cars but not people from falling off. I implored him not to do such a foolish thing, but he hopped up to the railing.

I peeked through my fingers as he walked along in the wind and whoosh of the passing cars, absolutely terrified he'd fall. What would I do if he did? Dave calmly walked the entire length of the bridge. Tears filled my eyes as he jumped down to the road. I was both angry and relieved at his foolhardy showing off. Dave just laughed and twirled his eyes.

On another adventure, Dave and I hiked up Mount Manuel. We made camp on top at dusk. After putting my sleeping bag in the shelter of scrubby bushes, I washed my underwear and hung my dripping panties on a manzanita bush. Dave picked them up, put them on the end of a stick then waved them back and forth vigorously to dry faster. He stuck the stick upright, undies on top, by the fire. I must have looked perplexed as well as embarrassed, so he explained. "Hey, I'm just showing you a trick I learned from my mother. I come from a family not overly concerned about modesty."

Modesty. I didn't consider myself overly modest, yet here I was, flustered by Dave drying my panties. I pondered this fault line in my character: shyness and shame about my body and sex. I felt this not only with Dave but with Bill and every other man I'd known well. The Underpants Incident made me aware I was a long way from integrating sex into a relationship. Could I keep Dave as a male friend without sexual insinuations? I could hear Nathan laughing at me.

Meeting people, mostly strangers, let me surf the waves of Big Sur in those tricky 1960s currents. I tried my best to be sociable at the café, parties, the hot springs, barbeques, dances, and gallery openings. I made few connections that way, but one encounter did lead to a special friendship. At a celebratory party thrown by one of Big Sur's sculptors, I went alone. Keeping to the edge of the group, I tried to be my unobtrusive observer self. A young pig was being slaughtered for the feast and I moved away. When it began to scream like a human in agony, I shrank back, slid sideways down a gravel slope, and bumped into a man.

"Steady on, girl!" said he, putting his arms out to hold me up. He led me away, saying in crisp English, "I know how you feel." Turning to look at him I saw a leprechaun with a receding hairline, full cheeks, and kindly smile. I felt genuine gratitude for his empathy. "Pig shrieks tear at your soul," he murmured.

My supporter introduced himself with a little bow and a self-mocking smile. "Eric Barker, at your service."

"Thank you," I said. "I'm Jeannette Hanby, and very glad to meet you." Thus began our lively and sporadic association.

Eric was an elderly poet and the caretaker for a house in Coastlands. This was a more densely populated part of Big Sur on the coastal side of Highway One. British by birth, Eric retained his accent even after decades of living in the USA. He twinkled when he talked about life in Big Sur. Eric became a valuable feature of my social world. I'd go to readings of his poems; he gave me copies of his poetry books. I'd drop by to see him at his cabin in Coastlands, where he made me traditional English cups of tea. And so, Eric also became a friend.

Eric Barker

My most earnest efforts to attach myself to a friendly spirit balloon were with Claire. She stayed in a cottage on the ranch while overseeing the building of her house. When I arrived there, she'd give me juice to drink or a variety of teas. We chatted, then usually walked over to the site where her home, studio, and showpiece took form. I enjoyed watching it grow. The house's skeleton was composed of enormous redwood beams settled onto several levels of the hillside. Then came the roof and sides. Each stage in the construction was fascinating.

Claire intrigued me on other levels. Her father had done exceptionally well managing Lockheed Corporation, building airplanes during the war years and afterward. The family was extremely wealthy. Claire's parents owned land in Monterey and had recently bought Rancho Rico, about 500 acres of priceless Big Sur coastal property. Despite their wealth, every Chappellet I met was approachable, never grandiose or lordly.

Claire gave me tangible things, like *Roan Stallion*, by Robinson Jeffers, and a book on coastal plants. She gave me new experiences, too, such as showing me striking photographs of Big Sur, family recipes, her paintings, or an article on sea otters. My mind continued to stretch. Claire not only provided me with insights and beauty, she also modeled a grace I found myself trying to emulate. I also began to imitate her clothing style by sewing loose-fitting dresses decorated with a colorful band of embroidered braid or edging.

As we walked along the ridges or roads, we shared world views. Claire asked me what I wanted to do with my life. I mumbled something like, "Travel, see the world, learn more about nature and people." My words sounded mundane and vague. I had no idea yet what I would do with my one, short, precious life.

"You know, Jeannette, I don't really need to travel. I've got such a large family and lots of friends. And I love it here in Big Sur. In my new house, I'll have space to decorate and paint." She sighed, paused, and turned to me with a serious look. "But what I want most of all is a secure family, with children." While the idea of being tied to a place and family didn't appeal to me, I was glad people like Claire could—and probably would—produce a worthwhile next generation.

Because of friendships with Claire, Dave, Eric, and a few others, I began to feel more stable. My introverted-extrovert parts tottered back and forth as I worked to build relationships. And yes, it was work. I'd have to talk myself into what I thought of as intrusions on the lives of the people I liked.

I'd screw up my courage to see Claire at her house site and feel embarrassed or hurt if she was curt because she had to tend to some building arrangement. That, in turn, made me feel immature because I knew she was just busy, not angry with me. I'd avoid Dave when I saw him at the post office because I'd feel uncomfortable by having to say no to a hike or meal with him. I'd pass by Eric's cabin, telling myself he wouldn't want me to interrupt him. I found it hard to be the easy-going person I wanted to be. But I kept trying, smiling my smile full of teeth, with a dimple in my cheek.

My growing bond with Bill remained the biggest challenge in building friendships. I seemed to have opened some channel in his dammed-up heart. He poured his feelings into words and the words into letters. They alighted like cooing flocks of pigeons at a cote in the Big Sur post office. He wrote them from his mother's home in the Salinas Valley, from his father's hardware shop in King City, from wayside stops, coffee shops, gas stations, and the Feather River canyon.

The letters alighted like cooing flocks of pigeons...

> I FEEL AS THOUGH I WERE POISED ON THE BRINK OF AN INCREDIBLE ADVENTURE, AND WOULD LIKE SO VERY MUCH TO SHARE IT WITH YOU.

His letters usually started with an avalanche of words that I came to think of as Bill's "unbearable torrent of love." After the torrent came comments about his current jobs and the gold mining project on the "Fabulous Feather River." In every letter Bill implored me to come to visit him at the mining camp in the High Sierra Mountains of Northern California. "You must come, it's so special. You'll fall in love with the place!"

His descriptive letters about the project did give me an enticing overview. In one long letter he wrote: "I'm in a strategic spot, writing to you in a steep ravine. It's halfway between the roadhead on the ridge top and the river at the canyon's bottom."

I tried to imagine the setting: the roadhead and ridge, the ravine and river. I read on. "A mile of ¼-inch plastic tubing traverses the whole route. My mining partner Mike is on top of the ridge, ready to put gasoline through the pipe. I'm going to follow the fuel line down to the river and divert the gas into 55-gallon drums on the ledge above the Big Pool."

More questions and images flowed through my mind. Who was Mike? What were the drums on the ledge? What was the Big Pool? I read on.

"I feel as though I were poised on the brink of an incredible adventure and would like so very much to share it with you. Our lease is a square mile of land, bounded on all sides by national forest. The Middle Fork of the Feather River runs through it from north to south. The area is known as Bald Rock Canyon."

His description aroused my curiosity. I went outside to get a map of California from my car. I could easily locate the Middle Fork of the Feather River in the High Sierra Mountains. One section was labeled Bald Rock Canyon. I read on.

"To the east are granite cliffs rising to wooded ridges high above the canyon floor. To the west is a steep sidehill down which our trail drops to the river. To the south, about a mile downriver, is a side stream. It flows in from Feather Falls, a plume of water that drops hundreds of feet over a cliff."

I consulted my map. Feather Falls was where Bill described it to be. Those falls would be worth seeing, I thought.

"The view to the north is truly magnificent. Rising three thousand feet above the river, and completely dominating the canyon is Bald Rock Dome. It is a massive monolith of curved granite, not unlike El Capitan. The whole canyon rivals anything in Yosemite."

Bald Rock Dome, seen from the river

Having been to Yosemite, I doubted anywhere else in the Sierras could be so dramatic. The next part of Bill's letter described following the gas line downhill to a ledge above what he called the "Big Pool," where the empty fuel drums sat. Upriver was a grassy bench named Evans Bar with "roughly two acres of level space and our cabin."

Bill gave a bit of history. "In the 1860s, miners worked the flat with hand tools in the dirt and rocks. When underwater suction dredges came into widespread use, modern miners could finally look for placer gold on the bottom of the river."

He went on to explain that a group of men from Las Vegas and Lake Tahoe took a dredge into the canyon. "They started with the biggest and best equipment available. The outfit was too small for the job, but the assays of the gravel they recovered proved that treasure was there."

I could envision what happened next, namely dredging with disillusionment. If they'd gotten a lot of gold, Bill would have told me. His next paragraph described the disaster that followed the winter storms. "The roaring river gobbled up their equipment as well as their hopes." So, after two years of loss, the Vegas-Tahoe crew gave up. One enduring member of that team, a fellow named Mike, took over the lease. Mike tried to get Bill involved and easily snagged him.

Bill wrote, "I took out the ol' slide rule and worked on the math, then went to see the place." His reaction: "The fabulous Big Pool was alive and sinister, brooding and implacable, serene and smug; completely magnificent, an adversary worth challenging."

I mused on Bill's hyperbole and response to such challenges. He loved framing his "adversary" in dramatic words. And to meet the challenge Bill spent a year preparing what he called his "giant hydraulic killer—namely twelve tons of engines, pumps, pipes, tubes, hoses, sluices, jets, drums, and compressors. All that plus nets, ropes, cables, chains, hooks, bolts, winches, tanks, wires, pulleys, belts, and gallons of blood, sweat, and tears."

Bill's long list of bits and pieces going into a "killer machine" was hard to visualize. Even so, the team installed it in late July of 1963. Bill, and a buddy, Larry, took most of the gear down the trail into the canyon themselves. A helicopter lowered the engines to the sand bar by the pool. Finally, the men put the thing together. The team made one successful, short test, followed by a few days of working out the bugs.

Then came a night of heavy rain. "The next day, the river was reddish-brown, rising, and ominous. We used the crane I made on the cliff to hoist the equipment to the ledge out of reach of the river. But the guys didn't want to wait for the river to calm down. Mike left for the taverns in Oroville. Larry stayed another day to help me pick up tag ends then fled."

Of course, that left Bill alone, wanting to see the power of the raging river. He stayed over that winter and rebuilt the cabin. He also proudly claimed he'd tamed several wild ringtails, relatives of raccoons. And he managed to witness "the river rise to full snarl in a fantastic white fury that chewed everything it could to shreds." He bragged that the river never reached the array of hardware he'd mustered. I could easily imagine this knight in shining wetsuit waiting for me to applaud.

As autumn cleared the Big Sur air, traffic slowed, and tourists diminished, I grew restless. The lure of the canyon tugged me. Though I was busy and happy for the most part, I was curious, too. Bill's letters continued to perch in the post office. He told me that the team had no success again because, "We are too few and started too late." The crew was already packing up and leaving. Bill wanted to stay on again. "I need to clean up the place and do some jobs for the locals up top. Also, I want some time alone to enjoy my special friends, the graceful ringtails. You must meet them. You'll love them. And the canyon!"

I'd planned to go south to see my family in December. I also wanted to see Perky who'd recovered from the accident and appendicitis attack. But first, I decided, I'd go north to that fabulous Feather River Canyon. I was ready for another adventure. I wanted to see Bald Rock Dome, Evans Bar, the Big Pool and the ringtails. And William Hawley Hargis, too.

Bus traveling through fruit orchards

CHAPTER 9

Merrimac Stage
Late Autumn 1964

I'm going to grok a canyon, in a corner of a planet.
I'm going to be a stranger in a mountain land of granite.
I'm going to a wild church, to stand in awesome grace.
I'm going to the mountains and hope to find my place.

—Genetta, "Stranger in a canyon"

The bus skimmed through the autumn mist cloaking the highway that stretched through the Sacramento Valley. I raised my eyes from my book, *Stranger in a Strange Land*, to see flickering, fanning rows of fruit trees shivering into the distance. The word "grok" in the book came to mind as I tried take in, or grok, the scene. I just couldn't grok the groves, the farms, the trees, houses, or road. So, I dozed. I woke when the bus quivered to a stop in Marysville. The small town crouched just north of the joining of the Feather and Yuba Rivers.

I peered through the tinted windows into the haze of afternoon. Outside was typical bus station squalor: ugly used car lots, neon signs on squat decaying buildings, and a sulking post house. The sight disappointed me. Coming so far into California's historic gold rush country and being confronted with this decrepit scene was depressing.

Marysville had once been a jumping-off place for lusty miners seeking gold. Now here I was, a modern-day pioneer, leaping off the bus to meet the ghosts of those raucous men and their parasites: thieves, hurdy-gurdy girls, gamblers, pawnbrokers, shopkeepers, and preachers. Alas, these picturesque characters had vanished from the modern Marysville. I was toileted and back on board the beast of a bus within minutes, eager to leave Marysville behind and get onwards to Oroville.

We sat waiting for the bus driver. I watched as a scrawny woman with greasy, gray hair boarded with huffs and puffs. She shuffled down the narrow aisle, talking to herself as her parcels and bags banged into passengers. I stopped staring too late.

She met my eyes, plopped into the seat next to me and started stowing her stuff. Baskets and bags went above, below, and beside while she muttered half-audible comments on space and modern conveyances.

I helped as best I could and was rewarded with an unwelcome string of questions and comments. "Where ya coming from? Oh my, where is this Big Sur? Who was this Sir? A knight? Ha, ha. On the coast? Never been there. Never been anywhere much. Lived near here mos' ma life. Where ya headed?"

The bus motor started up. I was glad we were moving on.

"I'm going to Oroville," I said grimly, wanting to end the conversation.

"Oroville. So, you're goin' ta Oroville? Lived in Oroville for centuries, it seems."

"Oh?" I said with a degree of warmth equal to an icicle.

"Oroville, well, dam it!" she said, smiling and poking me with her elbow to make sure I got her little joke. In case I hadn't, she added, "I'll be damned, you're goin' ta see the dam!" She chuckled then droned on about how nice old Oroville used to be, a tight community, where everyone knew everyone. "Full of good folks back then. Now, this here dam is comin' along. Damn those people; they're building over everythin', tearing the whole place apart, bringing in all sortsa speculators and no-goods."

Barely listening to her tirade, I gazed out the windows at the rows of peach trees. I wondered how long it would be before California lost its famed fruit farms to strip malls and tract houses.

Enormous piles of stones alongside the highway seemed to mark our approach to the town of Oroville. My seat companion pointed to them. "Those rocks are left over from all them dredgers and gold seekers. Look, those machines are collecting them." I looked. Huge yellow monster machines were picking up jaws full of rocks and dumping them into the open cars of a train. "Them trains go up to the construction place and get dumped into the damn dam." She laughed again at her joke.

Helping her off with all her possessions meant we were the last to get off the bus. I bid Mrs. Dam goodbye, thinking she was an example of the "local color" that embellished Bill's life in the Sierras. I was sure to meet others.

I walked into the station, wondering how I'd find my next ride. The lady at the window told me, "The only easy way to Berry Creek is to get lift on the Merrimac Stage, the mailman's bus. Unfortunately, he usually leaves Oroville early afternoon. You might have to stay over in town."

I sat down to contemplate that depressing thought. I'd sent a telegram to Bill telling him I was finally on my way to see him and his mining site. He wasn't here to greet me, nor was the Merrimac Stage. Now what?

I went back to the window to ask for advice, but before I opened my mouth, she pointed behind me and said, "Well, I'll be! There's the stage now. What's it doing here so late?"

Relieved, I turned to see a thin man with white hair and a large reddish nose walking into the station. "Hello Miss. You're probably the gal Hargis told me so much about. I'm Andy Kala, your gallant escort into this low side of the High Sierras." He grinned and swept an imaginary hat off his head into a bow. I smiled with relief as the fear of the unknown night took off like a bat from my mind.

Gratefully, I followed Andy out to the van and boarded the Merrimac stage. Yes, I was literally on the next stage of my adventure and eager to go. The romantic Oroville mining town was long gone, and I wasn't interested in learning about the new, ugly, modern one. But Andy insisted on taking me on a tour. He handed me a brochure about the new Oroville. Bright pictures urged me to invest in all the services needed to cater to the hordes who'd be coming once the big dam was finished. Oroville was the future, invest now, the dam will bring 'em in.

The eponymous center of this prophecy was on Andy's itinerary, a tour of the Oroville Dam site. We leaned out over the railing to be dazzled by man's overpowering of nature. Gigantic machinery bumbled to and fro, collecting, and depositing rocks like super huge yellow and brown beetles copulating, then laying eggs.

The Aztecs and Egyptians, with all their monumental sacred rock piles, would have looked in awe or horror at the earthworks. This heap of earth was no inspiring temple to glorify the gods or a tomb for the dead. The massive construction was solely pragmatic. Each stone contributed to the edifice designed to confine the waters of all three branches of the mighty Feather River in a vast lake.

The immensity and noise of the operation made me feel out of focus, intimidated, and repulsed. I stepped back from the railing. Andy gently took my arm and

D-9 Quad bulldozer and bucket wheel excavator working on the dam site

pulled me towards the visitors' center. Inside, I was surround by pictures, maps, scale models, diagrams, and showcases. A slide show flickered on one wall with a rasping recorded voice spewing facts about the construction: "a mile wide, 770 feet high; using gravel from tailings where $80 million in gold was recovered in the early 1890s; the highest embankment dam in the world, to be completed in 1968, providing water for the ever-growing state of California."

I couldn't take in the amount of information. I didn't like dams. I understood why humans built them for irrigation and hydroelectric power, but they worried me. I'd become aware of their faults from reading Sierra Club books, at a time when the Sierra Club was fighting to protect the Colorado River from more dams. The Oroville Dam would impound the waters of the three Feather Rivers. Lots of trees, farms, and villages would drown. I wondered when the lake behind the dam would silt up or the dam itself split apart. I didn't trust dams. (I was right: In 2017, the spillway started to crack and decay. It took two years to restore the dam at huge cost.)

Back in the Merrimac stage, we left the dam site. Andy gave me factual snippets as we drove along. "This is the Star Route of Oroville-Quincy highway. It follows the old pioneer route leading from California's Central Valley into the mountains. It connects the post offices where I drop and collect mail."

We drove up what he called Kelly Ridge, contouring around slopes, in and out of ravines as we ascended. Andy's commentary continued. "This road was the main artery of travel back in the old days. All the miners, stagecoaches, merchants, settlers, and," he paused to say in a creepy, low voice, "bandits used it!"

He patted my arm to reassure me or make sure I was awake and listening. I blinked and murmured encouragement.

"Black Bart would rob the treasure from the old stagecoaches. Everything had to go slowly uphill from Oroville. Black Bart and his band would stop them almost anywhere, grab their booty and disappear into the thick brush, the forest, and canyons."

Robbers disappearing with their loot became almost visible as I watched the deepening gloom steal the color from meadows and hillsides. The canyons were already dark and forbidding. I shivered, a defenceless stranger in a new land, without skills or weapons.

We followed the old route through pastures and over ridges, passing the stage stops of Harts Mill, Canyon Creek, and Berry Creek. Andy leaned over his steering wheel and said, "Now we go up Joe Moore Hill. Once, I hit a snowstorm here. It kept me snowed out, and Hedy, my clever wife, snowed in. The snow lasted a few days. I always carry enough food, and of course, Hedy has all the supplies she needs right there at home with her goats, chickens, and all."

I opened a window for bracing air and to see the scenery better. The light was fading, the silhouettes of firs and pines poked up like a cut-out scene laid against the glowing skyline. The sweet resin-scented air flowed in with that crisp, cold tang of late autumn. I breathed deeply and shivered. We turned off the narrow, paved road onto a gravel track passing the ranch where Black Bart allegedly hid out. Our

CHAPTER 9: MERRIMAC STAGE

modern 100 horsepower steed pulled into a yard full of barking dogs, bleating goats, and a braying donkey.

Hedy appeared wearing braids, jeans, and a plaid shirt. She looked plump, warm, and friendly. Taking my hand, Hedy led me into her kitchen, cluttered with pails and bottles of goat's milk, sacks, jars, cans, cloths, and odds and ends. She took me into a confused but comfortable-looking living room with birdcages, dusty-looking pots of succulents, and drooping plants. Rugs of varying colors and designs brightened the scene. The hide of a huge black Angus bull dominated the floor space. My eyes took in the old dark furniture, the clear plastic dust covers used as curtains, the many knick-knacks, and, best of all, the big black wood-burning stove radiating welcome heat at me.

My brain had such a swallow of sights that it took a while before I could start to absorb sounds. I tried to tune in on what Hedy was saying in her Austrian-accented English. She practically sang, "Bill will be up tomorrow. He'll take you from here into the canyon. Tonight, you will stay upstairs in the guest room. And eat with us first, of course."

I was so relieved to be warm and safe after such a long journey that I almost went to sleep over the hearty dinner Hedy served. I did my best to stay awake through Andy's dissertation served along with a dessert of apple cobbler. Hedy cleared the table and Andy spread out maps. He pointed out places as he described them.

"Tomorrow you'll be going to Evans Bar. It's one of the many places around here named after people who lived there. Whoever the Evans brothers were is fading, along with the names of other places in the Sierra Nevada like Long's Bar, Bidwell Bar, Potter's Bar."

Through bleary eyes, I tried to locate the names on the map while listening to Andy's lecture. "There are a lot of deserted settlements and mining camps around these here parts. But their locations are almost as lost as their names. Bagdad was lost, but Ophir became Oroville. Other towns will get drowned, like Enterprise, originally called Mountain Spring. It'll go under when Lake Oroville gets goin.'"

"Well," I said, "I'd better get goin' too. I'm all tuckered out." Hedy laughed, chiding Andy for not noticing how I was fading. She ushered me to the bottom of the stairs and said, "You rest up now. Tomorrow will be here to fill up with more stories."

I gratefully retreated to my cozy room, paved with goatskins. A high spring cot piled with feather-filled comforters beckoned me. Slipping between the sheets, I tried to read Stranger in a Strange Land but soon put it aside. I opened my ears and tried to grok the strange new world around me. Somewhere close outside, chickens chuckled, geese honked, then the donkey brayed and farted. Profound silence followed. I fell asleep smiling. This world was full of surprises and it had a sense of humor, too.

Clucking hens, honking geese, and the braying donkey invaded my dawn dreams

CHAPTER 10

Bald Rock Canyon

Late Autumn 1964

Cloud continents surge over high pines,
Colliding above the ramparts,
Rising up in mighty mountain ranges,
Melting and melding,
Tearing and ripping.
Their snow blood flows cold
Drifting down over granite scarps
Anchored to the sacred land
Where I stand,
In awe.

—Genetta, "The Sierras"

Clucking hens, honking geese, and the braying donkey invaded my dawn dreams. Where was I? Ah yes, Hedy and Andy Kala's farm somewhere in the High Sierra Mountains of Northern California. I reached out to the chair beside the bed and pulled socks, sweater, jeans, and jacket under the covers. Struggling into all the clothes, I still shivered as I got up to put on my shoes.

The warmth of the kitchen was welcome. No one seemed around. I assumed Andy had already gone on his stage run. The cacophony of livestock outside was a vocal vote for Hedy's whereabouts and popularity. Hedy moved through a quacking, hissing gaggle of ducks and geese on her way to the chicken house. I greeted and followed her. She instructed me to look at her hens, "I like all their colors, especially the sheen on the bantams." Releasing the milling mob into the yard, she handed me a tin of grain to strew around.

Next was the goat barn. "And now, meet my most precious flock, the goats." Hedy grinned as she introduced each one, then settled on a stool. While Hedy was milking her favorite goat, Mandy, I heard Hargis' Volkswagen approaching. I hid in Mandy's stall as Hedy blithely went out to greet him. "Oh, so sorry Bill, Jeannette couldn't make it after all." I peeked through the boards to see the expression on his face; would it show disappointment, concern, or relief?

He saw me before I could decide because the hay dust tickled my nose and I sneezed. Putting his face up to the boards Bill said an amused voice, "Well then, who's this?"

I stepped out, smiling. We fell into an awkward embrace. Bill pulled me closer to him and held me tight. I smelled the wood smoke on his sweater and felt the bristle of his unshorn beard. He whispered, "I love you," into my ear before he released me. I stepped back and looked at him, feeling a rush of emotion, happy to see him, apprehensive about being loved by him.

We helped Hedy carry the milk to the house. While Bill and Hedy chatted, I went to gather up my things. Hedy forced delicious coffee, scrambled eggs, and toast on us. Grateful and promising to return, we were off with a bag of supplies, including fresh eggs and goats' milk. The missing rear window made it easy to find a place for my little bag among all the things crammed in the back. Bill's beloved Hesperus, that mashed, bashed Volkswagen, roared along the driveway, the hole in its muffler making it hard to talk.

The Hesperus trotted like one of Hedy's goats over the old logging roads. The load of gear clanked and bonged as we bounced over rocks and ditches. We scraped over a high hump between two deep ruts. Hargis wriggled Hesperus around till one wheel was on top of the hump, the other in a rut. I was pushed into the door with an "oomph!" of protest. Bill couldn't resist giving me a lesson in bush driving. As we tilted into or straddled the ruts, he said, "Any good driver on dirt roads should always put a wheel on the hump in the middle. If everyone did, the hump

"Always put a wheel on the hump in the middle…"

CHAPTER 10: BALD ROCK CANYON

would flatten, and cars wouldn't high crown." I duly took note, and I drive that way to this day.

Soon the road straightened out and the sky unrolled overhead. Bill stopped, wound down the window, and waved his arm at the curving sweeps of granite. "That's the top of Bald Rock's head. This spot is locally famous. The Maidu Indians lived here. They left their acorn and corn grinding holes in the rock. I'll show you on our way out, or next time you come." I did want to explore Bald Rock's head with Bill, but wasn't sure if I liked him assuming I'd return.

We drove on through stands of tall trees. Finally, we came to an eroded track leading off to a grove of what I knew were ponderosa pines. The shadows of the trees covered us as we came to rest on a carpet of pine needles. All around were the remains left by careless miners: a torn-apart car, rusty machine parts, piles of yellowed newspapers, cans, bottles, boxes, boards, barrels, and dirty socks. Bill unpacked his lanky frame from the car, stood, and stretched. I clambered out and scanned around. He saw me looking at all the debris and said wryly, "Miners aren't known for neatness."

Long-crested blue jays screeched at us as we hunted for mushrooms among the manzanita bushes. We didn't find any, and I was relieved that poison oak also seemed absent. Little nuisance flies darted at our eyes and ears, urging us to get going. We harnessed ourselves into packs and set off into the canyon along a well-worn trail. Bill kept ahead of me, muttering comments. I found it hard to hear him as the space between us increased. I called out, "Slow down please, I can't keep up with you. What are you saying?"

He turned and swept his arm from me to beyond, "This is our easy trail. It follows an old ditch the miners used to bring water down to the workings at the bottom of the canyon. They took some care to contour the ditch properly. It makes a good trail now."

I was glad to be on the easy trail. It gave me some time to take in my surroundings. A distant murmur of the river floated up with a cool breeze. The pine trees and chaparral plants exuded a tangy, fresh smell in the sunlight. I took a sniff of a nearby plant. Bill leaned down and fingered the leaves, saying, "This is a mountain type of ceanothus. Wild lilac. I showed you another scrubby kind in Big Sur. This one has nice flowers and smells good in the spring. Makes a tea, too, but not to my liking."

I tried to recollect the thick clumps of ceanothus in Big Sur. California's chaparral plants were a complex assortment. I wondered if I'd ever get them sorted out. Bill may have heard my thoughts because he said in his patronizing voice, "I'll teach you the plants, just pay attention." *Thank you very much*, I thought..

The granite dome of Bald Rock loomed over us as we switchbacked down the trail. Bill slowed down long enough for me to catch up at a turn in the trail. He pointed, saying, "Good view of the old balding fellow. Note his Mohawk haircut of trees." I could barely see the top of the dome but was glad to stop and admire the scene. We lingered, adjusted our loads, and set off again.

Walking into the canyon

Bill got bored with the easy switchbacks; he wanted to give me yet another test, or maybe just wanted to show off. Without a word, he headed off from the middle of a contour straight down into the canyon. He went loping downhill with ease and speed, sliding on his heels. I followed dutifully and carefully. Bill only paused once to turn and call out, "This is the skid trail. We bring most of the gear down this way."

The trail was well named. Unless I kept my footing, I ended up skidding, sliding, and stumbling down the steep hillside. To keep my balance, I needed to jump and run sideways, almost dance downwards, as fast as possible. I had to trust my body to move clairvoyantly around obstacles.

The fall clutter of slick black oak leaves covered the trail. If those slippery carpets didn't cause a hasty sit down, the treachery beneath would. Rocks, roots, crumbling granite, and holes could cause a headfirst plunge. If the underfoot treachery didn't get you, the low and cleverly placed branches would. Being overly careful meant near paralysis, so I ran and slip-slid down.

With a final slide on my bottom over the pine needles and oak leaves, we left the terrifying skid trail. I caught my breath as I stumbled to a stop behind Bill. He turned to look at me, noting my trembling body and sweaty face. He chuckled in his amused, irritating way and beckoned me on. I reckoned I'd passed his test and gratefully followed as we resumed the last gentle switchbacks of the easy trail.

My wobbly legs grew more stable and the blood on my scratches dried as we telescoped down towards the vaguely glimpsed camp at the bottom. The roar of the river steadily increased, rich and vibrant, with moans and melodies. Bill stopped

CHAPTER 10: BALD ROCK CANYON

in the middle of the second switchback above the shelf of ground. I looked at the flat as he waved his long arm at the scene. Huge ponderosa and sugar pine trees dwarfed the small wooden cabin bordered by a garden plot. An old-fashioned outhouse lurked behind some oak and manzanita trees further away.

My gaze roamed to the cliffs opposite. A massive wall of granite rose up, "about twice the height of Bridal Veil Falls in Yosemite," Bill told me. The sheer, smooth rock ended in a jagged edge at the blue autumn sky. A few trees clung to this backdrop. In contrast to the immense rugged canyon, the little open space at the bottom looked benign and welcoming.

Coming out of the trees and onto the flat, I followed Bill to a rough, wooden table under a white-barked buckeye tree. He took off his pack, then helped me get mine off, and carried the packs into the nearby cabin. It looked humble and old from the outside, but inside, it was remarkably airy and light. I looked up and noted that most of the light in the cabin came through a Plexiglas sheet. Bill noticed my gaze and said, "Yes, I added the skylight and repaired the roof each season. Built the lean-to as well."

He'd papered the inner walls with cardboard and re-shingled the outside of the cabin, too. Bill was obviously proud of his improvements. He pointed to the stone-built fireplace, mortarless, but upright and intact. "That was built maybe a hundred years ago. I've done a few fix-ups. Still works, most of the time."

"Is the cabin old?" I asked.

The cabin, with Bald Rock Dome beyond

"Some bits might be, but most of it's been rebuilt over the years."

While the main light came through the skylight, the open door helped illuminate the place as well. As my eyes adapted, I focused on a well-ordered array of boxes and dishes stacked along a wooden shelf. Pots and pans hung from hooks and various sacks and bins were assembled on top of chunks of wood. A mattress wrapped in plastic hung suspended from the ceiling. Preparations against floods and rodents, I guessed.

"I always check our supplies when I come," Bill told me as he took down the mattress and started to paw through the metal trunks and boxes. "Mike and the boys are pretty good about keeping our stores in order, but we get incompetent idiots who come down without their own supplies and make a mess of ours. And we get tourists who steal, burn, damage, and deface stuff."

While he rummaged and grumbled around inside the cabin, I went outside. The lone camp table with two benches stood companionably under the buckeye. The naked little tree had already lost all leaves, but its deep amber "horse chestnuts" hung suggestively from the branches. Further away from the trees, some rocks were arranged in a circle, either a campfire spot or the place to cook, or both.

Buckeye nuts and leaf

CHAPTER 10: BALD ROCK CANYON

To the side of the campfire spot, two long shelves sagged between wooden blocks. Scattered over the rough boards were the remains of a summer's half-hearted attempt to keep a clean camp. Plates, pots, pans, cutlery, and a big black kettle huddled together as though afraid of parting company. A variety of cups dangled from nails on the edges of the boards.

An ancient, square icebox stood nearby. I opened it and sniffed the inside. It was clean and dry, crammed full with bags of flour, oatmeal, rice, and spaghetti noodles. Near the icebox was a wooden-framed, three-tiered contraption covered with hessian sacking. Its short metal feet stood on a huge metal tray. I opened the door, wondering what it was for.

Bill came out of the cabin. He stood watching me, hands on hips, that amused smile on his face. He offered the answer to my puzzle, saying, "That's the cool box. We put fresh vegetables and fruits in there. The hessian soaks up the water poured in the tray and the wind's evaporative power keeps the stuff cool." I thought that such a simple solution to cooling food in the wilds was brilliant and said so.

He smiled at my praise and said, "Let me show you my pride and joy." He led me behind the cabin to a small gulley, with a rusty contraption tucked into the crevice. Smiling, he looked at me and said with head held high and a sweeping bow, "Meet my smoke house."

A small door into a rusty cast iron stove was the firebox. Out the back went a pipe that led under a canvas sheet or tent. I could see that the tube directed smoke into the tent where screens were tiered inside. Bill commented, "It doesn't look like much, but it sure does make salmon melt in your mouth. I use it to smoke deer meat too. Even use some of Hedy's goat meat when she needs to thin her herd."

I turned to Bill and took a good look at him. He could cook, as well as a having many other skills. He cocked an eyebrow at my stare then took me in his arms, giving me another hard hug that squeezed the air out of my lungs. I caught my breath, squirmed away, and said, "Show me more." He gave me a tour of the garden. Ruffles of lettuce, purple eggplants, and dark green chard outlined wilting zucchini clumps and tomatoes trained up on sticks like leafy tepees. The weather had been benign, no hard freezes yet. He started a fire in the pit, waved a hand at the bench, and said, "Sit there while I make coffee."

I sat, listening to the roar of the river and the bang of the grate being settled over the flames. Then came the clank of the old percolator style coffee pot. I realized that almost every time Bill and I had shared a meal, he'd had to have coffee, too. While waiting to go through the coffee drinking ritual, I made use of preparation time to ask questions. "Tell me something about the history of this place. I know you've written to me about it, but I'd like to hear more."

"OK," he said, "brief history lesson. Obviously, the Indians were here first. They lived hereabouts for hundreds of generations. The remnants are the Maidu. They still live up top, around Brush Creek. They've left their grinding stones and other clues, too. We've found arrowheads in the middle of the flat."

He paused and gestured towards the distant granite face saying, "The Maidu have legends about that dome; they call it *U-I-No*." I repeated his words in my head as "You-I-know." I was puzzled by the name. Bill saw my bemused expression and drew the word U-I-No in the dust. I nodded. He continued.

"U-I-No is the guardian of the canyon. People aren't comfortable here. I've heard local Indians tell tales of red men, as well as white, who ventured into this canyon and never returned. Some people think that Ishi lived here while he was hiding out after his family and most or all of the Yahi tribe was wiped out."

I said, "I've read that after many years living alone, Ishi was picked up in Oroville, trying to steal meat. That puts him in the North Fork area. We're in the Middle Fork. Do you really think that Ishi lived here, or even saw this canyon in his lifetime?"

Bill cocked his head. "Ishi was 50 or more when he came out of the mountains. He may well have come through Bald Rock canyon. He could hunt and trap and keep out of sight. This canyon is a great place to hide."

The story of Ishi fascinated me. I'd learned about him at Berkeley and read the book *Ishi in Two Worlds*. In 1911, the lone Indian was found starving outside Oroville. He was rescued from jail by anthropologist Alfred Kroeber, who then kept Ishi as a friend and living relic in the museum in San Francisco. Ishi died there. He

Ishi

became a symbol of the wrong done to indigenous Americans, reminding us how they were persecuted and killed off. His story made me deeply ashamed and sad.

Bill poured coffee. I sat mute at the table, thinking. How did that lone man survive? Hordes of vigilantes, miners, military, and police hunted down the natives, drove them off their land, enslaved, and killed them. The day seemed more somber, the flat lost and lonely, as I thought over what my white tribe had done to the indigenous peoples.

I gratefully took the warm coffee cup from Bill. He sat down opposite me at the table and loaded his coffee with sugar. "Do continue your history of this place," I said, wanting to lure Bill back into a less disturbing conversation.

He sighed. "Well, after the natives, the second set of residents were the miners. They came during the gold rush. We've found their debris as we dug the garden. Things like square nails and hand-made turnbuckles, bits of rubber and old shovels. I even found a broken china pipe bowl, beautifully painted. I gave it to my mother, but I don't think she appreciated it. The history of western USA never has interested her as much as the eastern."

Hargis paused, drank his coffee, and hurried through the rest of his history lesson. He told me about the Chinese who came with and after the '49ers. By the end of the 1800s there wasn't much left and the flat was an eroded mess. Then came the Great Depression during the early 1900s. A mix of miners and local Indians came back. "They reworked the whole place, sifting through all the old piles of gravel, looking for the tiniest pieces of gold."

Bill's cadenced voice slowed as he said, "Then, Cousteau developed the aqualung in the 1940s. Underwater dredging came along. And so, here we are."

He got up from the table, signaling the end of his short history of Evans Bar. He took out a cigarette and lit it. Yuck. That was my cue. I stood up and headed towards the river's roar.

Big Pool in flood

CHAPTER 11

Ringtails
Late Autumn 1964

Quick, fur-footed, and furtive.
Quiet, nimble, and neat,
Comes a big-eyed, fuzzy-eared ringtail,
Fierce predator, looking for meat.
I hold out a morsel to tempt it,
It stares but a second and leaves,
The big-eyed, fuzzy-eared ringtail
Smells of musk and slides under the eaves.

—Genetta, "Ringtails"

"I just have to go see the river," I told Bill as I walked away, not sure where to find a trail. My feet found the rocky path. Soon I stood at the edge of rapids watching the thrilling sight of water boiling over boulders, dashing at rocks in feathery sprays of water. I had an urge to jump into the nearest pool. Bill came up behind me and said, "Don't try it, it's cold, really cold." I stuck my hands in the water and splashed my face. It felt good but stung like melted ice.

I stood and turned to look upstream. The sight stunned me. U-I-No's shining face loomed above the river like an outsized sculpture of a god frozen into stone. The dome dwarfed cliffs, boulders, stately trees, and humble cabin. I stared. Bill chuckled. I looked at him. Was he amused at my childlike awe? He attempted a joke: "Yep, you're face to face with Mr. Bald Rock Dome. He's the dome–inant feature of this canyon." I groaned at the pun.

Bill's comment didn't diminish my sense of wonder. The dome and cliffs created a backdrop that made the whole place seem unreal, too dramatic for us tiny humans. Hargis attempted irony next. He lifted his bushy eyebrows, saying, "Pretty, ain't it?" His tone told me he loved this place so much it hurt. I mumbled a quiet "Yes." Pretty indeed, an inadequate word, a word like a butterfly on the face of the moon. The canyon was much more than pretty.

I now understood that Bill's effort to build dredging equipment wasn't simply to win a fight with the river. A chance at getting gold, yes, also a chance to show off his skills, too, but mostly because the venture engaged his whole being. Bill was fitting his odd lifestyle to a landscape he loved

Looking at U-I-No's granite countenance, I felt a premonition that Bald Rock Canyon would defy all the treasure seekers in the long run. The canyon's grandeur put our puny pecuniary ventures in perspective. I looked at Bill, filled with appreciation at being in such a wondrous place, with such an amazing man.

Bill gave me another curious look as I stood staring at him. He turned me around and pointed to the trail ahead. "Here is where the trail forks. To the right the trail goes up the cliffs. See the hoist up there?" I looked and saw a wooden device with pulleys, and a crane with two 55-gallon drums dangling from it.

"Now look down the left trail," he commanded. I looked and saw the trail continuing downwards through piles of pumpkin-sized rocks. It disappeared under the foaming water. The old song rose into my head and out of my mouth:

"In a cavern, in a canyon, excavating for a mine, lived a miner, forty-niner, and his daughter Clementine."

I pictured a miner like Hargis trying to rescue his daughter from the foaming brine. I could imagine the girl thrashing about, Bill watching to see if she could pull herself out unaided. I mentally helped her out in my mind as I finished singing the song, then laughed.

Bill gave me a puzzled frown and beckoned me on. We crossed through boulders to a pool where the water ceased its roiling plunge to lap quietly at a curve of sandy beach. I gazed out at the expanse of jade green water. Obviously, this was what he called the Big Pool. The placid basin was framed by sparkling white cliffs splashed with golden light by the midday sun. I took a deep breath, taking in the cold mountain air and striking scene.

So, this was the place where so many men had lost time, effort, money, and equipment. I could see why the miners were so determined. The rushing water from the upstream rapids would bring gold-laden sand and deposit it behind the cliff at the pool's head.

Hargis pointed to the cliff and said, "We know that gold is down there. U.S. Treasury records reported three million dollars' worth of gold taken from Evans Bar alone. We think there is probably even more in the pool."

So far, none of the dredging crews had been able to get much gold out of the Big Pool. The most recent crew had included Bill, Mike, and Larry. As far as I could tell, Mike brought Bill into the operation in the hopes of using Bill's creative and technical genius. Bill got sucked in like one of the rocks sucked up by his ingenious dredge. Now, it was my turn to get pulled in. Maybe.

As Bill had told me in his letters, they'd started too late that season. When the weather turned cold, the crew had called it quits. They'd hoisted the two VW engines that drove the dredge up to the cliff tops. Then Mike and Larry hurried away, leaving the final clearing and storing of equipment to Bill. Knowing Hargis, the outdoorsman, I reckoned he hadn't minded much when his partners departed. He loved having the place to himself.

Dinner was smoked salmon on a bed of spinach, potatoes fried with onions, mixed garden vegetables, and the crunchy apples Hedy had given me. Bill bounced around cooking, serving, and cleaning up. He let me chop the onions and did all the rest himself. Flooded with curiosity about the place, I floated questions about the project and the canyon's wildlife. "Is the venison from a local deer?" I asked, trying to keep judgment from my voice.

That question brought a pause in Bill's activity. He turned to look at me, frowning. "Yes, but don't think we go killing just any deer that comes through. We only shoot the ones that are raiding the garden or are wounded. And we take very few."

He lifted his chin, saying with pride, "Of course, we use all the meat. We smoke, freeze, or dry it. And you saw the hides tacked up on the outside of the cabin wall." I hadn't noticed them. But I felt satisfied that each sacrificial deer had been thoroughly appreciated and used.

Deer hide on cabin wall

Bill's knowledge and respect for wild animals were epaulets on his character. That he was a crack shot and knew how to skin out and cut up a carcass didn't surprise me. But I wondered when he'd learned those skills. Maybe as a kid on his folks' ranch? Or in the Navy? As a World War II fighter pilot, Bill had to take off and land on aircraft carriers. Using guns in an airplane wasn't how I envisioned learning to shoot deer with a rifle. I knew that if I asked him about shooting, hunting, piloting, or the war years, our conversation would grind to a stop. He was in a good mood now. I didn't want to ruin it by turning his attention to the war and his past.

The weather was mild, so I told Bill I'd like to sleep outside. Secretly I also wanted to avoid a sexual encounter in the small cabin bed. My affection for him didn't include feeling aroused when he was near. I loved him as the wild, inventive, skilled man he was. Unsatisfactory sex would lessen rather than enhance my feelings for him. But Bill was not the man for a platonic relationship, and sex was ultimately going to be part of the deal if I stayed with him.

Without a word, Bill went out with frontier-style gallantry and cut pine boughs in the moonlight. He stacked and pulled them into a bed-shaped pile in a spot with an open view to the sky. When he finished the bough-bed I laid out my sleeping bag on top of the springy structure. Bill smiled and said, "Join me for a drink in the cabin. I'll sleep inside tonight. It's not that you aren't sexy and appealing, or this fragrant bed isn't inviting. It's that I have special friends coming to visit."

Caught off guard, I responded with, "Friends? Visitors at this time of day? In the dark?"

"You'll see," he said, with a devious look in his eye. I knew he was teasing me again. I also knew who his friends were. He called them ringtails or cacomistles, the creatures he'd extolled in his letters about the canyon.

His friends did come. As soon as we sat down in the cabin, a ringtail head appeared in the canvas gap. A fox-like face, with circles of white around huge eyes, peered cautiously into the dimly lit interior. Without a sound, the slender creature flowed inside and circled the perimeter of the walls. It avoided stepping on the rifles laid out on the spring bed and leaped to a shelf. So graceful!

The long, low-slung body was the color of a California late summer hillside, with black hairs sprinkled throughout the fur. Following the body like a banner was a fluffy black

Ringtail face

CHAPTER 11: RINGTAILS

Ringtail

and gray ringed tail. The animal wasn't the collage of fox-cat-coon I'd expected, just its unique self. I whispered with enthusiasm, "A ringtailed cat!"

"My friends are *not* cats," snarled Hargis, with exaggerated emphasis on *not*. He was being pompous on purpose; I got the point. In a softer voice, he told me, "They are ringtails or cacomistles. They're related to raccoons and definitely not cats." I tried imitating the word he'd said, "kack-o-missels," with a question in my voice. He laughed and corrected me, "It's a Nahuatl word, probably pronounced something like Thah-co-mixz-le."

I decided that I'd call the creatures ringtails, much easier to say. I leaned back in my chair and held still as I watched the ringtail glide around the cabin. Hargis' voice smiled as he said with warmth and admiration, "Our first visitor is Shatze. She's become really tame, the friendliest of the bunch. See, she'll come close to take this bit of bacon."

Shatze continued to explore the cabin, ignoring Bill's bacon. I had to smile at Bill's boast. The ringtail brushed past me and paused to look intently at the flap where she'd come in. Her ears were erect, and her body poised. She darted silently through the flap. We waited, but Shatze didn't return.

Bill started doling out more facts. "Going back to their names," he said, "the variety of names bestowed upon these dainty beasts shows how confused people are about them. Many unenlightened people call them ringtailed cats." He looked at me with such exaggerated disdain that I had to laugh. "I've also heard names like nocturnal cat, coon cat, civet cat, coon fox, band-tailed cat, cat squirrel, mountain cat. One of the most common names hereabouts is miner's cat, for obvious reasons."

I nodded, prompting more facts. "I like the scientific name best. It's *Bassariscus astutus.*" The word *Bassariscus* is from Greek meaning little fox, and *astutus* comes from Latin. It means astute, wily, clever, and attentive. So, Shatze is an example of a clever little fox. Sorta fits, doesn't it?"

Ringtail takes food

"Well…" I began, ready to agree when a smaller ringtail came in through the flap. It ducked under the shelves, darting behind the bags and barrels. Hargis kept his voice low, saying, "That one is Juniper, a youngster; she's shyer. Most of the cacomistles come in and check out the place first. I hope they're looking for mice. But I ruin their appetites by giving them goodies," he said as he laid out a small piece of bacon. "Keeps 'em around longer."

"A lot of old miners and trappers call a cacomistle a mobile mousetrap. They welcomed ringtails because they really do keep down the mice. But for me, I think of them as special friends. They are a joy to have during the long, lonely nights down here."

I could easily imagine Hargis sitting alone by the stone fireplace with a crackling fire waiting for his cacomistles to show. I'd already fallen in love with ringtails, so I was delighted when another one slipped into the cabin.

I asked, "Who is this one?"

Bill gave his low chuckle, watching the ringtail sniff my foot. "Well, since he seems to recognize a friend, why don't you give him a name?"

"Let's name him Ponder, as in Ponderosa," I said, "since we already have a Juniper." Ponder promptly disappeared as I sat up and stretched. I realized that all my energy had leaked away. The morning with Hedy and her flocks, a day trying to absorb the magnificent landscape, the antics of the ringtails, and the endless ping-pong of feelings about Bill left me overloaded. I needed to sleep. A hug and a "goodnight" and I staggered off.

CHAPTER 11: RINGTAILS

In the morning over coffee, Bill told me, "Today I want you to see more of the local scenery; it's some of the best, too."

"Better than here?" I asked, pointing to the dome of Bald Rock.

"We're goin' to hike to Feather Falls," he said pointing downstream.

We made a picnic lunch. At the head of the Big Pool, we launched the little raft, floating swiftly to the split rock at the end. Pulling the raft to the side, we started to boulder hop, definitely not my favorite travel mode. One must be very focused, carefully placing each foot and balancing while aiming for the next rock. All too easy to miss, trip, fall. Dippers and ducks fled before us as we walked, hopped, and jumped our way to the junction of Fall and Feather Rivers.

We stopped at an immense cliff where rapids plunged into a pool. To get closer to Feather Falls, we had to get around or through the pool, then tackle the huge boulders piled where Fall River joined the Feather. Our options were to act like monkeys and crawl up the cliff or leap like mountain goats over the boulders. The least appealing option was to swim like fish in the cold river water.

Long-legged Bill chose to leap. I tried monkey style, tiptoeing across some rocks, eyeing the rapids below. Pausing to watch Bill, I watched him jump onto a slippery rock. He fell but managed to get to the shallows where he waded through the chest-high water, clutching the pack above his head. I realized I wasn't going to be able to climb the moss-covered cliff base; I'd inevitably slip off. I looked at the river, jumped in, and swam. The cold water shocked me as the river's power pushed me down and around. I fought to swim to shore, frightened that the current would smash me into boulders.

American Dipper

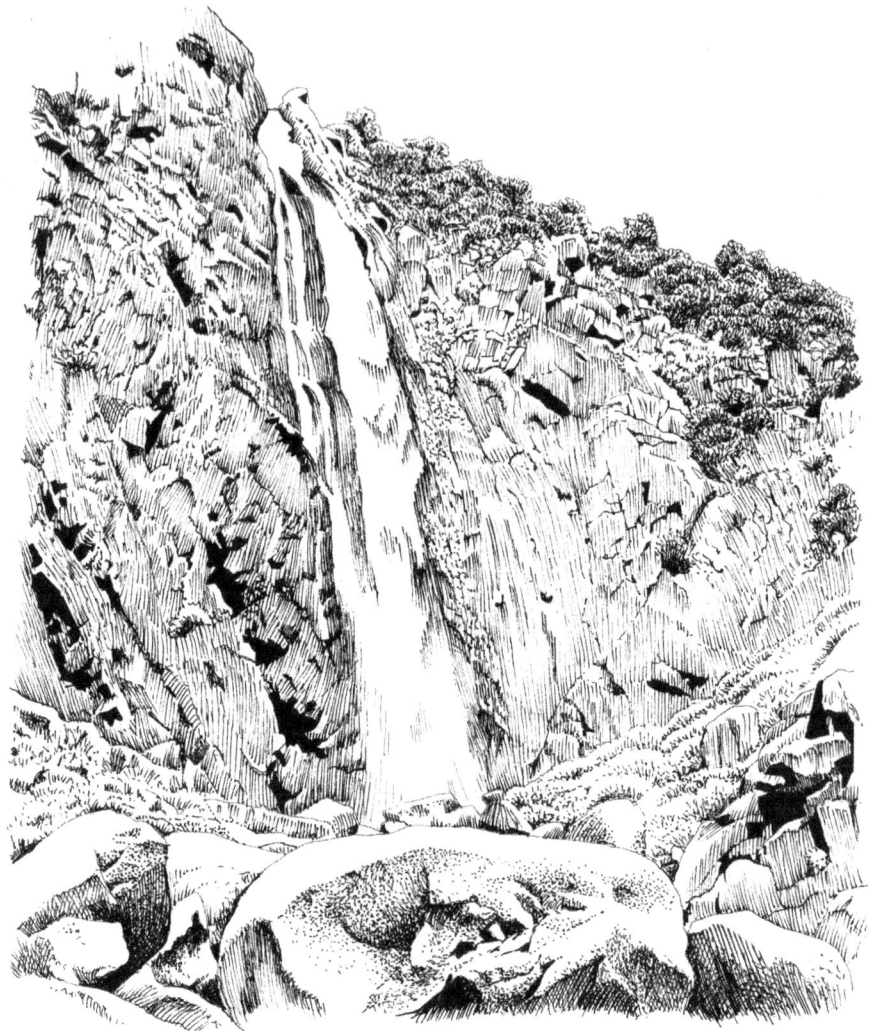
Feather Falls

Bill clambered over rocks, extended his hand, and pulled me out. I shivered in my wet clothes, but warmed up as we climbed in the sunlight, following a series of small waterfalls and rapids. We clambered up and up, finally coming around a bend to see Feather Falls above us. Standing at the bottom, we let the shower of rainbows surround us, breathing in the mist. I looked at Bill, drops of mist beading his salt and pepper hair. He looked back, beaming.

The pause made me realize I was hungry. It was already late afternoon. We retreated to a sandy flat backed by a ravine with a waterfall of vines. Munching on smoked venison, carrots from the garden, and the last of Hedy's apples, we felt renewed. Neither of us could face descending to the pool and rapids. We chose to climb a ravine opposite the falls.

Scrambling and slipping, we crawled up the crevices. Slowly we rose above the reverberations of Feather Falls. Near the top, we spooked two deer and entered a cluster of trees. I stopped suddenly, having noticed red flags following a contour on the slope. "Forestry Service," grumbled Bill. "Looks like they're going to put in a trail up here. Another unwelcome 'improvement' for John Q. Public."

Beyond the trees, we encountered thick manzanita brush and had to crawl under to get to a cliff that dropped into the river. Bill recognized some landmarks. He oriented himself like a bee heading for the hive, looked at me and slid downwards. I had no choice but to follow through leaves and stones to a ledge near the Big Pool. Over we went, finally reaching the little raft where we left it. We pulled ourselves to the beach at the head of the pool and trudged back to camp, exhausted.

A cacomistle came out of the cabin to greet us in the fading twilight. U-I-No glowed in the light of the rising moon. The smell of smoke and sap seeped into me as Bill built a fire. I was pleased with our adventure and realized Bill had been testing me again. Whether on purpose or inadvertently, Bill had been assessing my willingness to follow him. For months he'd been checking my endurance, courage, and adaptability. I'd accompanied him around Big Sur, found my way to the Feather River, and now, managed to get to Feather Falls and back without disaster or complaint.

Being tested made me feel good, noticed, included. I'd been seduced, not only by Bill, but the ringtails and the canyon's overlord, U-I-No. I sat at the buckeye table and sighed, weary and happy. A ringtail paused to look at me before disappearing into the cabin. I followed as the first drops of rain hit my head.

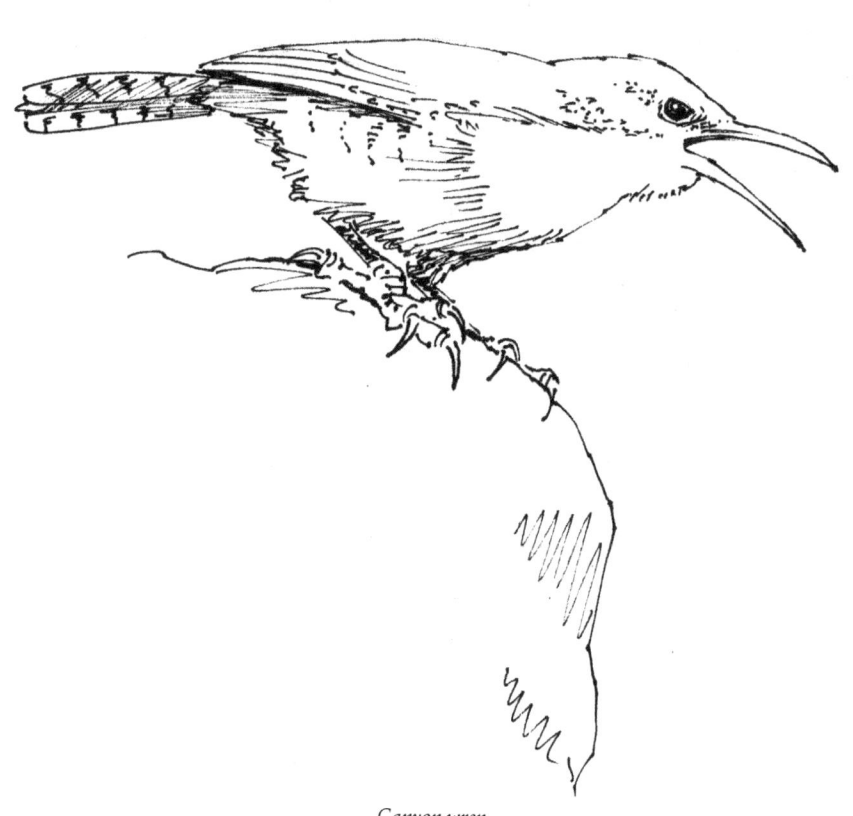

Canyon wren

CHAPTER 12

Big Pools and Old Miners

Late Autumn 1964

Water, water, here and there,
Carving canyons without care.
Water falls and rivers run,
Rainbows shimmer in the sun.
Ripple, glide, gurgle and giggle,
Pool and spray, surge and wriggle.
Thunder rumbles and clouds burst –
Water, water, quench my thirst.

—Genetta, "Water"

Rain leaked from clouds rolling over the canyon rim like soggy blankets. The patter of drops on the skylight lightly drummed a wet day tune as I awakened in the morning gloom. I'd slept poorly after clumsy lovemaking on the spring bed and woke groggily. Bill was making a fire in the cabin's fireplace. The crackle of wood and flickering flames cheered me. I stretched, relieved to find I was only mildly stiff from all the hiking and rock-hopping to and from Feather Falls the day before.

A bird trilled a long, bright, descending song. I smiled, recognizing it as a canyon wren, a perfect vocal symbol of the place. Good morning, I said to the bird, then aloud, to Bill. We nibbled stale bread and drank coffee while the wind pushed the rain blankets away and shook them out somewhere else. We emerged to find the earth soaked, the sky clear, the air cold. Bill and I went to the Big Pool and got on the transportation raft. We let the current sweep us out to the big raft. I clambered aboard, scanning around, trying to fathom how the whole operation worked. I decided to sketch it later.

From my view on the raft in the middle of the Big Pool, I could see that a lot more work needed doing. The set-up was partly taken apart, leaving a mess. Some 55-gallon drums floated at the far end of the pool; tools and pieces of equipment lay scattered about. The two VW engines had been lifted onto a cliff where they sat under tarps surrounded by various new and rusted spare parts. A couple of drums hung from the crane, waiting to be positioned and secured.

"And they've left me to get the tools off the bottom of the pool," grumbled Bill. I wondered why, as project boss, he couldn't he get his crew mates to help clear up. "And they left me to hoist the lift bag, too." Lift bag? What was that? I wondered. Hargis sounded only mildly annoyed as though they'd simply left their plates in the sink for him to wash up. He said, "We'll tackle all that after a better breakfast."

We? I guessed right away that if I joined this operation, I'd not be just a girl friend and team diver. I'd also be an organizer, picker-upper, washer-upper, meal-maker, a sort of super Girl Friday. Would I like or endure that role? Was I that interested? Yes, I was tempted, but not drawn to the role of underling.

After a quick brunch of oatmeal and smoked salmon, we went back to the Big Pool. I took along my paper and pencils. Sketching the dredge would keep me out of the way while Hargis tackled the clearing up. We boarded the small raft, drifted out, and tied up to the big raft. Bill started up the compressor and wriggled into his dive suit. He put the regulator to his mouth and jumped in. The long air hose followed him down, underneath the raft.

Bubbles and Bill came up. He handed me a dripping crowbar. Down he went again, bringing up a pulley and a wrench. Finally, he pulled up the lift bag. I clutched the top of the heavy rubbery thing while Bill's head appeared above water. "Hold onto it and climb on the transportation raft. I'm going to paddle us to shore."

Bill Hargis in wetsuit

CHAPTER 12: BIG POOLS AND OLD MINERS

Dredge operation

We stretched the bag out on the rocks. I admired it silently for several moments. A great deal of craft had gone into the design and making of the ingenious boulder displacer. The bag was shaped somewhat like a version of the balloon from "Around the World in 80 Days". It was made of neoprene with wire sewed into its seams. Those shroud lines met at the base of the balloon, to be fastened to boulders. I fingered the seams and was genuinely impressed at the workmanship. I could easily imagine how tough it had been to sew.

As Bill peeled off his dive suit, I commented that the bag was an amazing piece of work. I asked, "Did you buy this bag, or have it made?"

He shot me a look as if to say, *Silly girl, I expected more from you.* "I made it, of course!" he said, then added, "It can lift huge rocks that weigh tons."

Back on the small raft, Bill pulled us to a shelf under the rock cliff on the far side of the pool. He used the ropes strung across the water that served as towlines. I sat on the warm rock and tried to sketch while he answered questions and picked up tools and odd bits. I asked about the way it all worked.

He looked around at the setup and said, "Basically we have two engines that pump water through a tube that sucks in rocks, gravel, and the black sand. The sand holds gold. We reach it about 20 feet or more down. Gold is heavy so the sand with gold flakes drops down to the bottom of the tube. Sand plus gold gets brought back up and dumped into an open box with riffles. Riffles are like a long washboard; they trap the heavy elements, exposing the gold we want."

Bill sat down beside me. "You need to draw the primitive pans we use to swirl out the gold from the sand." He handed me a miner's pan, the same kind all gold miners use to this day. He told me, "We don't spend all day panning for gold, you know. Or dredging. Things go wrong; need fixing. There is fuel to fetch, supplies to get."

I mentally added all the camp chores to his list: wood to chop, the garden to tend, meals to cook, camp clean up, furniture to repair, and so on. I asked Bill if they took time to have fun. He snorted, saying, "Sure. We all like fishing. We even get to laugh at ourselves sometimes, like the day Mike, Larry, and I were coming through the rapids up ahead. We were pulling ourselves upstream when the water was high. The main rope broke. You can imagine what happened."

Indeed, I could, and almost put it in my sketch, all three men being thrown backward into the water. I laughed. Bill deigned to chuckle along with me. The sun hid again behind a veil of smeary clouds, and the air suddenly got much colder. I asked to call it a day. We pulled ourselves over to the sandy shore and headed back to camp.

Coming up the trail to the cabin, we were startled to see a man descending the last switchback onto the flat. He walked hunched forward with a pack on his back, looking at his feet, his face hidden in the shadow of his hat. He straightened up and raised his hand in greeting when Bill called hello.

Alonzo

CHAPTER 12: BIG POOLS AND OLD MINERS

Bill lengthened his stride to meet him with a loud, "Alonzo, good to see you!"

Alonzo's appearance was somewhat off-putting. He carried a .22 rifle and wore baggy overalls with a worn-out jacket and stained hat. Alonzo turned his craggy brown face and dark brown eyes to me as Bill introduced us. "Alonzo, meet Jeannette. Jeannette, this here Alonzo is one of our rare locals who really belong to this place."

Alonzo took my hand in his callused one. He nodded at Bill, saying, "Yes, I am part of the Maidu clan. But don't know why Bill thinks that makes us more entitled to be here."

Bill said, "Ah, come on, Alonzo, your people have lived around here for generations. I think of you as owning the place. I'm sad the railway people and politicians stole it away. Anyway, I feel it's our privilege to come to work here for a while. Glad you put up with us."

Alonzo didn't respond, but his eyes roamed the clearing. It took several requests to get him to take a cup of coffee and sit down on the bench. He put his gun and pack on the table, took off his hat, and scratched his head. We chatted a bit about the loggers ruining the forest up top, the lack of deer, and berries that should be around in autumn. He finally loosened up enough to talk of old times.

"I was all grown up when we were mining here at Evans Bar in 1918," he said. I reckoned that made Alonzo between 60 and 70 years old. He looked older.

"I mined here with my father and three brothers. We used an old Maxwell engine. Had to make a trail from the saddle up above. Then we hacked on down through the ravine between our ridge and the old Zink ridge trail. It was a fairly easy trail. We walked in every morning and out every evening."

"Didn't you stay in the cabin?" I asked.

"No, it was a ruin, just some old shingles and a rock pile where the fireplace is." He pointed at the cabin. "Bill here has done a good job; built it up again. Taken out a lot of trash. We didn't want to stay down here. Too dark. U-I-No, that head up there, just staring at us, daring us to take anything out of the canyon."

We all gazed up at the great Bald Rock, the granite top glowing in the burst of sun through the clouds. Alonzo continued. "Those were the Depression years. Money and jobs hard to get. We made a living even though the price of gold was low. Still is."

Both Bill and I nodded and frowned in agreement. We were always amazed and annoyed to think that the official government price was $35.35 for one ounce of gold. It was worth at least ten times that on the black market.

"Has your family always lived here?" I asked.

"I can't tell you much about my ancestors, but I think we've been around for a while. We still have gatherings and ceremonies at the burning grounds."

I wanted to ask him about the intriguing burning grounds but didn't want to interrupt him.

He continued, "Our customs have changed a lot these days. But we're still here. My father, Johnny Johnson, is about 100 years old. Always lived here. He knew the Evans brothers who mined the bar back at the turn of the century. The Evans brothers are the ones who built the first cabin up in the saddle; it's pretty much disappeared."

Alonzo pointed to the cabin nearby, saying, "They also built this one here on the flat. They get the credit for the fireplace. As a boy, I got the impression those Evans brothers were masons or stoneworkers, in addition to being miners."

He stared at the cabin, sipped his coffee, then said, "After the Evans left, us folks came during the Depression. After us, there came the Nottingham brothers. They made those cuts in the slopes above the flat to drain rainwater away, so it didn't wash away the overburden."

"Well, well," said Bill. "So those cuts aren't natural. I've always suspected they were dug deliberately. Even in the hottest part of summer, that cleft is damp and cool. We sometimes store carcasses or perishables in the shadows. I found a cache of bolts and nails, pulleys, and such in the rocks there. We've even used some of 'em in our operation."

Mrs. Nottingham

Alonzo nodded as though approving Bill's thrift. "Those Nottingham brothers did a lot of work down here. There's a trail going from the flat here up to their old dam and around the cliffs. It goes down to the river. They stretched a cable across the river to an old oak tree. Used it to ferry people and buckets of stuff back and forth. Built a cabin there, too."

He paused to drink the last of his coffee. "The men worked the bar and other places along the river. All the men died off, but ol' Mrs. Nottingham is still alive, up there at Brush Creek."

"Do you think she'd talk about old times with me?" I asked.

"Hmmm, she might. Have to ask her yerself."

I made a mental note to try to track down Mrs. Nottingham as I watched Alonzo scan around the flat again. Bill was starting to cook some venison steaks with potatoes. He invited Alonzo to join us. "No," he said. "Can't stay for supper. I just wanted to check on the place. See if anyone around. Maybe I can catch my supper on the way back up the hill."

He hoisted his backpack, slung his rifle over his shoulder, and disappeared up the first switch back. My thoughts trailed Alonzo. Luckily, unlike Ishi, Alonzo wasn't the last of his tribe, he was still a hunter and gatherer of the Maidu.

My last morning in the canyon was crisp and very cold. Bill made coffee and

CHAPTER 12: BIG POOLS AND OLD MINERS

omelets while I sat and inhaled the smell of food and wood smoke tinged with tangy pine sap. I worked on my sketch of how the operation might look: the serpent-like dredge gobbling rocks, gravel, and sand, the men panning for the gold that came through the riffles on the raft. I imagined the great granite overlord of the canyon watching with amusement or dismay while the engines roared over the trill of canyon wrens.

Yes, I'd fallen in love with the canyon. Even so, I was eager to get back to Big Sur. I reminded Bill we needed to leave soon. I had a bus to catch in Oroville. My Renault waited for me in Monterey; my job, and friends, in Big Sur.

Bill wiped the frying pan, sat down with his coffee cup, and put his hand on my arm. Looking at me with his head tilted sideways, he said firmly, "No worry, I'll drive you back to Monterey. It's only 300 miles or so. I need to tend to some chores at my mother's place and get some paying jobs. It's nonstop trying to earn enough to feed this project here on the Feather."

"But what about all the equipment, the garden, the fence, the cabin?" I asked. The amount of work still needing to be done worried me. Bill assured me he'd soon be back to do the rest. We rounded up some more pieces of this and that, dismantled and secured the undercurrent box, and carefully placed tools and small equipment in the rocks above the pool. The big raft and compressor stayed in the pool. Hargis would need more than my help to get them out of the water. He and I managed to pull the air reserve tanks and the lift bag up onto rocks.

Bill said, "We can leave them here; it's above the high-water mark." A born skeptic, I pursed my lips with doubt. *Not my project*, I told myself, but I worried, nevertheless.

In the late afternoon, we loaded up and started up the Easy Trail. As we plodded along the switchbacks, Bill kicked away stones, shored up gullies, and cleared some drainage ditches. I followed his lead, pushing rocks aside and placing stones and branches alongside the trail's outer edges. My mentor rewarded me with a gruff, "Good girl. If everyone helped, we'd have a really good trail. But guys like Mike tell me, 'Trails are a luxury, don't waste energy on 'em'. He's the one who started the Skid Trail, straight down that slope. Useful but ugly, and it erodes too. It's becoming a scar and soon it'll be a gully."

I sang "Clementine" while I trudged uphill, merrily kicking rocks away, glad to be an apprentice trail maker. As the roar of the river diminished, I felt I was emerging from a healthy, wild world into an unsettling modern one full of noise, roads, dams, and diversions.

I knew I would come back to the land of U-I-No. How could I resist returning to this canyon full of pools and waterfalls, ghosts of Indians and miners, cacomistles, and the glissading song of canyon wrens? I wanted and needed the challenges it offered. I looked at the old dome looming over the canyon and smiled. I felt its ancient brooding presence watching me, waiting to teach this young woman more lessons.

"They'd work all summer making things, then burn them in the fall."

CHAPTER 13

Transitions
Winter 1964 to Spring 1965

A seagull flew over us, its voice running with the light, its voice passing historically through songs of gentle color. We closed our eyes and the bird's shadow was in our ears.

—Richard Brautigan, *A Confederate General in Big Sur*

Before setting out on the long drive south from the Sierra Nevada Mountains to the coast, I persuaded Bill to help me find Mrs. Nottingham. I wanted more history of Evans Bar and the Maidu. We asked at the Brush Creek Store and were given directions to her cabin. She was nearly 90 but sharp and savvy, sitting on her porch in her nightgown. After introductions, she told me about the raccoon family under her house. She obviously found them more interesting than the two husbands she'd outlasted or the area where she'd lived all her life. Failing to extract local history, I tried to find out more about the local Indians. I asked her about their traditions, especially their burning grounds.

"Well, the Maidu, yes, that's the name of this tribe hereabouts." She pursed her lips and shook her head as though trying to see back through the mists of time. "I was a youngster. We went to the Indian burnings every fall. That's the place near Bald Rock. Drove over in a spring wagon with two horses, taking blankets and sleeping in the back. Indians have queer customs. They'd work all summer making things then burn them in the fall."

Leaning forward in her rocking chair, she scratched her back. We waited for her to continue. "Those Indians made song poles like flag poles, put on pants, shirts, blankets, stacked them up and set them on fire. They believed the ashes went to heaven. The old women would wail and cry. At some point, one of them would throw in a devil made of feathers. It looked like a scarecrow. She'd throw it in at dawn. When the dipper was overhead, they'd throw in the devil to burn, then wail and moan."

She shook her head at the memory and closed her eyes. We shook her hand in farewell. She sat her rocking back and forth in the sunlight as we left.

While we wended our way down the wiggly mountain roads, I tried to summarize what I'd learned about the history of the area and Evans Bar. First, the resident tribal natives, the ancestors of Ishi and Alonzo. Then the pioneer types, mostly from Europe, who pushed them out. In poured various homesteaders, hunters, explorers, and, of course, the miners. They dug, cut, destroyed, built cabins and trails, leaving their refuse and names behind. A lot of history would fade into the forests when people like Alonzo and Mrs. Nottingham faded, too.

The thought saddened me. Their stories, that once burned as brightly as the Maidu fires, were passed on to my generation as dying flames. They would cool to dull embers in our lifetimes. I was quiet for a long while driving from Oroville down California's central valley. Thoughts of the canyon and the people there, both the living and the dead, filled my mind. I didn't expect to die there, but had the certain feeling that I would be tested.

Bill broke into my musings with comments and questions, "Hedy and Andy were really nice to pack lunches for us. What do you think of that wonderful pair?"

Before I could answer, he followed with, "And Mrs. Nottingham, a pioneer relic still here. And Alonzo. An Indian still living on ancestral land. You have to agree that he is really special."

Without responding to my affirmation, Bill plunged on. "Too bad we didn't have time to stop and look for the acorn grinding holes on the dome's pockmarked

Ringtail - Bassariscus astutus

head. But our trip to Feather Falls, really an adventure, yes? The canyon itself, isn't it incredible? Don't forget our cacomistles, our precious ringtails. Really priceless!"

He continued to wax enthusiastic about the wildlife, the setting, and the lure of gold at the bottom of the Big Pool. Finally, he stopped talking. With a sideways glance at me, he asked, "How about joining the crew this coming year? You'd really be a great asset. You can garden, cook, dive, and organize. Really, think about it."

I allowed a pause before responding with a deliberately drawn-out word, "Re-al-ly?"

I paused, smiling, and looked at Bill. I hoped he realized I was teasing him about his overuse of the word "really." But he didn't respond to my effort to lighten things up. His many blandishments seemed pushy and swamped my enthusiasm. My adventurous side responded positively to the idea of the river challenge, but how much and what was I 'really' willing to do?

Bill took me to Monterey, where I'd left my Renault. It didn't start, so he towed me to a mechanic friend. While my car was being fixed, Bill and I went to eat at a diner. We talked about the river project. He seemed reluctant to let me go. When my car was ready, I was eager to head on down the coast. Bill was on his way to what he called the "home ranch," his mother's place. I expected to see it one day, but the thought of meeting his mother made me apprehensive.

I got into my toadstool car, dingy white with its red top spotted with seagull droppings. I thought of naming it Amanita in honor of the poisonous mushroom. The Renault had cost a lot to repair. At least it would get me back to Three Acres and my job.

Days later, Bill stopped by Big Sur briefly before returning to the Feather River. He told me he would be preparing the project for winter, as well as doing some jobs for the locals. From the Feather, he continued his Love Campaign. His letters flew into the Big Sur post office and roosted in piles. When I'd met him, I had no idea how much he liked to express himself by writing. The salutations on the letters continually changed, like bright gifts of a bower bird: Dearest Kleinchen, My Dear Peanut, Darling Mite, My Precious One, Dearest Flea, Squirt, Enigma, Baby, Termite, Runt, Silent One, My Personal Pandora.

Bill sent letter after letter. They followed me like hungry birds, pecking away at me, reminding me of his existence, his overwhelming love. On Thanksgiving he wrote, "I'm spending this evening with Hedy and Andy. She is plucking ducky bachelors and he is cleaning them for dinner. Both send you warm greetings. I'm taking some time to relax up here, been working hard and late, so super tired. Miss you madly."

Bill wrote a letter each time he went down to the flat, on his trips to Oroville, to Brush and Berry Creek. In one, he mentioned he shot a buck on the way up the hill. In the frenzy of loading the carcass in the Hesperus he left his pack with letters behind at the trailhead. It rained. He promised to send the water-soaked bundle to my folk's address in Covina where I planned to spend a few days.

The postman must have been intrigued by the pack of wrinkled letters he put in my parent's' mailbox. My mother and father were curious about the man who wrote so often. I was relieved they accepted my explanation that I'd gotten to know the mad letter writer in Big Sur. I added that Bill and I were thinking of doing a mining venture together with others on the Feather River.

When I got back from my short trip to Southern California, I found a new stack of mail that caught me up to date with Bill's doings. He wrote: "The River has risen. The engines and compressors are OK, but the raft was straining at the anchor line. I managed to climb aboard and pull the whole thing to the shore just as the raft broke up under the impact of the roiling froth. I've tied the wreck of the raft to the big rock and secured the drums that got loose."

I was relieved he'd rescued some things but wondered why he was still there in the cold canyon. He could be in Brush or Berry Creek with friends, at his mother's, or in Big Sur with me. Instead, he kept making repeated trips into the canyon, presumably to make improvements. He told me he'd hauled in some sinks and installed insulation panels. Every letter made sure to mention the ringtails.

"I'm here inside the cabin with Shatze on my lap. Ponder is peering out from the woodpile. Owls are hooting. I admit I'm feeling lonely. Tomorrow I'll go out to see the Morgenroths. You haven't met them yet. They are fairly well off and plan to develop the residential area around Brush Creek. I do some odd jobs for them. They let me stay in one of their A-frame cabins when I need to stay up top."

Besides making sure I appreciated all he was doing on the Feather River, Bill's letters always mentioned his other jobs. He seemed to be hired often to survey land, put in water systems, advise on building houses. I realized all his jobs earned him companionship and self-esteem in addition to a little cash. But I did wish he would come to Big Sur and spend time with me.

Bill phoned one day when I was waitressing in the Big Sur café. He said he was calling from Tex's store. I asked where it was. He said, "Berry Creek. Next time you come, you need to meet Tex. But now I'm coming south. I'll make a flying visit to Big Sur to see you. I miss you so much."

Our reunion was brief. We snuggled, made love, and talked about the canyon and ringtails. I tried to tempt him to stay so we could get more used to one another. I needed time with him to let me untangle some of my sexual hang-ups and build a friendship. But he was eager to be off and headed for his father's shop to do various jobs.

After Bill left, he took the long twisting back road from Big Sur over the mountains to California's interior valley and King City. He wrote about an event that gave me an insight into his character, as well as the wide-spread Big Sur coastal community.

"It was Tuesday when I left you about 10:30 at night and drove down the coast. I started over the Nacimiento Grade, that potholed road snaking from Highway One, over the Santa Lucia Mountains. On one of the steep turns, my headlights showed a fellow sitting in the middle of the road. He was shivering, with a look of utter despair on his face. He said he had cerebral palsy. I tried to decipher his mumblings while I put my jacket around him. He told me he was hitching, and someone had given him a ride. The driver left the main road, went up this winding side road, and pulled his hitchhiker out of the car. Then he stole all his stuff."

"I put the cold and dispirited fellow in the car, turned around, and went back down to Highway One. I drove on south to Lucia. Lu Harlan, an old friend, and herself a cripple, met me. She gave the man a key and put him in a guest room. The whole episode made me wonder about humankind's bad and good behavior while I drove alone over the mountains."

More letters came. He'd taken some bits of equipment to the canyon. He wrote that, despite the cold, he mostly went around nude midday. He was hoping to brown the fish-white legs and bottom I'd teased him about. He told me other things he was doing to please me, including trying to cut out cigarettes and his nightly habit of having wine before bed. Most of all, he wrote, he wished he could be with me in Big Sur, seeing people we knew. "How many familiar faces have you seen lately? I hope you're having fun."

Indeed, I was having fun. I enjoyed my routine of part-time work at the café, solitary walks, and some socializing. There were the friendly familiar faces of Claire, Eric, and others. I exercised my social self by joining various parties, poetry readings, square dances, and trips to the hot springs. To earn a bit more money, I took on small jobs such as cashier and stocker of shelves at the Big Sur grocery store. Altogether, those activities made me think I was having fun.

But in calmer moments, I pondered about Bill and the project on the Feather River. I knew I'd already made the decision to join the team in the coming summer. The situation was irresistible, and I was ready. I was uncomfortable about my role but realized Time's own wisdom would give me answers.

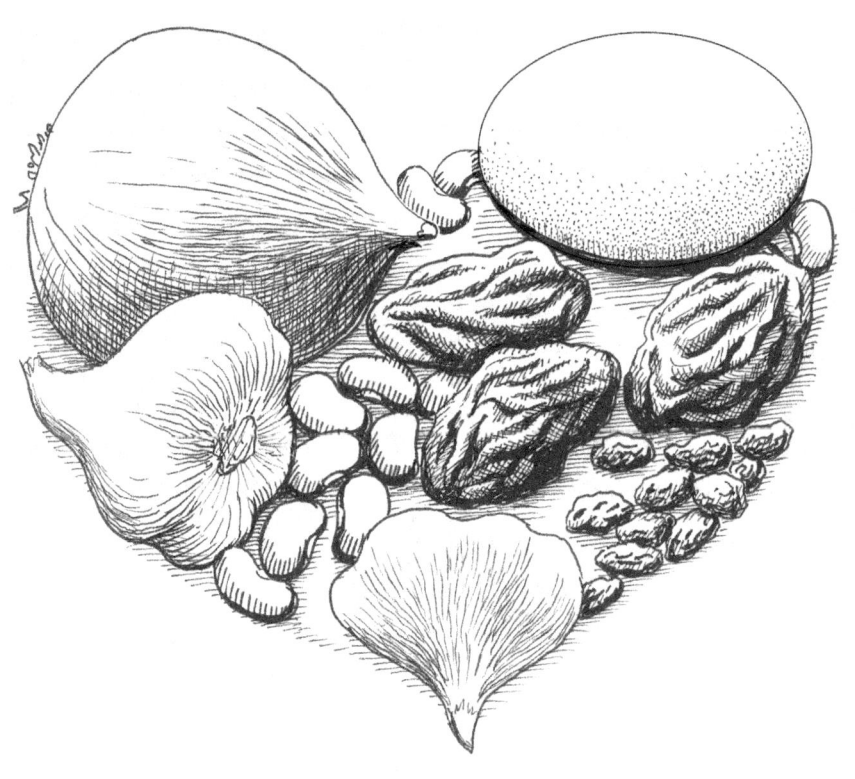

CHAPTER 14

Proposals

Winter 1965

Can you love me as much as I love you?
Can you share some years, more than a few?
I need you to light up my life.
I want you to make sense of my strife.
You are my crutch and my tether.
Can't we be happy together?

—Genetta, "Bill's lament"

Early in the new year an intriguing and worrying letter arrived from Bill. "I told my mother about the gal who came to the canyon. She asked me why we didn't come by her place on our way back. That was a surprise. My mother is a strong, competent, and proud woman. I was afraid that introducing you to her would be like putting you on the chopping block. But after talking to her, I think my apprehensions were unfounded. She seems genuinely eager to meet you. Lord knows it's been decades since I brought a woman home."

He went on to say that when meeting his mother, I should be prepared for her treatment of her only offspring. "She has a knack for reducing me to a jelly. One of her favorites is looking me in the eye and saying, 'William, straighten your eyebrows.' That usually makes me blink and shut up right away."

The thought of mother and son confronting each other that way made me smile, then cringe. How would she deal with me? I was soon to discover the answer. On a stint back in Salinas, Bill phoned me at the café. "Time to meet my mother. I'll pick you up in three days at your place." When he arrived, I was nervous, dressed in my newly sewn conservative dress with my best smile in my deep pocket.

On the coastal road and through Monterey into the Salinas Valley, Bill was oddly quiet. His hands gripped the steering wheel as he stared at the road. I tried to ease him up by getting him to tell me more about his early years. He glanced at me as if to determine I was sincere, then grimaced and spoke.

"I grew up as a single child with a doting mother. My father was away a lot. He owned several hardware stores; still owns the one in King City. We had the big spread in the Salinas Valley where I had lots of room to explore. In Pacific Grove we had a house next door to the Steinbeck family. I collected turtles for John Steinbeck. I was lucky to get to know a famous person and a genuine one. He even gave me the nickname 'Firefly' that he used in one of his novels. He told me I was one of those people who grasp at the moon."

Bill turned to glance at me again. I nodded, affirming that I understood he wasn't just name-dropping. He was making sure I knew what a deep impression Steinbeck made on him as a boy. He faced the road again saying, "Mostly, I was left to roam, maybe too freely. I was a real outlaw. I loved horrifying my parents and doing pranks."

One particularly memorable prank involved a friend. They captured a sack full of bats and released them into a movie theater. People fled while the boys watched in glee. Bill seemed proud of that caper, telling me: "We got caught as we tried to sneak out of the theater, laughing so hard we almost peed our pants. Reprimands and threats didn't stop me though. I really enjoyed putting creepy crawlies in desks and cupboards. People are so predictable, their fears of insects and amphibians so ridiculous."

Bill swiveled his head to see if I agreed. I nodded. "Another thing I really liked to do was ride on buses and trains, farting away people."

"Farting away people?" I asked, puzzled.

"Yep, I ate prunes, raisins, beans, boiled eggs, garlic, and onions in various combinations. They made a marvellously bad smell!" He chortled. I grimaced but had to laugh at the image of people holding their noses, gagging.

"Besides doing outrageous things you must have had to go to school. Did you have good teachers, a good experience?"

"No," came the short answer. "I was bored. The other kids were mostly stupid and silly, wasting time fooling around. Teachers and the blah blah of grown-ups were irritating. Lessons clogged my mind. I've mostly taught myself what I've needed to know."

I accepted that Bill was an independent learner. Obviously, he'd bullied his way through life acquiring many skills on his own. He was, to me, a storybook "Rugged Individualist." I admired those qualities. Even so, I wasn't sure Bill's personality would foster a good working relationship. And what about our more intimate involvement?

I put my hand on his knee and gave him a squeeze, indicating I wanted to hear more. He went on to tell me about mixing with people in society, upper-crust sorts. In a tight voice, as though admitting misdeeds, he said, "I did sports such as skiing at a time when few skied, polo when few knew what that was. I flew planes at eighteen, played golf and tennis, and went sailing at a private club."

CHAPTER 14: PROPOSALS

I was surprised he'd done all that; somehow it didn't fit the Bill Hargis I'd come to know. I asked him if he still did any of those things. He huffed, saying "They all seemed so superficial, snobbish. But at least it helped set my benchmarks for determining real values."

Bill gave me another look as he slowed the car. He seemed to be trying hard to make me understand him better. Yes, he'd been exposed to a fancy lifestyle, yet in his opinion, he had chosen a more admirable and challenging one.

"Go on," I said, "tell me why your mom and dad split up."

"My father fell in love with another woman. He moved out, got a divorce, and married her. My mom was deeply wounded. During the divorce, they sold the big house and some of the land. She's stayed on the ranch in the small house."

Bill drove into the gravel driveway towards that small house. He parked; I turned to look at him. He sat still, his weather-beaten visage with a lost look. I put my hands on his cheeks and turned his face to mine. I looked into his hazel eyes. With the sternest, most severe expression I could muster, I held his gaze. In a low, slow voice, I said, "William… straighten… your… eyebrows."

We both laughed 'til our sides hurt. We hugged, and I felt the tension leave his body. He was ready to take me to meet his mother.

Mildred Kellogg Hargis came to the door wearing a strand of pearls, a pale cream blouse and fawn-colored cashmere sweater that complemented her mid-calf-length tailored brown skirt. Nylon stockings covered her trim legs ending in shoes with low heels. She was the very image of a well-to-do, well-bred, respectable matron. I almost curtseyed as she took both my hands in hers, not shaking them, but pressing and patting them.

"I am so glad to meet you, Jeannette. William has told me about you, of course." She smiled then continued while directing her gaze at her son, "I'm glad William has a companion in his nefarious expeditions. I'm happy he has brought you to meet me at last."

I felt uncomfortable, not knowing how to behave correctly in her exalted company. She did her best to put me at ease, giving me tea, fruit, and cookies. Afterwards we walked around her small garden. She invited me to stay overnight and let Bill go on to King City to do some night work at his father's workshop. I noticed that whenever she mentioned her former husband, she called him William's father.

Staying overnight allowed me to get to know Mildred a little. She seemed somewhat withdrawn but gracious and kind. She took me to a small room with a bed so high I needed to bend over onto it and swing my legs on top. It had a silken Chinese coverlet I came to love. She showed me the volumes of history about her extended Kellogg family and alluded to her desire to have grandchildren. I wondered what she thought of Bill and me as a couple. And children? I hadn't worried about that yet, relying on the pills I took to prevent pregnancy.

Bill returned, relieved that his mother and I liked one another. He took me back home to Big Sur. We spent only a couple of days before he zoomed off again to do jobs that earned a pitiful amount of money. Being alone on Three Acres allowed me to have solitude interspersed with occasional visits from family or friends. They brought the outside world to me.

My college friend Nathan showed up again, fresh from a trip to Bali. His descriptions of the beaches and beautiful people captured my full attention. A gift he gave me of an original Balinese painting has charmed me for more than five decades.

Nathan's stoic face broke into an amused grin when he learned I was still living by myself. I caught him up with descriptions of the river project and my confused feelings about Bill.

"So why aren't you living together?" he asked me.

"Well," I said, trying to answer honestly. "Bill is always dashing about doing his many projects. Right now, I'm glad not to have a live-in lover. I'd rather have a more platonic relationship, a friend, like you or my hiking buddy Dave. But Bill isn't that type. With him I need to get deeper, more physical, and that scares me."

Nathan laughed heartily, saying, "Platonic male friends, ha! Scratch a male friend, and you'll find a potential lover. Get physical woman, you need a mate!"

Sea otter

I didn't want a mate. I loved the freedom to roam by myself. I could walk into the damp redwood canyons where the forest floor had a carpet of feather-like leaves. The trees looked poised to lift off into the sky and lifted my spirits, too. And those skies, full of sunlight, clouds, mist, fog, stars. I bathed in the glory of it all.

I also liked having time to spend with friends like Eric and Claire. Eric's gentlemanly manners made me feel ladylike. He was a chubby elf with a sweet smile and a soul full of kindness. As a caretaker for a house in Coastlands whose owner was seldom there, he could potter around the gardens, think poetic thoughts, or sit in his cabin by the wood stove and compose his lines. He always greeted me warmly, his English accent as crisp as a newly minted five-pound note. "Jeannette, how good to see you, please do come in. Tell me all about what you've been up to." Once, he shyly told me he'd been awarded the Shelley Memorial Award of the Poetry Society of America.

Even though old enough to be my grandfather, Eric seemed full of spirit, with a young heart. He and I went to parties together. He took me along sometimes when he gave readings of his poetry. We'd give each other lifts to the grocery store and post office in Big Sur. One day he invited me to see a film, a musical, in Monterey. I disliked going out at night as well as musicals so must have made a sour face.

"Don't worry," he said, "I'll drive. I know you don't like to drive at night. And I can promise the movie is exceptional." My role as a friend meant I had to keep Eric company. How could I refuse? I was rewarded with the surprise that the movie, "My Fair Lady," was delightful.

Claire and I grew closer, too. We bonded over our mutual love of all things marine. We were both concerned about the fate of the sea otters. The otters needed protection from fishermen, abalone divers, and people after their soft fur. Claire's devotion to conservation projects made me envy her links to powerful people in the area. She could actually do things to help, whereas I, the Curious Observer, was too transient and shy to get directly involved.

Claire

Claire gave me insights and interests. What did I have to offer her in return? At the least, I could listen when she revealed her private concerns and appreciate what she valued. For example, one lovely day, Claire took me along to see her parents at their luxurious house on the rocky coast at swanky Pebble Beach. Their home resembled a museum of modern art, full of paintings, sculptures, textiles. Even the "powder room" at the entryway had carefully chosen adornments and the softest towels I'd ever touched.

Looking out the open doors onto the terrace, I could see the ocean teasing the rocks with spray. The setting was so nearly perfect that anyone might think a sculptor and Japanese gardener had been at work. We walked down to the water across lawns and flowerbeds graced with sculptures and laced with shadows from the Monterey pine trees, carefully pruned like bonsai plants. I tried to imagine the demands on these people as well as the opportunities. I was grateful for Claire, my interpreter, my window into that world.

Claire shared another valued experience. This one gave me a lifetime interest—monarch butterflies. She took me to Pacific Grove, where a stand of eucalyptus trees allowed butterflies to shelter. I stood gawping at the flickering clusters of black and orange monarchs. They dangled and fluttered like scarves sewn with hundreds of thousands of bodies, living ornaments. It was a stunning sight. I'd seen monarchs on trees around Big Sur, but in this grove, there were cascades of them. Claire told me they arrived in the autumn, stayed over till spring, then went on an astonishing journey over the western USA.

My mind filled with the usual questions: Where did they go? Why did they

Monarchs clustered on branches

come back to Big Sur, to Pacific Grove? How long did they stay? Monarchs were a great mystery. They gave me another glimpse of the wonders of the natural world.

Into this idyll came a bombshell. Friend Perky wrote, "After seeing you in December, I realized we'd better get to Mexico before our tickets expire. Guess what? I've finally managed to get a chunk of time off! Let's go in March."

I phoned her back immediately, "Yes! Let's go!" I booked my ticket. The owners of my house in Three Acres wanted to do some repairs, so I moved out. With Claire's approval, I moved my stuff to an empty wooden chicken coop on Rancho Rico. Bill helped me clean and give the coop a coat of paint. Claire came to see me while I piled my boxes with books and clothes into corners and under the bed. She laughed and teased me about setting up house in such a small space.

Although Claire had encouraged me to move into my coop, the very conservative and religious ranch managers took umbrage about Bill staying there with me. They called me into their house and scolded me for my immorality. I was an unmarried woman, "living in sin." Their disapproval made me feel like a whore, or Hargis a villain who had seduced me. I took their negativity with what grace I could, knowing I was leaving for Mexico soon. But what would I do when I returned?

When I told Bill about the encounter, he said, "While you're in Mexico, I'll find a better place to live. And I hope you'll agree we can share it." That was an invitation I felt able to accept. We needed time together. But the next invitation stunned me.

He took my hands in his and asked, "Will you marry me?"

Shocked, I said the first thing that came to mind: "I'll think about it in Mexico."

Jeannette at the Tepotzotlán aqueduct

CHAPTER 15

Mexico

Spring 1965

Just when the caterpillar thought the world was over, it became a butterfly.

—*Anonymous*

Ta dah! The trip was on again. My nipped-in-the-bud adventure outside the USA burst into bloom at last. This time we'd meet up in Mexico City. Perky told me she was bringing along two friends. I planned to arrive before the others so I could find an apartment where we could stay. I packed a few things, eager to be on my way. I needed to be free of personal decisions for a while. Travel decisions were bound to occupy all my mind. I'd let my subconscious mull over Bill's marriage proposal.

Mexico City immediately challenged me. The huge city squeezed itself into a tight valley, choked with people, buildings, smog, and noise. In comparison to the peaceful beauty of Big Sur and the Feather River, the city was hellish. From the airport I got a taxi to my hotel and a small room smelling of mildew and cigarette smoke.

In the morning I went to the desk. A man with owlish glasses endured my high-school Spanish then answered me in perfect English, "I am sorry your room is unacceptable. You are interested in finding an apartment to rent? I might be able to help you."

Jorge told me, "I'm the agent for both the hotel and other rentals. Let me show you a couple of places." Off I went with this helpful man. He showed me one apartment that seemed ideal for the four of us: two big airy bedrooms, a sitting room, a kitchen, and one shared bathroom. I moved in right away and started exploring on my own. In 1965, Mexico City still rocked in a slow-moving rhythm, buses sometimes showing up on time, often not. I walked a lot.

Jorge became my advisor. One of his suggestions made the entire Mexico experience more worthwhile. He told me with emphasis, "You must go to the National Museum." I dutifully went. The newly finished Anthropology Museum in

Chapultepec Park astounded me. It changed my worldview. I had never suspected, let alone learned about the myriad cultures of Mexico. Sure, I knew native peoples lived there and Spaniards, too. But now I became aware of the many different Indian tribes, different European groups, their mixes, lifestyles, music, architectures, and histories.

Overloaded by information, I exited the museum to sit on a bench outside. A woman carrying a basket of wrinkled, purplish orbs came up to me. She took one, cut it in half, and held it out. I took it, sniffed up a delightful fragrance and looked a question at her. She silently raised her hand to her mouth. I put my lips on the fruit and sucked up the strange gooey stuff studded with seeds. It looked like snot but tasted like ambrosia. I bought her bag full, becoming an instant convert. I've adored passion fruits forever since.

While savoring my passion fruits and lessons from the museum, I was accosted by a man who looked like a film star. Tall and trimly bearded, wearing a suit and natty hat, he came to sit by me. My Spanish wasn't up to much, so we switched to English.

I extolled the museum and offered him fruit. He offered me his views of life in Mexico City. At the end of our conversation, he invited me to accompany him to the evening's Ballet Folklorico. He added an offer to have dinner afterwards at a sidewalk restaurant with a good mariachi band. I accepted with only a bit of worry about an evening with a stranger.

I dressed for my date in the "Claire style" dress I'd sewn for the trip. The soft cotton fabric was my favorite cherry-red. I'd made deep pockets plus a wide band of black and white trim on the square neckline. I hoped that my fringed black shawl added a touch of elegance since I wore no jewelry or makeup. The night soaked my senses: amazing dancers in colorful costumes, spicy food, loud music, and soft conversation.

My companion was charming. And no, I didn't invite him up to the apartment afterwards. I remained vague about meeting again. The next day I wanted to be ready to welcome my three traveling companions without a strange man in tow.

In they came, Perky looking smart in charcoal gray trousers and jacket with a bright pink silk scarf that made her chocolate brown skin glow. She introduced me to Elaine—tall, dark, and slender—dressed in loose dark blue pants with a turquoise tunic top. Juanita was a contrast to the elegance of the other two. Her short stature and plumpness were accentuated by an ill-fitting dress, rucked at her middle. Her sweet smile drew my focus away from her overall appearance. I was glad to meet her.

We settled into our rooms, Juanita and I in one bedroom, Perky and Elaine in the other. When Jorge came to see how we were doing, we thanked him profusely. We gave him tea and buns while asking advice about where to go in the City. He suggested a visit to the pyramids and offered to guide us to Teotihuacan. I loved trying to pronounce the name, *Tay-o-tee-wa-khan*. There, among the many tem-

CHAPTER 15: MEXICO

With Jorge at the Pyramid of the Sun

ples and pyramids, was one of the largest in the world—The Pyramid of the Sun. I wanted to climb it. I wondered if cacomistles lived in the rocky ruins. I'd ask Jorge.

The trek to the pyramids revealed a lot, not only because I learned about archeology and ancient culture. I made two other important discoveries. First, my companions and I were doomed to differ. They walked around looking bored and hot. They decided they wanted to go back to the apartment, so got a taxi. Very expensive; not in my budget. I wanted to explore, read signs, climb. I stayed.

Second, I learned that most artifacts at such sites are fakes. Jorge introduced me to some artisans producing pots and shards. The craftsmen made them look old and sold them to tourists. Since that lesson, I've delighted in trying to guess which "artifacts" are real or fakes. Neither Jorge nor I saw cacomistles, but he told me he'd do some research about them.

When I dragged my weary self into our apartment, I found the gals all gussied up, ready for a fling in the Mexico City night scene. Night-time isn't my best time. I went to bed. The next day we planned to visit a site I'd learned about in high school Spanish class—the floating gardens of Xochimilco. Yes, *Sow·chee·meel·kow*, a wonderful sounding word. We four set forth. But once again, my companions weren't keen. They didn't like the bus. They didn't want to take the unstable looking boats across the scummy, smelly water. Instead, they hired another taxi and went back to prepare themselves for another evening on the city.

After a few days in Mexico City, my friends and I parted company. They wanted to enjoy nightlife and towns, could pay for good hotels and taxis, and rent cars. I wanted to explore, to wander everywhere by train, bus, or on foot. I wanted to mix with Mexicans and learn to speak some Spanish. I had a travel book of $5-a-day options and consulted it often, as well as seeking Jorge's advice. I simply couldn't afford to travel with Perky and friends. Already I was running low on money.

They decided to leave Mexico City to travel to Guadalajara. I said that I needed to stay on to wait for a loan from my folks. Staying a couple more days also gave me time to plan out a clearer itinerary for myself. We agreed to meet up in Oaxaca at a certain hotel in a week or so and stay for a few days.

While I waited for funds, Jorge told me about aqueducts and colonial ruins. "Would you like to see some of them?" I did. The beautifully engineered Tepotzotlán aqueduct with its graceful arches surprised me. After seeing the sights, we shared a meal at a little café, and I drank my first Mexican beer. I soon learned beer was the best drink available, bubbly, refreshing, and safer than water. I also chose huevos rancheros as my mainstay meal. Eggs, beans, rice, salsa, and tortillas made a filling, delicious dish I could order anywhere, at any time of day.

Jorge's mentoring and my own discoveries were a good introduction to Mexico. But I yearned to get out of the big city. Money arrived. I said "Hasta la vista" to Jorge and took a bus north to Guanajuato. This was a special expedition on behalf of my mother, to buy her opals. After buying several lovely stones, I backtracked south through the countryside on noisy clickety-clack trains and crowded buses. Each stop offered free cultural performances: different costumes, accents, foods, and music.

People swarmed onto the train selling eggs, nuts, watermelon and pineapple slices, scarves, shawls, and baskets. Such diversity delighted me. My enthusiasm made me careless. I bought a sliced smile of watermelon from a tray of melting ice and fell horribly sick for two days in a village I can't remember.

I headed towards the Pacific Coast, stopping at Lake Pátzcuaro, where fishermen threw their circular nets. I found a small hotel at the top of my budget in the surrounding volcanic highlands. It was the best place I stayed in Mexico. I had a snug room overlooking bright flower gardens and dark green coffee bushes. Right behind my room was a swimming pool dotted with floating gardenia blossoms! Each morning I woke to the aroma of freshly roasted coffee beans and picked a fragrant flower to put in my hair.

On I went to Acapulco, where I did touristy things like go out on a little boat and watch high divers plunge off cliffs. But I felt restless and uncomfortable among the many suntanned, wealthy, lazy Americans. In Oaxaca I got a room in a hotel near the central square. The city was my fantasy of real Mexico, with attractive buildings and nearby ancient ruins.

My friends did not appear. I took the chance to explore. A kindly man at my hotel offered to take me over to the west coast, so off I went to Puerto Escondido. We walked along a wide curve of sandy beach where someone stood by a little fire, cooking turtle eggs. I tried eating one. The rubbery ping-pong ball-sized egg filled my mouth with a slimy, moldy-tasting goo—ugh!

CHAPTER 15: MEXICO

In the afternoon, my ride said he wanted to get back to the city. I wanted to stay, so found a room and enjoyed a quiet night eating fresh pineapple slices while working on my Spanish. The morning was bright and clear, tempting me back to the beach. A woman carrying a large yellow net bag over her arm walked up to me. She held what I thought was a fishing net, saying to me in Spanish, "Senorita, you are traveling. You need this hammock. It is made of silk." I examined the golden hammock. Though it was woven with nylon, not silk, I bought it. I still use it, memorabilia of the best kind, even as it unravels with time.

Oaxaca had many attractions, so I stayed a few more days waiting for my friends. They didn't appear. I checked at several of the hotels, markets, and plazas. No messages came to my hotel. I wondered if I'd see them again. Thinking about how they spent money reminded me I was running out of cash again. With disgust at my lack of foresight, I decided I'd have to go all the way back to Guanajuato. I'd beg the gemstone dealer to buy back some of the expensive opals.

Reluctantly I backtracked to Mexico City. I stopped to say hello to Jorge, went on to Guanajuato, and got most of my money back from the surprised opal dealer. Feeling guilty and inept, I kept only one pretty opal for my mom. Yes, I'd thoroughly learned a few lessons about proper preparation for trips.

My itinerary from then on included a long train ride to Mexico's east coast. From the high, cool country of middle Mexico, the train rumbled down and down to the humid coast. Palm trees and a new day waited for me at the Veracruz station. Excited, sleepy, and unsure where to go, I got myself to a seaside bench. I watched the rosy fingers of dawn tickling the waters of the Gulf of Mexico and smiled as I thought of that phrase so often repeated in *The Odyssey*.

While I waited for the sun to rise, I pondered my own little odyssey. I'd made it from one side of the country to the other. I'd seen the sun set on the Pacific; now I watched the sun rise over the Atlantic. I awarded myself the New World View achievement award.

A few fascinating days in Veracruz primed me for my next destination: the Yucatan peninsula. On the way I went into jungle-covered Palenque, where archaeologists were still uncovering temples. I sat and sketched, all the while feeling amazed by the works of the Mayan peoples.

After Palenque, I went to Merida, the city closest to the famous Mayan site of Chichén Itzá.

Before visiting the ruins, I decided to give myself a break. I wanted to visit an offshore island called Isla de Las Mujeres. A bus ride, then a boat trip, got me there. A woman offered me her teenaged son's room where I hung my golden hammock. The family seemed a bit shocked by an unmarried young woman traveling alone. They were protective as well as kind. The mother made her ousted son take me around the tiny island showing me the best places to snorkel.

Packing my golden hammock to leave Isla de Las Mujeres, I realized that I had not yet thought much about Bill's proposal. Travel let me live outside my head and left minimal mental or emotional space for pondering marriage. Like Scarlett O'Hara in *Gone with the Wind*, I told myself I'd think about it tomorrow, or at least, some other day. Events got in the way.

Returning from the Isla to the mainland, I got off the boat at dusk. No buses. To get back to Merida I needed to get a taxi. This became a turning point for me, literally and figuratively. I was starting my journey back.

The taxi driver went slowly along the unlit road, unnerving me. When he swung into a little row of motel-like rooms, my mind slipped gears. I asked in a slow low voice, "Porque detemos aqui?" I didn't want to stay there. I wanted to go back to Merida. He said, "Un ratito?" I didn't know what he meant. Did he think I needed a pit stop or a short break for food or drink? No, he made it clear he wanted a "quickie."

Appalled, angry, fearful, and defensive all at once, I sat numb, my stomach and jaw clenched. When he stopped the car, I threatened to jump out and scream if he didn't take me to my hotel in Merida immediately. He drove on. The experience shocked and humbled me. I knew traveling alone had risks but had mostly ignored them. Back inside my Merida City hotel I felt safe and undaunted. The "ratito" incident made me more alert and careful, but I was still determined to visit the ruins of Chichén Itzá.

My guidebook described the ancient Mayan city in detail: its architectural styles, cenotes, and ball courts. My main aim was to climb all 365 steps of El Castillo, the central pyramid dominating Chichén Itzá. I also wanted to see the temple inside; it held secrets. In 1935, the excavators discovered a Chac Mool statue as well as a red jaguar statue with jade eyes and jade inlays for spots. I really wanted to see that jaguar.

Chac Mool sculpture, Chichen Itza

CHAPTER 15: MEXICO

Red jaguar sculpture, Chichen Itza

The morning was already hot as I walked first to the sunken wells called cenotes. I gazed into the depths of the green pools, thinking of sacrifices made there. Next was the Ball Court, where I walked to the temple at the far end. Sitting in the shade of a wall, I observed the scene. Voices from the tourists echoed clearly from the court. Some clustered together like herded sheep, their guides moving them along with gestures and shouts. I noted that most the Europeans dressed with care and panache. The men wore hats, nicely pressed trousers, and shirts with collars. The women wore dresses and scarves. In contrast, Americans looked dowdy in their t-shirts, shorts, or rumpled pants. Gaggles of black-haired Mayan people stood out among all the others, wearing colorful clothes and expressions of wonder.

As I sat musing on the mix of cultures, a whirlwind swept into the ball court. Swirling over a tour group, the little devil snatched a hat off a tall, thin, pale-skinned man. The hat flew towards me. I bounded down to catch it. The man bowed as I handed his hat to him. He thanked me profusely in a sing-song accent I guessed was Scandinavian. When I just stood there mute, he also thanked me in French and Spanish. The encounter was another lesson in humility, reminding me not only that people of other nations were often more skilled in languages, but also in courtesy.

Feeling inept, I made my way to my ultimate goal, El Castillo. A line of people stretched around the base, so I climbed to up and down until I completed the 365 steps. On top, I scanned the site. Multiple hues of jungle green shimmered in the hot sun's glare as I watched the different colors of humanity below me. I felt overwhelmed by our diversity, numbers, and impact on the planet. My brain went numb and sweat started trickling down my back and between my breasts.

I descended the Castillo to take my place at the tail end of the line, one humbled human. Finally, my turn came to go inside. I entered the narrow passage, my vision obliterated by darkness. Pulling myself up the steps one at a time, I fought to breathe the hot, humid air. The smelly and uncomfortable tunnel made me claustrophobic. People pushed me from behind to go up and squeezed me aside to pass down. I gritted my teeth and wiped my wet face. Slowly I pushed on and up.

At the top of the stairs, people started squirming sideways to see into the chamber where the sculptures reposed. I stared at the statues of the Chac Mool and then the Red Jaguar. But sweltering in the heat and gloom, among the press of bodies, I couldn't fully appreciate them. I desperately wanted to get out.

Turning to go down the stairs, I stopped in shock. Staring back at me was a dark but familiar image. There at the top of the stairs was Perky! Behind her, like a darker shadow, stood Elaine. I fell into Perky's arms and hugged her. We gabbled hellos and how-are-yous, totally flummoxed with surprise. Who could ever have imagined this chance meeting inside a pyramid? A final, momentous coincidence at the end of my trip. It was a tale within a tale, ancient and modern, old and new, friends and strangers—complete culture shock!

Perky said they wanted to see the statues; I said I had to get outside. I'd wait at the bottom. Outside, I was so stunned, I simply stared around until Perky and Elaine came out. They wanted to leave immediately and asked me to come with them to their hotel. I agreed with mixed feelings. I longed to get to my hotel and digest my experiences, not go to a fancy resort hotel. By this time, I'd reverted to my introverted self and did not feel very sociable. But heck, these were friends, and fortune had brought us together again.

We went to the palm-festooned, multiple-pooled hotel. Juanita lay in a lounge chair outside their spacious rooms. They ordered drinks. I listened to their accounts of all the places they'd been. They planned to head home soon. I was glad they'd had a good time, but not at all happy with their complaints about the squalor, dirty people and places, poor service, and so on.

I kept refusing more drinks and wondered if they'd been drinking so much each night. I tried to leave and get a taxi, but they kept pressuring me to stay with them for the night. They offered me the lounge chair outside.

I rejected the idea of trying to sleep with the mosquitoes in the humid night with traffic and merrymakers. My eyes kept closing; I wanted to go. I tried to think of a gracious way to leave while Perky and Elaine went to put on their swimsuits for a dip in the pool.

It seemed an opportune time to escape, but Juanita pulled me to her side and onto the recliner. She kissed me on the cheek, held my head, and gave me a solid smooch on the mouth. "Ah, Jeannette, stay the night, sleep with me here. We could make love and have a good time. I've always found you attractive. Won't you stay?"

CHAPTER 15: MEXICO

A mix of emotions flooded me: surprise, understanding, sympathy, fear, and weariness. Out of that blend came a sound, "No." I repeated the word with greater emphasis, "No. I'm sorry." I paused and tried to look at her with a kind face, she looked so lonely. I told her, "I can't stay, I simply must go. Bye, tell Perky and Elaine goodbye, too."

I returned to Mexico City. Jorge handed me his notes about cacomistles in Mexico. Yes, they were well-known, but somewhat different from our northern ringtails. Jorge treated me to a Mexico finale; he drove me a long way to see the monarch butterfly roost in the mountains west of the city.

Shimmering masses of orange and black wings hung from the pine trees, creating an overwhelmingly beautiful sight. Clustered in thousands upon thousands, they clung together and flickered. Those living draperies were composed of many more butterflies than I'd seen at Pacific Grove or anywhere else in California. I simply couldn't fathom how those delicate millions could fly so far—from Mexico to places north in the USA.

Jorge expressed concern. "I don't know how all these butterflies will survive the cutting down of their trees. I wish somehow we could protect this place."

"I truly hope you can," I said, thinking of the sea otters recovering from slaughter on the California coast, the whales still being slaughtered, birds and fish vanishing. The monarchs were trying to hang on too, literally. And in Mexico, at least one Mexican, Jorge, was concerned for the monarchs and their winter home.

I bought rugs, baskets, a pair of huarache sandals. I rolled my golden hammock tightly full of memories and thanked Jorge for all his help. Off I flew on my own migratory route back to California where Bill waited for an answer to his question.

Red-tailed hawk

CHAPTER 16

Hawks and Happiness

Spring and Early Summer 1965

"The most difficult thing to adjust to, apparently, is peace and contentment."

—Henry Miller, *Big Sur and the Oranges of Hieronymus Bosch*

Flying back to the USA from Mexico, I thought about monarch butterflies. They would be making the same trip with tissue paper wings. The contrast with my metal flying machine was mind boggling. As I soared high above the earth, I mulled over my adventures in Mexico; they seemed almost a fantasy—the astonishment of finding my friends inside the ancient pyramid being the most unreal. My first major trip outside the USA had soaked me in lessons about another country, its people, and myself.

Being immersed in the "now" of travel had made me feel fully alive. As the plane descended, my mood declined with it. I dreaded having to cope with much more than just the ugly Los Angeles airport. I had to get myself to Covina, meet and greet the family. And I finally had to try probing and pondering my feelings about Bill and his marriage proposal.

Culture shock rattled me immediately. Southern California was overwhelming. I cringed at the noise, freeways, shopping malls, dirty air, and zombie-eyed people. I wanted to escape; Big Sur beckoned. I gave my mother her opal plus apologies for not bringing more and promises to repay her. She gave me a stack of letters from Bill, shaking her head. She said, "He must like you a lot, or he's writing a book."

Bill's letters were full of love and endearments, with a sprinkling of descriptions and updates. He had the usual array of jobs: working on hydraulics in Berkeley, installing sprinkler systems in Salinas Valley, making ski bindings, and polishing jade slabs for tables in King City. He wrote that his biggest challenge was making what he called "a 'watzit' to end the battle of water on Partington Ridge in Big Sur."

The watzit water job intrigued me. Partington Ridge had a reputation for conflicts and touchy people. It was easy to image a water wrangle there. Henry Miller, the author of banned books Sexus, Nexus, and Plexus, was a central figure living on the ridge. Miller had moved away, so maybe his departure facilitated Bill's work. He said he'd invented a "wild gizmo to partition water accurately into set portions for each of the warring factions."

That sort of work earned Bill more self-esteem and admiration than cash. But it certainly cost him physically. This time, Bill was working in his father's shop on the gizmo when he fell through the flimsy floor of the loft where he slept. The fall twisted his shoulder and cut his chin wide open. "I got a tetanus shot when they stitched my chin. Next, I got a high temperature and had sweaty nightmares thinking I'd die and never see you again."

Bill's most recent letter told me he was in Big Sur working for Nepenthe. "I need funds for the river project, but also to buy new clothes."

I frowned and reread the words. New clothes? Bill never worried about clothes. I read on and was taken aback by his reason. "To meet your people, I must at least be clothed acceptably. Confrontation with your father frightens me a little. With your mother, it's somewhat more. Educated mothers are all too few. If she raised you, she must be amazing."

Bill meeting my parents was hard to imagine but he obviously expected to. He phoned, saying he'd be arriving in two days. With a feeling of dread, I waited for Bill's flying visit. He rented a car and drove from the L.A. airport. He arrived looking very unlike his usual self, fitting effortlessly into the figure of William Hawley Hargis, Jr. I was surprised to see him all spiffed up in clean navy-blue trousers, pale blue shirt, and dark blue sports coat. I was glad he wasn't wearing a tie. The added formality would have unsettled me even more.

We hugged, and I felt the crispness of his new shirt, the smell of aftershave. I reached up and tenderly straightened his eyebrows. We laughed and kept on hugging, my fears floating away momentarily.

My father took my mother and the two of us to lunch, a meal that made us all feel awkward. I introduced Bill as the man I intended to work with on the Feather River, the man I'd come to know and love as a mentor and companion in Big Sur. I left it to my parents to make their own conclusions about our deeper connection.

Bill drove off that same evening with the excuse of meeting some people from his War years. My parents and I didn't discuss him much after he left. I knew Bill hadn't the opportunity, or perhaps the courage, to ask for the father's traditional blessing for marriage. I felt relief and pushed the encounter to the back of my mind. I could continue to float on down life's river without being anchored to an old-fashioned engagement.

In a way, though, Bill and I were already engaged, as working partners. We had

CHAPTER 16: HAWKS AND HAPPINESS

agreed to live and work together. During his brief stay, he told me how he'd organized our living arrangements in Big Sur. He'd made a deal with a couple who had a cabin near Coastlands. They worked and stayed at Esalen Institute most the time so were happy to rent.

"It's called the Stone House, and yes, it's built of rocks and stones. The house sits high on a ridge above Highway One. The setting is stunning, with incredible views plus privacy. It's perfect for us. You'll love it!"

Bill explained he paid for leasing the Stone House by fixing it up, improving the water system, and the trail. Trail? Was the house that remote? We agreed on a day and approximate time to meet up at the Stone House. He and I avoided any discussion of marriage, content to wait for our reunion in Big Sur.

I drove up the California coast with my ephemeral friends, Joy and Anticipation. The open car windows sucked in the intoxicating smells of warmed sage sweeping up from the salty surf. I made frequent stops to watch hawks and clouds soaring above, and the sea lions (not seals) honking and snarling below. Here I stood, in the "Real" California, unspoiled so far. I was so glad to be back in this grand and less human-hammered landscape that I twirled around and shouted out, "I'm back, amen!"

I stopped at Nepenthe to ask if anyone had seen Bill. The waiter who once thought me a phony because I smiled so often, said, "Ah, Hargis, yes, he said you'd be coming by. Got you in his clutches, does he? Or is it the other way around? Ha! Anyway, he's doing some work on the trail down by Pfeiffer Burns cove."

I didn't think Bill would be trail building because he told me he was working for Nepenthe. I drove on to Coastlands and found a side road leading away from the main highway into a canyon full of sentinel redwoods. On a curve where the track disappeared into the canyon sat Bill's VW. I felt a stab of anxious delight. I parked next to Hargis' wreck of the Hesperus and got out of my barely-functioning Renault.

The road ahead led into the redwood canyon. Beside me, a grassy slope with a trail led uphill. I breathed in the unique scent of redwood duff and earthy mold slathered by sun. I stood silently for a while, just absorbing, then ambled into the canyon. I needed to decompress from the long drive. The tall redwoods cast feathery shadows that landed on me with feelings of solace.

A deep quiet filled me. I turned back with an overwhelming desire to lie down on the grass in the late afternoon sun. I chose a spot on the slope, lay on my back, and looked at the clouds gliding by. My mind followed them, floating along, totally in the moment. I dozed. A gentle whisper on my forehead told me Bill had materialized.

"Welcome home, my love. I saw your dust trail as you drove up the road, gave you a moment to orient, and now, here I am to greet you."

He grabbed me up from the ground and swung me around like a little child. I felt helplessly happy. We hugged and kissed then picked up my gear to lug up the steep trail to the house.

Inside the Stone House

The Stone House enjoyed a solitary view on the ridgeback surrounded by a sward of grass brimming with colorful wildflowers. Here and there, a few dark oaks dotted the hill, accentuating the slopes. I stopped to appreciate the scene; it seemed a painting especially done for me. Looking up, I saw a red-tailed hawk floating above the house as though Bill had positioned it there as a banner of welcome.

My man paused at the doorway. I half expected him to pick me up and carry me over the threshold. I was relieved when he stepped aside and waved me inside. Uncluttered space greeted me. The room had a table with wooden barrels to use as chairs, a small sink, and a wood stove. A bedroom was tacked onto the back with a small area devoted to a toilet and shower.

There were kerosene lamps here and there, and candles. I assumed we had no electricity and was glad to note the faucets with running water. I wondered where the water came from. Bill could find water and channel it anywhere. I looked at him, his face beaming with pleasure at my delight with the house. I couldn't help but grin back.

I settled in. The Mexican rugs I'd bought stretched themselves out on the stone floor, my new baskets embraced fruits, my huaraches clasped my feet protectively. Wildflowers found their way into jars on the table. I breathed in smells of green grass and blue skies, finding smiles on my face as I adjusted to my new home. Bill watched me with a twinkle and went off to do his odd jobs.

At Rancho Rico, I collected my things from the chicken coop. After loading the car, I went to see Claire. She was still occupied with building her gorgeous, multilevel house. Like some angular, prehistoric bird, the house perched on the ridge overlooking the ocean, far too heavy to take off and fly.

CHAPTER 16: HAWKS AND HAPPINESS

Claire had named her place "Hill o' the Hawk," and hawks did indeed soar over the ridge. They were mostly red-tailed hawks and Cooper's hawks, or, as Hargis cautioned in his educator's voice, "They could just as well be sharp-shinned hawks. Hard to spot the difference."

Claire gave me a warm hug and showed me around, all the while asking questions about my trip to Mexico. "Meeting your friends like that, in the middle, literally the middle of the Chichén Itzá pyramid, that must have been incredible!"

She was also amazed by my getting to the monarch butterfly roosts west of Mexico City. She spoke with real enthusiasm, saying, "Your description of the masses of monarchs stuns me. You were so lucky to see them in their winter roosts just before they migrate away. What a lot of striking adventures you've had."

Claire caught me up with Big Sur and her own family news. She was delighted that Bill and I now lived in the Stone House. She expressed sympathy about my dilemma over the idea of marrying him. I felt deeply grateful to have her as a friend.

I left Hill o' the Hawk feeling good. I was where I wanted to be on the planet. Twenty-four years of living and I'd been given a big box full of little boxes, each containing glowing, bright gifts. A significant one was good health. Another was having family and friends. There were adventures to look forwards to and the trip to Mexico had given me many marvelous experiences to digest. Even the challenge of my developing relationship with Bill was a gift. Finally, I was growing up, stretching my spirit wings.

My positive mood buoyed me as I explored my surroundings. The steep trail to the Stone House kept me in shape. I could walk up and down to see Eric at his house in Coastlands. I also made a deal with the Posts to borrow one of their horses from time to time. With a horse, I could carry supplies up the hill and enjoy rides to explore ridges and valleys, flushing rabbits from the grass, watching hawks soar above.

I particularly enjoyed going to the Big Sur Hot Springs, now called The Esalen Institute. The place continued its transformation from a local hangout to an expensive retreat for "alternative humanistic education." The place upgraded itself steadily, morphing into something unique. The Institute offered seminars in mindfulness, group therapy, retreats to develop human potential, gestalt therapy, existential philosophy, zen, body awareness, yoga, and tai chi. Performers and celebrities, such as Joan Baez, came to entertain the clients and promote the new age.

Our "landlords" at Esalen sometimes traded places with us. Pete and Micky returned to the Stone House to find peace and solitude, while Bill and I went to Esalen to indulge in the hot baths and enlightenment. Sometimes when Bill was gone, I went alone to visit people and enjoy a soak. I learned practical things at Esalen, as well as new ideas. For instance, the Institute catered to a varied clientele with different diets. I learned about cooking delicious meals to fit the palates of vegans, vegetarians, and omnivores.

One cooking lesson that I modified became a lifelong staple. I call it Hot Springs Bread: My recipe includes a mix of whole wheat, regular white, and rye flours, plus wheat germ and molasses. Later, when I made this bread in England and Africa, I added raisins and seeds to the mix. With crunchy peanut butter, few foods are as delicious and filling. And the bread lasts for days on safari.

I wrote to my "trauma friend" Nathan of UC Berkeley days: "Here I am at Big Sur Hot Springs, while the owners of the Stone House take a break at what I call The Hillside of Happiness. I'm soaking up spring, both in terms of the season and hot water. Also, I'm imbibing what Esalen people refer to as positive 'vibes.' Come visit me sometime and get new vibes!"

Nathan didn't visit right away because he was traveling. He sent me postcards from exotic places. He'd spent time in China and India. One card showed an ornate Hindu temple which reminded me of some of those built by the Mayans. Mexico had been just a starter, Nathan's photos and cards kept the coals of yearning for travel glowing inside me.

Meanwhile, there was Bill and the river project. In a few weeks, we'd go to the Feather River to start the garden. I was eager for the adventure awaiting in Bald Rock Canyon. In the meantime, Bill came and went from Big Sur doing jobs. The arrangement suited me perfectly. During stints when he was working in Big Sur, we shared space and time in harmony. Our lovemaking improved a bit, mainly because I loved him more than I loved having orgasms. We laughed more often; his face was soft as he puttered about the house fixing things.

I smile to think of that season of love, spring flowers, hawks, and happiness. My experiences in Mexico, exploring, absorbing, and learning had made me more confident. I was ready for more adventures. My ebullience flowed over Bill, and he too seemed unusually content and happy.

Alas, under the currents of love and well-being, swam Inner Skeptic. It snidely

CHAPTER 16: HAWKS AND HAPPINESS

intoned with its usual drone: with every up, there's a down; light has dark; yin has yang. Beware, happiness is but foam on a transient tide. Mr. Puritanical Work Ethic also rose up, hands on hips, chastising me: You haven't even resumed work at the café or looked for jobs. You let Bill pay for most everything.

As usual, these shadows in my soul brought introspection, and with it, depression and questions. What about my long-term future? What could I do with my fruitcake mind? Get a job? Marry Bill Hargis? Feeling adrift on a sea of choices, I floundered and pondered.

Jeannette on horseback at Stone House

Misty redwood canyon

CHAPTER 17

Feathered Canyons

Spring into Summer 1965

Grant me deep roots.
Solid branches.
Let the fires pass me by.
Let generations of squirrels and blue jays
hop on my limbs.
Let me breathe fog, chew sunlight, and look down
over centuries.

— Joe Cottonwood, "Redwood Prayer"

During my season of hawks and happiness, my mother and older sister Betsy came to visit me at the Stone House. My sister remembers struggling up the steep hillside hot and sweaty, with her infant in her arms, plus a bundle. I ran down to meet them and help with their bags and baskets. They brought gifts, one of which—a book—changed my life, but not at the time. They also brought good company, angst, and a chance to reconcile with my mother.

When I came to Big Sur and tossed my symbolic wedding ring into the sea, I let the memories of my traumatic pregnancy go with it. Or so I thought. But when my mother arrived, so did the memories of my last year of college. That was when I birthed a daughter and gave her up for adoption. My mother didn't know of my pregnancy until my graduation. I'd told only my father when I found out that my carefully installed diaphragm had failed. I asked for his help to finance me through the ordeal. We agreed not to tell my mother. We feared she'd become hysterical.

Alas, she found out at my graduation. My mother saw the tears running down my face when I talked on the telephone to the father of my unborn child. He was still trying to convince me to marry him. I just couldn't face marriage then, let alone to this self-important but brilliant graduate student.

My mother watched me sob and argue. She figured it out and indeed became hysterical. "So, you've got yourself pregnant. How could you do this? Didn't I rear you to be more careful?" Her words stabbed my weakened spirit. I couldn't understand why she felt harmed or hurt when I was the one who was pregnant.

After our confrontation, my mother and I didn't speak for months. I leaned on Nathan for emotional support, and my father supported me financially. He paid for my escape to Santa Barbara. There I could hide my pregnancy from the rest of the family while I took the course in marine biology. I let the matter lie dormant for three years.

When my mother came to the Stone House in Big Sur, I tried to talk to her. I still didn't want to tell my siblings that they had an unknown niece, so I tried to find time when I could be alone with my mother. Finally, on a walk into the nearby redwood canyon, I brought up the subject.

"Have you reconciled yourself to my having a baby out of wedlock and giving her up for adoption?" I asked.

Her response, "Well, I hope you've learned your lesson. And I hope you'll find the right man and have grandchildren for me."

"What do you think of Bill Hargis as a 'right man'?"

"Well, isn't he a bit old for you?" she replied, glancing at me with raised eyebrows.

I felt she'd just dipped my heart in vinegar. I never thought of Bill as old. To me, someone's age wasn't much of a factor in my feelings about them. As for the grandchildren gambit, my older sister already had a daughter and was pregnant with a son. My mother didn't have to pin her grandmothering hopes on me. Also, my younger sister, Stephanie, had presumably found her "right man" and would contribute descendants as well. I let the subject drop, sighed a deep, sad sigh, and walked my mother back up the hill to the Stone House.

Childrearing didn't attract me, with or without Bill. I'd formed a strong opinion while working with the abused and abandoned children in Los Angeles County. Children had a better chance in life when growing up in a stable environment with stable caregivers. Bill and I were in no position to provide a child with stability in either sense.

My disappointing talk with my mother reminded me of Bill's marriage proposal. Thinking about marriage made me uneasy, eclipsing this sunny period in my soul. I pushed it firmly into my mental shadows, along with anxiety about my abilities and goals. Someday, I'd take a closer look at all those concerns.

To give my restless mind a break, I'd learned to get outside. I walked the hills, rode horseback, visited Claire and Eric. Then I turned to reading books. Some gave me entirely new perspectives, such as Rachel Carson's *Silent Spring*, about poisoning Mother Earth, and Betty Friedan's *The Feminine Mystique*, about how society had warped women, including my mother, who, in turn, had warped me. I loved reading and learning but wished I could be more of an activist. My society frightened me. Police were attacking peaceful marchers in the south. Negroes

CHAPTER 17: FEATHERED CANYONS

were still persecuted everywhere. Young men were being sent off to fight an unjust war in Vietnam. Big Business continued to rape the land. I often dissolved in tears when reading about what humans were doing to our planet. Did I have any positive role to play in this crazy modern life?

I tried to pin down my feelings by writing to friend Nathan. "I'm reading a lot and thinking about jobs and careers. Having been trained to be a good student I'm wondering if returning to graduate school might give me a focus. For now, I have an important part to play in the Feather River gold mining project. I'm part planner, gardener, cook, and diver. If we get gold, Bill and I want to build a boat for a trip around South America, inventing ourselves as itinerant "Peace Corps" type workers. Even if we don't become millionaires, I shall not regret a pleasant summer in a beautiful wild canyon in Northern California."

I put books aside and enjoyed late spring in Big Sur. The sun shone on the slopes of the Santa Lucia Mountains and peered into the damp redwood canyons full of misty light. The grassy carpet surrounding the Stone House descended into a sea of fog. Under the foggy blanket, the Big Sur mayhem seethed. It was time to escape to the Feather River.

We left Big Sur for Bald Rock Canyon, staying overnight at Bill's mother's place in the Salinas Valley. Early in the morning we took the new freeway—Interstate 5. We were lured into thinking we could zip through the San Joaquin and Sacramento Valleys to Oroville. But as the mind-numbing miles rushed past, we found we couldn't stay on that lifeless thoroughfare.

Freeways were long boring sentences, so we broke the journey into phrases. Dropping off onto old Highway 99, we went at a slower pace. We drove through little towns punctuated with clusters of houses. We passed vast farms dotted with lines of fruit trees or underlined with rows of vegetables. Refreshing ourselves with periodic stops for coffee at roadside cafés and fruit stands, we bought spring strawberries and winter oranges.

Making one last stop on our route, we chose a café in the town of Gridley. Bill wanted a cigarette with his coffee. I complained. "You are doing so well. Don't start smoking again."

"Not even one?" he asked wrinkling his brow in a fake frown. "They're my lungs you know."

"Not so, they partly belong to me now," I said with a fake smile, patting my heart and faking a harsh smoker's cough in protest. Smoke did bother me. Living in smoggy Southern California, I'd endured years of hay fever symptoms. Smoke made me sneeze and my nose and eyes itch. To make my aversion to smoking clear, I added a threat, "If you don't abandon cigarettes now, and for as long as we're together, I'm leaving you right here in Gridley, California." I stood up, partly in jest and partly serious. I hated his smoking.

From that day, Bill quit smoking. I gave him the nickname Gridley. He retaliated by calling me Feezer. I liked it because it conjured an image of a feathery-furry-sneezer creature like myself. I'd acquired many names in life and none of them seemed right until a good friend gave me the name Genetta. That's the scientific name for the African genet that looks so much like the ringtail of America. Nicknames come naturally with best friends and family members, so Gridley and Feezer declared a closer bond between us.

By the time we got to Oroville, we could see the effects of the winter rains. Over Christmas and New Year, 1964–65, Northern California had been soaked in unusual rainfall. The storms produced one of the largest floods in California's history. The water draining from the slopes of the Sierras caused enormous erosion where timber merchants had stripped away the trees. Muddy waters sluiced down canyons into rivers and towns, over roads and bridges.

In the Oroville area, the new dam held back the water from the overflowing tributaries of the Feather River. The water covered the road to Berry Creek. Local residents and Andy's Merrimac stage had to be conveyed across the temporary lake on an ungainly, tank-like amphibious vehicle known as an army duck.

By the time we arrived, we found the road open but scattered over with litter and debris. We wondered what the free-flowing water had done to the flat and equipment in the mountains above. As we neared Berry Creek, I started seeing signs stuck alongside the road:

"Tired old apples, 5lb. for 25 cents."

"Rip Roarin' Red tomatoes 3 lb. for 40 cents."

'We got veggies, stop in and check 'em out."

"Fresh hen fruit."

At the end of the line of signs stood a low building with a very large handwritten sign: "Free! *Felis domesticus* desires habitation with *Homo sapiens*."

I pointed to the sign laughing, "About the last thing we need on the river is *Felis*

CHAPTER 17: FEATHERED CANYONS

domesticus." Bill laughed too, and said in his most pompous voice, "I certainly prefer our friends *Bassariscus astutus* and the felids *Puma concolor* and *Lynx rufus.*" In his normal voice he added, "And I trust they'd eat up any ol' domestic cat."

Bill parked by the shop entrance saying, "We need to stop here for supplies, not cats. And I want to introduce you to Tex Boone, the owner. He's a distant relative of Daniel Boone. Tex is a great character, real 'local color.' He'll tell stories 'til your ears fall off."

We walked in. A thin man in white jacket and dark trousers leaned over a boy, cutting his hair. The barber turned with a grin and said in a Texas drawl, "Howdy folks. Good to see ya, Bill. Be with y'all in a minute."

Bill started collecting groceries while I stared at the various horned heads tacked onto the walls, mostly deer with antlers but also horned animals from Africa. The cramped store had low ceilings accentuating its confines and clutter. I saw boxes of stationery, bolo ties, old Christmas wreaths, striped stretch socks, obscure California wines, earrings, books, vases, artificial flowers, and colorful rocks as well as buckets, barrels, and bags stacked around.

The barber finished with the boy. He turned to Hargis and grinned, "Well, Bill, been a long time ex-cet-er-rah. Ho hum... What ya up to? Going on up to that Feathered Canyon?" Bill nodded, turned to me and said in a mocking drawl, "Miz Jeannette Hanby, meet this 'ere hombre. Name is Tex Boone. He's the proprietor, repairman, barber, and more. Yep, this here Tex is a man of many skills."

Tex shook my hand, saying, "Welcome, welcome, welcome." He added with a twinkle and a wink at Bill, "Watch out for mean ol' Bill, he'll work ya to death on the river. For sure. Ho hum.. I assure you, all this rain will have made a real mess at your camp. You'll both be near death clearin' up."

Tex in his Berry Creek store

Bill chuckled and started to pile things in the only space available on the counter. As Tex rang up the total, he asked, "Do you want this on the tab? Bill answered, "Yep." I realized this was one of those old-fashioned stores that trusted customers to pay up periodically. Somehow, the idea pleased me.

Tex jabbed at the adding machine keys then turned to Bill to ask, "The usual? For both?" Bill nodded. I stood puzzled while Tex ushered in a plump young gal, dressed in a short pink dress. "This here is my granddaughter, Pixie. She'll get it." The questions bonging around in my head settled when Pixie handed Bill, then me, an ice cream cone.

The ice cream melted in my mouth like languid summer days. I studied Tex and Bill as they bantered words back and forth. Tex was a true old codger, with wonderfully wrinkled skin, laugh lines, and calloused hands. Besides being a barber, he kept groceries and mail for miners, sold gasoline, ran a pawnshop, and was generous with credit and gifts of food. He had a wide mischievous grin and a weave in his gait that make him seem a little drunk.

Tex became a symbol of mountain people, as well as a mainstay in our Feather River mining venture. He hung onto the mountains and his crumbling store like mistletoe clings to an old oak tree. I knew I'd enjoy getting to know him and Pixie. I envisioned the two in auras of colors: bark brown, lichen green, pretty pink, and vanilla cream. Local color.

Ponderosa pine on Bald Rock trail

Small photos from top: Manure pile, Hargis digging, Jeannette digging, garden crops.

CHAPTER 18

Gardeners of Eden

Spring to Summer 1965

Now in the spring, the heaving ground swell breaks
For future flowers and my heart awakes
And listens to itself below the ground.

—Eric Barker, "The Green Wave," from *Looking for Water*

We stopped to say hello to Hedy and Andy Kala but didn't stay over. We were too eager to get into the canyon. The sun settled over the western rim as we ran down the hill, reaching Evans Bar at dusk. I dropped my pack and rushed over the rocky staircase to the head of the Big Pool. Bill joined me. A great surge of water still rioted through its channel, white froth and foam hiding former sand bars and rocks. We stared. The hungry river had gobbled up much of the equipment. The list of what was lost took a couple of days for us to compile:

The boulder lifting bag
The reserve air drum
A set of barrels
A significant amount of the big raft
The entire transportation raft
The undercurrent box
Nozzles
Gold pans
Uncountable tools, fittings, pulleys, wire, etc.

The river left us a symbol of its power—a large iron lifting bar bent double in the rocks where Bill had stowed it. So much for leaving equipment above the high-water mark, I thought. I was reminded of a life lesson—never underestimate the power of nature—but kept my mouth shut. What a loss. Gridley tried to take a positive view, saying, "Now I'll have the chance to do it all better. I can work out the bugs in the equipment."

His statement tried to cover our disappointment. We both knew we had a lot of work ahead if we were to continue the project. I missed the lift bag the most. The time, money, and skill to replace it and the other items would be significant. We couldn't do much about the losses at the time except grieve. Our depression sank to a further low when the ringtails failed to appear.

Instead of being able to set up the equipment, we started fixing up the cabin. We also built a new bough bed under the pines, putting flexible, fragrant pine branches on top of an old spring bed. We put it in a sheltered spot downslope towards the roaring river. Our outdoor bedroom had both afternoon shade and open night sky. My golden Mexican hammock found a space between two pine trees nearer the river. It became my place to retreat for keeping notes, writing letters, and private siestas.

Our next major task was the garden, an expanse of soggy dead or dying plants. We started to build a better, bigger fence around the plot. Gridley set out to rescue old pieces of barbed wire from fields up top. We salvaged a large roll of hog wire from an old pasture. An abandoned house offered up several rusty rolls of wire tangled in years of weedy growth. Slowly our expanded garden area was fitted with hand-split posts linked together with odds and ends of wire.

Hedy gave me many varieties of seeds to add to those I'd bought at stores and from catalogs. We dug and spaded, pulled weeds, spaded, and pulled more weeds. I took a close look at the soil. So many living things crawled and wriggled there: worms, bugs and beetle larva, sow bugs. We found miner artifacts too: pieces of glass, crockery, and nails.

I planned the garden with care, then planted seeds in rows with labels: corn, lettuce, carrots, turnips, broccoli, eggplants, cauliflower, chard, tomatoes, and peppers. I planted as many squash varieties as I could find, mainly yellow, zucchini, and butternut, but also one new to me, spaghetti squash. An entire section went to melons: honeydew, casaba, and cantaloupe plus an oddity, banana melons.

For my role as chief cook, I added a patch for herbs: thyme, marjoram, dill, oregano, basil, sage, chives, and parsley. Hedy gave me some spearmint plants and a bag of Shasta daisies with roots. I carried them down in paper bags and planted them tenderly. On a trip out to Berry Creek, Tex gave me some shriveled peppermint plants that thrived and started me on a lifelong habit of drinking peppermint tea.

I soon tired of cooking over our campfire, so started selecting stones. I piled them carefully to make a platform, then walls with an open area on top for a wood or charcoal fire. Bill watched me skeptically as though the whole edifice would collapse with the addition of a teakettle. But my stove was solid. I added an extension with a big flat rock where I could put a little gas stove at the right height for short me.

We brought down a kerosene refrigerator on Hargis' sled-like invention and put it under the buckeye tree. He fixed up the outdoor table and benches. On our trips up and down the hill, Bill and I worked on trails. We were on the lower switchback clearing branches of manzanita when he said, "Let's tackle the water supply."

CHAPTER 18: GARDENERS OF EDEN

The rock stove

Off he went, as usual assuming I'd follow. And, as usual, I did. We walked up the slope into a pretty canyon above the flat. A lively waterfall giggled as it danced down a 12-foot cliff, then snuggled in among magnificent deep green *Woodwardia* ferns. Yes, I'd learned their name from my mentor and master, William Hargis. This was the cleft Alonzo had mentioned and where Bill had written me one of his long letters from the canyon.

Where the water emerged, we built a little dam; it would hold enough water in reserve to see us through a dry period. Bill had repeatedly warned me, "It will be hot in the summer, really hot. Be prepared."

Part of the preparation was the ingenious water system Bill invented to keep our garden flourishing. Starting at the little spring in the side canyon, a system of pipes and floats led to a 55-gallon drum with a self-activating toilet float valve. A simple float and string arrangement showed the water level in the tank. I dug furrows and placed hoses to lead the water into the plots.

The garden began to look like one, but there were setbacks. On a day we went out for supplies, we came back to find that deer had managed to get over the eight-foot fence. In their eagerness to get out they trampled and tore up many new plants. Bill tightened and strengthened the fence while I replanted melons, cabbages, marigolds, and herbs.

Birds took their toll on the garden, eating up seeds. They left their droppings and feathers in payment, the gifts enhanced by their songs. The squirrels were rampant destroyers of vegetables and Bill shot a few. Luckily, hungry insects left our food plot mostly intact. We had plenty of pollinators: honeybees, bumblebees, flies, ants, and butterflies.

Fence lizards became more abundant and tamer. They devoured insects, sunbathed, and did pushups on my rocked-up stove. We caught hoppers to feed them. Several lizards became so tame we treated them like pets and gave them names. Like a thoughtless child, I caught one to get a better look at the blue on its belly, but it slipped out of my hand, leaving its quivering tail. Tailless didn't seem to mind and was easy to recognize. He occupied a rock in the center of our eating area, lying still while I scratched his head with a stick, pine needle, or finger. He'd crawl into the ashes at night and scamper out when I laid the morning fire.

The ringtails reappeared, Shatze so tame she sat on our laps and tolerated being stroked. After touching her ears and neck, I smelled my hands, inhaling the erotic scent of musk. Ponder was now fully-grown and easy with us. He seemed especially adept at being the first to the food we put out. New ringtails came in shyly and became habituated easily, probably Shatze's offspring.

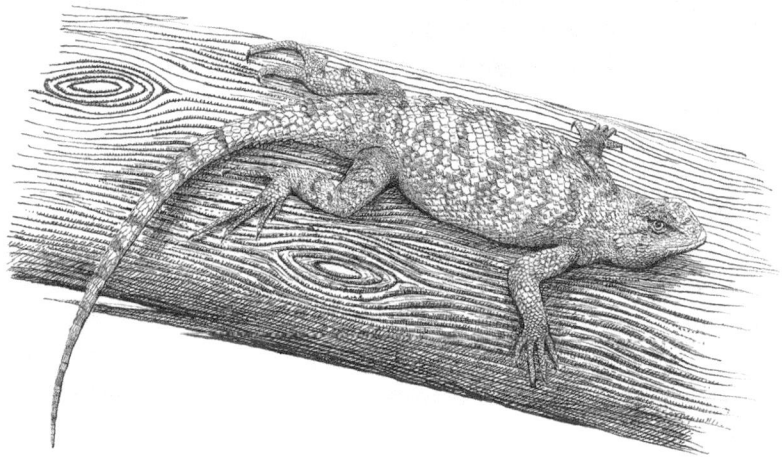

Fence Lizard

In addition to the canyon flora and fauna, I met a few more members of the human species outside the canyon. These people were important ingredients in the menu of our lives. Our mainstays were Hedy and Andy, Tex and Pixie. The proprietors of the Brush Creek Store also became fixtures in our out-of-canyon lives. Manuel Sousa was a heavy-set Portuguese; his wife Melba, a plump local gal. She sold groceries, doled out cheer, and managed the post office during daytime. Manuel tended bar. Brush Creek Store was essentially a log cabin with a bar and supplies for locals, tourists, and hunters. A big wood stove heated the place in winter, welcome even in the crisp days of autumn and spring.

Sitting with a drink on one of the few bar stools at Brush Creek Store, I could swivel myself around to refresh my eyes, too. I learned to check out a Hamm's beer ad, the kind with a light behind the picture, making the waterfall appear to flow, and the lake ripple.

CHAPTER 18: GARDENERS OF EDEN

The first time I went to the store, I'd noticed an oddity in the ad—fish swimming up the waterfall. Yes, Manuel had drawn the fish on the glass. I found the innovation delightful. After that first discovery, I checked the beer sign regularly to see other surprises in the waterfall or lake. Usually something new was there to amuse me, like Christmas ornaments on trees or a kid with a kite in the sky. I loved the whimsy and found myself smiling every time I went to the store.

The Brush Creek Store, a ranger station, and a couple of cabins constituted most of the village of Brush Creek. We often visited Mountain House just a couple miles up the road. The Morgenroths lived there surrounded by new houses built around the old hotel and stage stop. They were a well-off couple promoting developments in the Brush Creek area. They gave us a place to retreat and recover when we went up top.

The illuminated beer sign

I tried to describe the scene to pen pal Nathan: "The Brush Creek Store is fun as well as a supply and mail stop. Nearby, the Morgenroths have an old house with a beautiful grapevine winding around the veranda. They let me use their phone in the living room where elk and deer heads peer at me. There's a fishing pond (pay and fish year-round) and a few A-framed cabins. It's another bolt hole for us."

Before our mining partners appeared, we had a few visitors who were brave and clever enough to find their way to Evans Bar. Some were welcome, like Alonzo, the Maidu Indian, and local fishermen who often left fresh fish. Others were not so welcome, mostly men armed to the teeth with guns.

On a morning when warm breezes wafted through camp, another adventurous person appeared on the trail. He whistled a lively tune, stopping at the edge of the trees above the clearing. Bill had gone out to get supplies, so I was alone, scouring pots in the kitchen area. I was immediately alert to this stranger invading our realm.

A scrawny, suntanned older man stood surveying the cabin, the flat, and me, with intense interest. I stared back. He wore a floppy hat and one of those flimsy, sleeveless undershirts men wore in movies showing European immigrants on the summer streets of New York. Pausing to stand calmly in his thin shirt and khaki shorts, the man smiled.

I waved at him, a neighborly wave I hoped. He approached and introduced himself in a husky German accent, "Hallo, I am Valter Fischer. I lif at Berry Creek. I often hike down here. Is gut to see all the improvements you haf made."

He nodded at me, almost a bow, and extended a warm callused hand. I shook it and said, "I'm Jeannette."

"Ah, a French name, yes? But to me, you looked like an Indian girl with your long dark braids and that bandana around your head. I like the way you waved a hello, impartial, not off-putting, a special kind of wave." The compliment pleased me. I liked his tone, courtesy, and accent. And so, I met Walter Fischer, who became important to me in many ways.

Walter Fischer

River rocks and reflections, Bald Rock Canyon

In the canyon

CHAPTER 19

In the Canyon

Summer to Autumn 1965

"Ye miners all, ye weak and strong,
Who to these rivers swiftly throng,
Cast down your tools and fly amain,
To those at home, who cry in vain.
Give up the search, turn back I say,
And ye will bless that happy day."

— "The Aged Miner" by "A Mountain Bard"

Midsummer sauntered in with long days and short nights. Finally, the other members of our team arrived. Mike and Norm came sliding down the hill on the Skid Trail. "And Larry?" I asked. Mike frowned, "Oh, he quit, he won't be coming this summer."

With only the four of us, I wondered how we would fare. Mike looked fit and determined. Norm looked more like a student, rather soft, pudgy, and only mildly eager about the project. We conferred about what needed to be done. We agreed that the two of them would start to resurrect the rafts and lower whatever equipment had escaped the floods. Bill and I needed to go south on the long central California road to replace lost equipment.

After a week rushing between Salinas, King City, and Big Sur, Bill and I returned to the canyon. We found the place empty. The partly assembled raft floated in the Big Pool without engines. We couldn't find any note of explanation. A few days after we finished bringing down supplies, Mike and Norm appeared. Mike explained, "Had to get out to do odd jobs for people up top. It earns a little cash." He paused and smirked, saying, "And I like catching up with a few select friends." He winked at me to make sure I got the point about what sort of friends he caught up with.

Though we smiled, we were not amused. Bill and I had expected the dredging operation to be in full swing. Mike and Norm seemed unconcerned. In between trips in and out of the canyon, the men inspected and prepared equipment while I worked on the garden, fence, and cabin.

Walter Fischer came down a couple of times with fresh vegetables and news of the outside world. He also brought companionship to me. We'd talk and fish together. I was repeatedly impressed by his love of nature and humility. His company was a treat.

June rippled away into July, and, as Bill had predicted, it was hot. The canyon was like a solar oven as sunlight bounced between cliffs. I sweated as I dug, raked, weeded, picked, and pruned. I trained bean and pea vines, watered and fertilized plants. In between cooking and cleaning camp, I jumped into the cold river pools to revive myself. Even after the sun slid over the west rim, the rocks held the heat until darkness, breezes, and the river cooled the air. Then we rested, ate, and watched for the cacomistles to arrive in camp.

While the men fooled around with equipment, I stole quiet times in my Mexican hammock to write notes and letters. But free time was rare; there were always chores to do. My stubby fingers were grubby and dirty, fingernails broken from garden and kitchen work. Smoke and soot from blackened pots and dirty kerosene lamps tattooed my face. My bare feet hardened up like old leather; clothes became rags. I cut the legs off filthy jeans to make dirty potholders and wore the rest as shorts. I tore the sleeves off old shirts and tied the shirttails at my belly because the buttons came off.

At last, the men started dredging. Right away, problems pestered the project. On the first full day of work, the strong jets of water pumped through the underwater tube of the dredge caused sections to break apart. The tube needed welding, which meant taking it out of the river, getting welding equipment organized, and repairing it on the beach. On subsequent days, guy lines broke, the engines growled and quit, hoses broke, the compressor failed. The three men spent hours on the raft trying to cope with one issue after another. Days passed with no gold coming through the sluices.

July days slipped down the riffles into August. The men toiled. In addition to camp chores, I tried to promote cohesion among the grumpy males. Being cheerful and positive helped, but it was food that soothed. I used meal therapy to improve moods: I made tortillas, baked bread, concocted stews, and grilled fish.

I invented new items, such as venison rolls composed of deer meat rolled up with curls of onion and sweet pepper chunks, then tied with bits of cotton crochet thread, the kind I used to make potholders. Steamed in the Dutch oven on top of potatoes, carrots, herbs, and sometimes tomatoes, my venison roll dinner was filling as well as delicious.

Spending time cooking and gardening give me chances to enjoy the wildlife on the flat. Birds, reptiles, and insects made appearances at different times of day.

They alerted me to the hourly changes in sunlight and shadow sneaking across the clearing. I often looked up at the wedge of sky above the canyon to watch weather patterns. Cloud lines on U-I-No's ancient face or the sheen of moonlight on the granite cliffs made my spirit soar.

But the dredging didn't fill any of us with joy. The crew became as fluid as the river. On many days someone would go out to get parts to keep the show going or just take a break. I began taking a more significant part in the operation, learning to start the engines and the compressor, and run the underwater rig. I became more involved in soothing over the breakdowns and distractions that marred our days.

We persevered through August and into September, hope fading with the hours of daylight. Personal trips up the hill became more frequent. Norm went out to enroll in classes and didn't come back. Mike was prone to going out "scouting," meaning seeing one of his lady friends. With only three of us, dredging became even more of a challenge.

Mike and the Tote Gote

I was gardening one afternoon when Mike came down the hill, heralded by the horrendous growl of the Tote Goat. That was our three-wheeled motorcycle with a box on the back. The machine had been left under a tarp up top, waiting for some spare part. Mike got it going again and roared down the hill, skidding in with a flourish of dirt, a wild gleam in his eyes. He dropped supplies, revved the engine, and took off uphill. He'd brought along his dog that usually stayed with the Kalas. It romped through the open garden gate into my patch of melons and lettuce. Barking and yelping, the dog tore precious vegetable plants to bits before dashing off after Mike and the Tote Goat.

A horrible howling from behind the cabin added to the din as Gridley worked on cutting up a tree trunk. The whining chainsaw, combined with the roar of the

Tote Goat and the barking of the dog, echoed around the canyon. I couldn't bear it, so marched off, waving at Bill, calling, "Hey Gridley, want to go fishing?"

"Good idea, Feezer," he said, putting the saw on top of a pine round. "Let's go!"

Water ouzels bobbed away as we hiked upriver to enjoy some peace. The song of a canyon wren and hooking three salmon restored us to equanimity. Returning downriver, we passed by camp to leave the fish on the table. Wending our way to the Big Pool, we swam to the big raft. While Bill fished some more, I lay on my back and looked at the sky. An osprey flew overhead, swooping down to catch a fish its talons. In the last of the sunlight reflected from the canyon walls, I watched groups of bats flicker above me, flying higher and higher, whisking the remaining daylight from the sky. Dusk and peace settled on me. I fell asleep and woke abruptly when Gridley hung a big dripping salmon over my face.

In the morning, while the fish grilled, we three remaining miners composed a long list of needed supplies. Mike had his unemployment money and felt flush. Gridley decided it was his turn to get out for a supply run. He took the cash, loaded the Tote Goat, and left in a cloud of blue smoke stinking like the Devil's breath.

Mike and I were left to carry on with the dredging. Following our usual routine, Mike circled the cliffs to get to the transportation raft. Taking what I considered the easier route, I swam, holding our lunch above the water. We both clambered onto the big raft. I started the compressor and Mike primed the two VW engines. When the engines were pumping water, Mike suited up. He dove down to tie up a broken cable, check things over, and pull the suction tube into position.

I could hear stones rattle down the tube, the monster machine's intestine. Big rocks, little rocks, and sand bounced along and came out the end. The finer stuff

"I heaved the nozzle forward as it devoured rocks with a mind-numbing clatter."

CHAPTER 19: IN THE CANYON

came squirting forth from Hargis' ingenious undercurrent box. Gravel shot up through a hose and onto the raft to be sluiced down the row of metal riffles.

After nearly an hour, Mike came up and throttled down the engines. We sat on the raft in relative quiet to eat sandwiches. He speeded up the engines again and did another short stint while I put on my dive suit, hood, weight belt, and fins. When Mike came up, I added my facemask, put the regulator in my mouth, and slipped into the water. It was always a scary moment as the cloudy, cold water enveloped me. I sank slowly while air escaped from my suit, trying to clear my ears from the increasing pressure.

Trailing the air hose after me, I took hold of the handles at the front of the suction tube and positioned myself among the boulders. I heaved the nozzle forward as it devoured rocks with a mind-numbing clatter. Back and forth, I pulled the tube while the machine sucked up soccer ball-sized rocks, gravel, moss, sand, and haphazard darting bullheads.

I worked a big hole in the gravel and became worried about a huge boulder sticking out precariously at the edge. I was about to go up to ask Mike to help move it when a large rock went down the tube bonking and banging. And got stuck. I bubbled my way up, signalled Mike, and went down again. He joined me underwater. We pulled the tube to and fro, managing to coax the rock out. Then we heaved on the leaning boulder and pulled it aside.

I was shivering uncontrollably, so pulled myself onto the raft to try to get warm. Mike took another turn and got another rock stuck. We abandoned the effort to free it. He downed the engines and said, "Let's see what riches we've got." He emptied a portion of the sluices into the gold pan. Like any old-timer miner, he swirled the water around and around, so the lighter stones and sand got carried off. Soon we could see the gold flecks. There were also pieces of solder, mica, iron pyrites, and small glints of garnets. "Not much gold here," grumbled Mike, "maybe seventy-five cents worth."

We collapsed on the boards, disappointed and exhausted. Dusk shadowed camp when we returned to see what we could scrounge for supper. Our eyes lit up when Bill roared down the hill with a roasted chicken!

The next day Bill and Mike spent much of the day trying to dislodge the stuck rock. The boulders were just too big to handle. We needed the lift bag that the river had taken, the balloon that would float the rocks aside.

Alas, Gridley decided that in place of a lift bag, a dynamite charge was needed. It would separate the rocks as well as break up some boulders. After fussing around with the cap and electric wire, Bill went down to place six dynamite sticks. He came up and turned the handle. Once, twice, three times. Nothing. but when he touched the terminals of the battery, BAM! The sound of the explosion was picked up by the drums and echoed around the canyon. Then came bubbles, murk, and dead fish bobbing around in the jade green water.

I went underwater to look. Through the murk, I could see the blast had caused broken boulders and gravel to pile up. More dredging to do. Also, a thick wall of sand and rock needed breaking up. But we didn't have any more blasting caps. We didn't have much of a crew or energy, either. Mike decided to leave. He went up top to work for Hedy painting the Kala abode for cash. It was obvious he didn't have a drop of enthusiasm for the project.

Bill and I were dejected. Only the two of us and more work to do in the little time left to do it. The water was at a low point, and so was daylight.

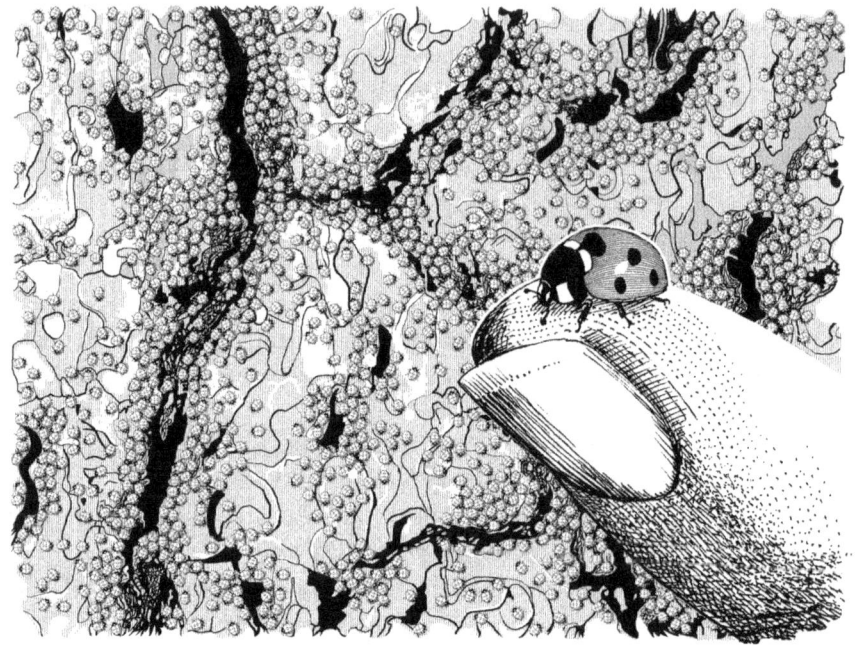

Ladybeetles on ponderosa bark

Autumn had snuck into the canyon. With it came ribbons of reddish insects that settled on the trunks of the ponderosa pines, among the needles and on logs. I was fascinated to inspect the clusters and find thousands of lady beetles squeezed together. In the spring, I'd seen beetle larvae eating aphids in the garden, and now the adults seemed to be settling in for the winter. I asked Bill, "Do lady beetles hibernate here all winter? Do they migrate seasonally, like monarch butterflies?"

"Well, to tell the truth, I don't know." My hero Hargis didn't know? Here was a chance for me to learn something new, even to him.

Bill figured that we would try blasting once more, do some dredging, then quit for the season. On a chilly October day, we went up the hill to get blasting caps. Bill's bashed up VW was parked on the incline because the starter didn't work reliably. We push-started it and drove to Kala's. We found a good place to park on a slope, greeted Hedy and went to look at Mike's painting job. In the cluttered living room with its huge black angus hide rug, Andy Kala lay on the couch, covered with blankets.

Hedy glared at him, hands on her hips. "You and Murphy sure got looped last night. Now, look at you, totally wrung out." Murphy was our local game warden, sheriff, and building supplier. Andy ignored Hedy and said with a silly grin, "Great fun we had, too, worth every moment of the wrunging out."

I listened to Hedy and Andy argue while Bill called around to locate blasting caps. He got a lead to someone named Harsy, who gave us directions to his place. We arrived at an open space among pines where five dilapidated pickup trucks were parked in disarray around a cabin. On the front porch stood wrinkle-faced Mr. Harsy, chewing something. He spat, wiped his palms on his dirty overalls, and extended his hand.

Push-starting a different kind of Beetle

Bill shook it and began a lengthy conversation about our mining project. The Harsy shack was like a theatre set. Through the open door, shadowy figures moved around inside. A little boy with an open flap in his fuzzy blue coverall came out, playing with his penis. A young girl with dark braids came out, too, peering over the boy's shoulder. She gazed at us sidewise with crossed eyes and stuck out her tongue.

Two young men emerged carrying rifles. They pushed the kids out of the way and drove off in one of the rusted trucks. A woman in a purple bathrobe flounced onto the porch complaining in a slurred voice, "Why da I hafta feed doze dawgs?" She kicked one of the two mutts lying on the steps. It yelped and slunk away.

That was enough local color for me. I put my hand on Bill's arm and tugged. He thanked and paid Harsy for the blasting caps. Finally, I was able to hop into Hesperus while Bill got behind then pushed me downhill. I popped the clutch; the VW sputtered to life.

I needed a normality fix, so begged Bill to go to Brush Creek Store for a beer. The beer sign at the store did not ripple, disconnected. But there was other entertainment on tap. A rotund, bearded young man and a toothless, smiling old codger occupied two of the stools. Bill launched into an exchange of mining tales. They were especially keen to chew the fat about a man named Carl Davis. He had a claim upriver from us and lured several groups of divers with their dredging rigs to his site. When the rigs or the divers failed, Carl Davis conned them into running his own equipment. The Davis effort failed, too.

"The suckers had to haul everything in by helicopter at a minimum of $150 for an hour," chuckled the old codger. "But since they didn't get any gold, they couldn't afford to get all the stuff out again. They had to leave barrels full of fuel!" We dutifully laughed. After various jokes about how we or someone else might get the fuel at the Davis claim, the subject strayed back to gold mining. Finally, the two men left the place to Bill, Manuel, and me.

Manuel turned on the beer sign. It flickered to life, showing the beautiful watery scene with a tiny fisherman in a boat on the lake. I pointed out the fluffy clouds with dark bottoms Manuel had drawn. I asked him if they meant a storm had passed or might build up. He smiled and told me, "You figure it out." He took his cloud chart off the wall and gave it to me. As we left, I looked up at the film of feathery cirrus above the canyon. The chart said those clouds often signified cold weather.

Indeed, the veil of clouds preceded a cold snap. We ignored the weather and used the blasting caps. Several days of hard work clearing debris followed. On a day when I was underwater dredging, I paused to clear my ears. Diving had become a real chore because of an ear infection. It took a determined effort to equalize pressure by swallowing and moving my jaw. Doing so, I hesitated too long, and the greedy machine sucked my fin into its mouth.

I went up and Bill went down to retrieve my fin. Just as he climbed on the raft, the compressor choked to a stop. I looked at the machine, then Bill. "Time to quit," I said. He just stood there dripping, fin in hand. I said more firmly, "Anyway, I definitely quit." He looked mildly shocked as though I was another piece of equipment that had failed him.

We dismantled the rig and the raft and hauled what we could onto the cliffs. Back at camp we found Walter Fischer, who'd come down to fish. He and I went upriver while Bill went up the hill. He was going to ask Mike to come help dismantle the operation.

Walter and I chatted while we waited for the salmon to take the roe bait. I realized how much I liked and trusted him. I decided to propose an idea that had been swimming around in my mind. I pointed up to the great dome and asked a question. "Do you think we could get through Bald Rock Canyon?"

He looked at me, puzzled, then asked, "We? Does that mean you, me, Bill, Mike, who?"

I said, "Could you, Walter Fischer, and I, Jeannette Hanby, go through the more challenging part, from Millsap Bar, down to where Feather Falls River meets the Middle Fork?"

Walter nodded slowly, then asked, "Are you saying we'd have to swim and climb rocks all the way? Get bashed around? Maybe drown?" His bemused smile told me he didn't know if I was kidding or serious. I stared back, letting him know I was sincere. He said, "Hmmm. Certainly, would be an adventure. But I...."

"But what?" I interrupted, determined not to let him say he was too old or would be a drag, a burden, or a deterrent. Or worse, that he didn't want to go with me at all.

"Well," he said, taking a deep breath, "I don't want to damp down your enthusiasm. I'll think about it. A river trek would be a challenge for sure. Maybe test us to death."

We were excited about the idea, but when we told Bill, that daredevil air ace scowled. He scanned our faces and said, "Too risky." That made me more determined. Walter and I exchanged a look. Regardless of our resolve, that sort of adventure would have to wait until another season.

The infection in my itching ears, the cold water, and short days told me it was high time to get out. I'd miss the cacomistles pitter-pattering over the bed and their sweet musky smell. I'd also miss the magical light in the canyon, the song of the wrens, and, sometimes, even the Local Color up top. But for now, I was glad to go back to Big Sur.

Anna's Hummingbird

CHAPTER 20

Turning Point

Winter 1965 to Spring 1966

Hummer oh hummer, so small yet so strong,
Hum me a message, wing me a song.
Hummer oh hummer, I hope I'm not wrong,
To sip from your flowers, and follow along.

—Genetta, "Hummer"

A hummingbird flew into the Stone House. I caught it and marveled at its long, nectar-probing beak, iridescent feathers, and tiny perfection. I released it. Where would it go in this cold weather with so few flowers? I wondered if hummingbirds migrated like ladybird beetles and monarch butterflies.

I felt like a fellow migrant wanting to fly free. But now I was captive. Bill had me in his hand. My emotions ebbed and flowed from devotion and love to dissatisfaction. I reckoned the winter in Big Sur would allow me to sort out how much of my life I wanted to spend migrating up and down California with Gridley. I needed time to consider futures and whether Bill would be a long-term element in my life.

Instead of pondering, practical demands distracted me. The most urgent task was to make another lift bag. Its loss had severely hampered our summer's work. The chore of creating a new bag was daunting. Bill had designed and sewn the first one. He vividly remembered how difficult it was. To duplicate the effort would be a real challenge. Industrial sewing machines that could sew leather and rubber were hard to come by. We'd have to rent one.

Bill didn't want to make another lift bag. He told me, "I have enough to do. I'm too busy. It's hard enough to keep up with other jobs. You do it."

I wondered if he said that to get me busy or keep me with him. I'd have to work by his side in his father's hardware store, his base while building equipment and tackling other jobs. After the second year of failure for the gold mining project, Bill needed extra money and the ego-boost from completing commissions and contracts.

My ego was OK. I was part of the mining project: making plans, finding seeds, fishing for funds, acquiring wetsuits and diving gear. My inflated ego was what caused me to take on the lift bag. I knew how to sew and loved challenges, didn't I? Little did I realize what a horrible job it would be.

To sew the bag, we had to live temporarily in King City. This town, not a city, sat astride the Camino Real, the 600-mile highway connecting the 21 old Spanish missions in California. I liked the historic road, now named Highway 101, but I didn't like the situation. To use the machinery, we had to work in the smelly shop during the dark hours when the workers weren't around. To save money, we slept on a mattress on the flimsy floor of the loft above the shop, hot and stuffy. But my ego told me I was tough, committed; I could do this.

Sewing another lift bag involved several steps that took me many wearisome hours and days to accomplish. To start, Bill laid out big pieces of paper and made arcs, then marks at the loci. He said proudly, "I've found that reason and logic are much faster than digging back into my rusty spherical trigonometry. Seeing basics beats the hell out of rote, and here you have an example."

My spherical trigonometry equaled zero, so I was glad he could devise patterns without help. When we had the designs for the individual pieces of the bag laid out, my job was to cut all those pieces and sew them together. The bag I sewed had a 24-foot circumference; the material 12-ounce heavy-duty vinyl-coated nylon. Bill reckoned the bag required about 180 feet of cutting to hack out the pieces.

Then the pieces had to be sewn together. All in all, there were 36 panels with 12 meridians of 11-foot seams. Sewing cables into the seams, strong enough to lift massive boulders, was the hardest part, and I had to ask Bill for help. Eventually, we had 12 shroud lines of 1,200 pounds tensile strength.

Holding the slippery material felt like wrestling with a giant squid. It was a behemoth, a giant sack, an intimidating black shroud. I gritted my teeth, cut and sewed, struggled, and sewed some more. Bill came to admire, sympathize, or tell me what to do better. In general, he annoyed me so much I told him to leave me alone. He growled his low laugh, saying, "I know just how you feel. I remember how much it irritated me when people came to watch me do the first lift bag."

I ignored both his empathy and his gloating. I sewed on. At last, the lift bag emerged with my own body embroidered into it. Hargis jokingly and disparagingly called it my little "pebble snatcher." Making the lift bag was like giving birth to an unwieldy devil monster. I was exhausted at the end. All I wanted to do was get away from King City. I retreated to Big Sur. The Stone House welcomed me, surrounded by grass and trees instead of highways and houses.

My senses opened again while walking into the feathered canyons laced with ferns and sky-pointing redwoods. My whole body responded to the open spaces of sky, natural sounds, and smells. The sight of ocean and grassy hills, plus the fragrance of chaparral, were soul-restoring tonics. My spirit soared to songs of birds swooping above and hummed along with murmuring grasses below.

Acorn woodpecker

I fell in love with grasses, in the plural. They brought me back to earth. I liked the shapes and subtle flowers of grasses like wild oats, fescue, and bluegrass. A sward was home for the many creepy crawlies that found shelter among the stems. When I lay in a summer meadow with my eyes close to the ground, a beautiful, mysterious, miniature world opened up to me..

Grasses were more than a world that housed and fed countless creatures. They provided other lessons, too. Bill showed me how the types of grass and other plants could indicate the quality of soil or the presence of water. Laughing, he told me, "Sometimes I pretend to be a water diviner with special powers. I use grasses and geology to help me find wells for people. It's not my occult powers, but the composite of vegetation, rocks, and soil that tells me where to dig."

Wintertime gave me time to read. I wanted to ingest some meaty books and get my mind going again. But after reading for half an hour, I'd lose focus, get up to stretch, pee, fix a meal, or wander the hillsides and canyons. I visited Claire when I could. Eric gave me a Siamese kitten that followed me up and down the hill and slept in my lap, a fuzzy companion.

Other diversions included welcoming visitors, descending the slope to get supplies, and attending gatherings. I still square-danced at the Grange and enjoyed sojourns at the Big Sur hot springs. Bill was always a distraction when he found time to visit. I tried to balance my need for solitude with sociality, my need for intellectual stimulation with physicality. My emotions rocked liked a boat in the cross currents of a riptide.

Then came my life-changing discovery. On a calm day, the winds of fate filled my flaccid sails and sent me sailing into my future. I decided to read something challenging. I pulled out the book my mother had brought me and looked at the title: *New Directions in Psychology*. Boring, I thought, an academic book composed of chapters by different authors. I looked through the contents. One title attracted my attention with a new word I'd never heard of—"Ethology"—written by Eckhard Hess. I plunged in and sank entranced, like a happy snorkeler onto a colorful coral reef.

The chapter was about animals studied in natural conditions. The European term "ethology" meant the study of animal behavior in the wild using careful observations. In the USA, psychologists had a tradition of studying animals in captivity under controlled conditions. My psychology classes in college used rats in mazes. The idea of using scientific methods to observe animals in the wild excited me. The behavior of ringtails, lizards, bats, birds, butterflies, even ladybird beetles, fascinated me.

As I read the chapter on ethology, I knew I'd dived into my intellectual home pool. The study of animal behavior was for me. Ethologists seemed to be fascinat-

Studying ethology, the science of animal behavior

CHAPTER 20: TURNING POINT

ing people as well, their lives full of adventure. They went to wild places where they lived close to animals, observing and learning about them. They studied essential behaviors like the four Fs I'd learned about in college: Feeding, Fighting, Fleeing, and—professors always paused here so you'd get the joke—Reproduction. And yes, it was the last behavior that most intrigued me. I had a special need to understand how sex and social bonding came to be so intertwined in humans, in me.

When I finished Hess's chapter on ethology, I started rereading it. I was surprised by how profoundly the chapter awakened my mind. For years I'd asked myself on my birthday what I wanted to do with my life. Now I could say YES! I know what I want to do: I want to spend my life trying to understand animal behavior. I want to listen, watch, and learn about living, breathing, jumping, leaping, sleeping, eating, fucking creatures.

I decided to go to graduate school. My decision was daunting, so many obstacles ahead. I felt like that hummingbird setting out on a new flight path. Where would I go? Would I have to take tests? Entrance requirements? Letters of recommendation? My mind whirled in the vortex of questions and snagged when I thought about the Feather River project. And what about Bill?

I did some research, wrote letters, and learned that not one university in the USA offered a graduate degree in ethology. A few offered a blend of psychology and biology that could be called "animal behavior." New York University had a course in animal behavior, but it was in a huge city; I cringed at the idea of living there. I kept searching.

To go to any graduate school required my taking the Graduate Record Examinations. Taking the test after years away from school would be like diving off a cliff into an opaque pool with hidden rocks. I was apprehensive but gritted my teeth, bought self-help books, and scheduled my exams. I had to take the tests in Monterey the next time they were offered. I had mere weeks to prepare my reluctant, lazy brain.

The early spring days were as soggy as my brain. Gray clouds flapped like wet, wool banners over Big Sur, splashing rain over the land. In between bouts of reading, I put on a hat and poncho and saddled up to ride the hills. I searched for edible mushrooms and took time to observe bugs, birds, rabbits, secretive deer, and soaring raptors. I realized how much I had to learn just to identify, let alone understand them.

I visited Claire on her windy ridge top to tell her of my decision to go to graduate school. Her magnificent house was nearly complete, embellished with treasures, including huge whale bones she'd found on the shore. We walked through the building, dwarfed by the beams and giant windows facing the ocean. Somehow the weight and size of the place didn't feel overpowering. The play of light inside the house amplified my feeling of awe. But the place was not very cozy, as I realized on a day when rain and drafts drifted through the windows while Claire and I tried to stuff cloths in cracks.

Most impressive to me was a large walnut table Claire had made herself. For "family feasts," she told me. Her kitchen was her prize place, with counters and cupboards, and lots of space. Claire was a terrific cook. I learned many little things from her that have stayed with me for decades, such as her basic salad dressing recipe: lemon juice, grated ginger, a trickle of honey, and a big squeeze of fresh garlic plus your favorite herbs. Claire also introduced me to The Joy of Cooking, an essential kitchen component and one I've kept as my guide to countless meals.

The days lengthened, sunshine sucked moisture from the storm clouds, grasses grew green, and spring tiptoed in with bouquets of flowers. When darkness curtailed my roaming, I'd write and read by a lantern. I studied; I took the stressful Graduate Record Exams. To my surprise, I passed, scoring well enough to apply to a few universities that would allow me to focus on animal behavior.

My brother and friends came to visit. No one cared that I was still living with Bill without getting married. No one cared if I mined gold on the Feather River or went to graduate school. I avoided any mention of marriage with Bill. He seemed happy enough coming and going from me as his base. Every so often, he'd talk about using the money from the gold to build a trimaran to sail away, exploring the world side by side. "We will escape from progress and wayward social developments." His dream drifted further away from me the more I anchored my thoughts to graduate work.

I received letters from universities. The University of Oregon was my first choice. They offered me a research fellowship for three years, an attractive offer, but I turned it down. I thought that being a teaching assistant would be better for my education. I also wanted Oregon because the department promised me a professor who was coming from England. He studied wolves!

My supervisor would straddle the biology and psychology departments. Perfect. The university would let me take all sorts of courses without having to get grades. I'd be able to explore different subjects such as anthropology, ecology, genetics, and evolution. And, of course, another attraction was the Oregon coast!

Signing on to graduate studies was a significant commitment. I'd been out of school for four years and needed a lot of catching up. Bill put up with my self-doubts, my reading, and scheming, but I could tell he was uncomfortable. What would he do while I was in school? What would we do if I got a higher degree? What about the dream of a boat and sailing away?

I tried to talk to him about possible futures, but he usually twisted the discussion into tirades about jobs, loyalty, and love. He consistently held the river out to tempt me, the link to the treasure trove of money that would induce me to follow his dreams. He was most verbose in the evening when I was weary and only wanted to sleep. We argued and I felt more and more exhausted despite the beauty of my surroundings. I needed a break.

CHAPTER 20: TURNING POINT

"Hill of the Hawk" perched high above the Pacific

CHAPTER 21

Going for Gold
Spring to Summer 1966

Gardening is good for the soul, or so the poets say.
Dark thoughts vanish as the mind strays away,
Playing with the earth on a golden sunny day.

— Genetta, "Gardening"

In late spring, I headed north, alone. I was exhilarated to be off to do something useful, namely starting the vegetable garden at Evans Bar. We needed to have it growing food before the arrival of team members in May and June. I felt stabilized. I knew what I was going to do: gardening now, gold mining in the summer, graduate school in the fall, then whatever wind pushed me onwards.

I sang to the wildflowers as I drove. Their medley of colors gladdened my heart: golden poppies, blue-green sages, white daisies, bright blue lupines. Spring had come early to the central California valleys. The San Joaquin Valley farmers were already plowing. The sight of tractors followed by flocks of blackbirds and sea gulls seemed a good sign.

The mild winter bode well for our mining season. Bill was still building equipment while doing local jobs. He said he was also raising money for the project. But getting Bill to ask a realistic amount for his jobs was like asking a mountain lion to trade its rabbit for a bigger pile of acorns. We were always short of cash. I pondered how we could get more reliable funding.

My Renault was as comfortable to drive as an ancient tractor. The seat wouldn't go far enough forward, so I had to wedge a pillow behind me and use my toes to reach the accelerator. My leg cramped from using the clutch. And of course, the car boasted no power steering or air conditioning or radio. I drove on, sang on, and stopped often for gas, at fruit stands for nourishment, and anywhere else to stretch or snooze.

As I got closer to the Sierra Nevada Mountains, I saw they were true to their name, snow covered. Although farms were being prepared in the lower valleys, I wondered about the mountains. I stopped at Berry Creek Store. Tex greeted me with a hearty, "Howdy there, Shorty. Goin' on up to the canyon?" I couldn't resist replying in my best western drawl, "Yep, I reckon I'll do just that." He laughed saying, "Just maybe you won't. I heard it's still hard goin' up in the mountains."

"Oh, no," I said, "is there still a lot of snow?"

"No darlin', not snow. It's all melted into MUD!"

That warning was repeated when I got to the Kala farm in late afternoon. Andy shook his head, saying, "Well, you can try to get in, but the loggers have been in there all winter. Those heavy trucks have gouged great ruts in the soggy soil. You shouldn't even try to get in."

Andy gave advice I ignored, and Hedy gave me eggs I accepted. I decided to carry on to the Morgenroth cabin so I could set off early in the morning. As soon as the sun peeked through the pine trunks, I drove to nearby Lake Madrone. I wanted to get a coffee at the shop and phone Bill. A man in a forestry service uniform was sitting at the counter so I asked about the status of the roads. He told me in an irritated voice, "The loggers have been ordered to stop working and make repairs. But they've done severe damage. Even with a four-wheel drive vehicle it's hard to get around now."

It was hard. From Brush Creek I struggled with gut-clenching slithers along Bald Rock Road. I toiled along, roaring or grinding through puddles, ruts, and churned mud. Reaching Bean Creek Road, I had to stop. A massive clearing with huge pyramids of ponderosa pine logs confronted me. The logging trucks had left an impassable mire. I parked my Renault on the driest side of the quagmire and prepared myself to walk the several miles to our trailhead. Packing myself with fortitude and gear, I headed through the trees at the edge of the former road. I carried a jug of kerosene in one hand and what seemed like 200 pounds of groceries, seeds, sleeping bag, and clothes in my backpack.

I trudged down the rutted road. In a curve of a small side canyon, I stopped to look at the showy whorls of wild azaleas in full bloom. Their honeysuckle-like fragrance was so rich I felt I'd drunk the elixir of life into my lungs. That sustained me on the march onwards. At last, I reached the trailhead, paused, readjusted my load, and headed downhill.

The granite face of U-I-No darkened as I slogged along the easy trail to reach the flat before dark. I tried going down the skid trail. I tripped on a root, and sprawled full length, my face flattened into the prickly oak leaves. Reaching the bottom with sore shoulders and trembling legs, I dropped my load in the cabin.

Back outside, I rested on the bench under the bare buckeye tree. The place seemed exceptionally quiet, only a little breeze tickling the pine needles, making them sigh. The soft purr of the river fit right in, inviting me to lie down on the table. I looked up and watched flimsy clouds lazily crossing over the wedge of darkening sky between the canyon walls. I fell asleep.

A loud crash made all my senses come alert. I sat up and scanned the moonlit gloom. A skunk emerged from under our makeshift outdoor cupboard. I relaxed, said a bleary howdy to the skunk, and crawled off the table. Inside the cabin, I fumbled around to find bread and peanut butter. I ate while I spread my sleeping bag on the bed and crawled in. The ringtails nuzzled me awake around midnight. Dutifully I wriggled out of my bag and hung some pieces of ham for them. Their fearless elegance as they casually patrolled the cabin made me feel welcome.

It rained in the night. Empty of moisture, fluffy cumulus clouds fled when the sun's eye peered over the canyon wall. I set to work with hoe and shovel in the bright sunshine, turning over clods with wriggling earthworms and curled black millipedes. Already, there were butterflies dancing around: violet ones looking like miniature boats with blue sails, white ones with spots, and some big gold and black swallowtails.

Western Tiger Swallowtails

The weather was much warmer on the floor of the canyon than up top. By midday I'd worked myself into a sweat. Taking off my shirt, a cool breeze slid out of the pine shadows to caress my bare skin. No sunscreen in those days. I wanted to acquire a protective tan all over my body, so stripped off my shorts too. Totally naked except for my hat, I hoed rows then planted vegetable seeds. I added flowers, including a border of Sweet Williams, especially for Bill.

That night as I waited for the ringtails, I sat on the bed playing tunes on my alto recorder. A rustle of the canvas made me pause. One look at an animal told me it

Candide the skunk

was most definitely not a ringtail. It was a skunk! Tail up like a whisk broom, the black and white skunk waddled in and thumped around, as clumsy as the ringtails were graceful. I kept still. Twice the skunk approached me, but it didn't spray. It finally wandered off under the back flap. I named him Candide because he was bold and ignorant and lived in the best of all possible worlds.

In the morning I woke to an uncomfortable feeling in my arm. I pulled up my sleeve and saw the hard body of a tick embedded in my flesh. I tried rubbing it out, gently pulling on it, holding a match over it, then pouring kerosene on it. The tick stayed tight. Finally, I gritted my teeth, put tweezers close to its entry point, and pulled. The entire body came out leaving me with a lesson: check all over my body and bedding every day. The tick could have transmitted a nasty disease. The thought made me realize that disease-carrying little critters were just as dangerous as any larger predators, including trigger-happy hunters.

Several dry days in a row were just right for soil preparation and final planting. I watered everything, checked the fence carefully and tied the garden gate shut. I packed up. Tangy pine fragrance mingled with the scent of manzanita flowers as I plodded up the hill. At the end of a switchback, I looked back at the flat with its fenced garden, the cabin, and curls of new leaves on the buckeye tree. When I returned in May, I'd have to share the place with others.

A newly graded, partly dried-out road greeted me up top. But the noisy trucks were already lumbering about. The angry whine of chainsaws made the din worse. The sounds brought back hurtful memories of my childhood watching my world disappear as developers cut the fruit trees and oaks, planting tract houses and suburbia in their place. I felt badly about our own messing with the Feather River. Even though we were trying to do as little harm as possible, I knew we would affect it. Passing by the Oroville Dam building site reminded me that the post-war economic boom in general was changing the California landscape in so many unattractive ways.

When I got back to Big Sur, I found Bill at the Stone House, irritated and irascible. He had warrants for his arrest.

A tick

"Unpaid traffic violations," he told me. "That means, Sugar Pie, I can't drive around to do all the things we've planned." It also meant Gridley needed to avoid the cops by driving back and forth from Big Sur to the Central Valley by way of the deserted Nacimiento road over the Santa Lucia Mountains. The added time, energy, and planning were stressing Bill out.

I knew he wouldn't or couldn't do all the necessary preparatory work himself. That's partly why I'd gone to the river to start the garden. Already we were approaching summer with much to do. Then we got a major blow: we were losing Mike.

He wrote to Bill from Las Vegas: "I'm not going to participate this year. It's near impossible to estimate the money, let alone the time and effort any of us put into the river project. We owe you and your dad money for materials. We all put in cash. I don't see how we can ever figure who owns or owes what. By bowing out I'm giving you my share. I'll come visit sometime to see how you are getting on."

Mike's quitting made me genuinely sorry because I liked him and he was a good worker. I was worried, too. Without Mike we would have only five people in our crew: three newbies, plus the two of us. Bill and I spent days discussing options, arguing, and annoying one another. Finally, I told Bill, "Go pay your fines; get the equipment together. I'll see people, and get funding and the lease renewed."

My priority was to visit Bill's geologist cousin, Dick Thorup. I thought he'd be interested in the project. He might even fund it or lead me to other supporters. I drove to the Monterey airport where stout, balding Mr. Thorup sat in a room full of boxes and maps. He gave me a warm welcome, then we perused local geological maps. Finally, I introduced the subject of the gold mining project. Dick told me, "Bill is a technical genius, but doesn't seem to know how to put it into the context of a venture with others. I have more faith in him now since you are guiding and working out details. He might even win through this time."

I was glad Dick liked and trusted me but felt a knot of worry tangled in the lines of praise. Bill seemed to have a reputation as an independent genius who didn't work well in a team. It was reassuring to know that Bill's family and friends knew his faults as well as his skills. I asked myself if I had the will and ability to help prod, push, and pull Bill into success. I'd try.

I had a list of estimated expenses to hand to Dick. He said he'd think about it. We arranged a time when Bill and I could take him to visit the Canyon. Pushing himself up from his chair, he smiled broadly and said, "My dear Jeannette. This has been most enjoyable. Now, let me take you out to lunch."

My next chore was not as pleasant. I drove to San Francisco to secure our mining claim. When the west was being "won" from the indigenous peoples, Southern Pacific Railroad managed to secure alternating squares of land over vast areas. We had to get a lease to mine in one of their squares in our mountain canyon. I parked in an alley behind an ugly building and entered a large bare hall with elevators, no stairway or people. Finally, on a third floor, I found a door labeled Land Office. I knocked. A chorus of voices answered, "Come in." A man rose and asked me what I wanted. I explained. He pointed to another door and said, "Wait in there."

I waited. Another man came in and told me he'd take me to see the accountant in another office. There I promptly paid the lease, all of $200. The man led me to yet another office and said, "Wait here, I have to check if this is all that's needed and get a receipt for your $200."

While I waited, I read the signs on the wall showing the forms needed for the kinds and amounts of timber on leased land. I chuckled and a man in the office asked why. I told him that the canyon where we worked was inaccessible to logging trucks, the hillsides way too steep. "There's no way timber could be taken out that would make it profitable."

Thinking of prices of timber, I had an idea. I asked, half joking, "Can I buy some wood for our stove and fireplace?" Laughing, he sold me two and a half cords of black oak at $1.00 a cord and one entire ponderosa pine tree for $2.50. The bill for all the wood we could use in the summer and probably winter, too, came to $5.00. Though the sum was absurdly small, the labor would be large. We would have to saw and chop, split and haul, involving many hours of toil to produce shingles, posts, planks, and stove wood.

After getting our lease renewed, I went to consult with an attorney about legalities, percentages, and how to handle any investments. We invented a contract for crewmembers, fairly useless legally, but it did outline the dangers someone was signing on for. Since we weren't a registered business, and had no wealth, no one could really sue us.

Bill and I picked up Dick at his office in May. The three of us set off for the Feather River. We expected to find Kevin, one of our new crewmembers there. Reaching the flat at Evans Bar at dusk, we couldn't see Kevin anywhere. There was no sign of his work and no note. I wasn't too surprised. When Mike had introduced me to Kevin in Monterey, I asked him what he expected to get out of the summer's work. He exclaimed jovially, "Work? Why I thought this was to be a summer vacation!"

CHAPTER 21: GOING FOR GOLD

Bill showed Dick the sprouting garden while I tied a red ribbon around the dead pine tree I'd paid for. We got Dick set up, supped, and bedded down in the cabin. The ringtails put on their best performance to charm him. The next day we took Dick to the Big Pool and let him be awed by the site. He seemed pleased with what he saw. He even left his mammoth sleeping bag as a token that he'd be returning. And yes, he told us he would deposit funds in the bank account I'd set up. He'd contribute a start-up sum of $1,000. I was thrilled.

As we escorted Dick out of the canyon, he expressed his dissatisfaction about Kevin, the missing crewmember. Bill and I were uncomfortable thinking our sponsor might conclude we were poor judges of character. We stopped near Brush Creek to show off Lake Madrone to Dick and found Kevin there. He looked only a little chagrined at being discovered. He told us he was staying at the home of his new friend Ivan, a crippled older man.

His excuse for not being in the canyon: "I was lonely. Kinda dark down there in the nighttime. That big Dome glares at ya all day. I didn't have anyone but those miner's cats to talk to. Radio doesn't pick up signals. And a skunk kept coming around. Scared me. Anyway, I'm up here with Ivan, helping him out."

What could we do? We weren't paying Kevin or any other crewmembers to work for us. Pay would be the gold—if we got it. We told Kevin a pine tree was waiting for him. If he still wanted to be a member of the team, he'd better get down to the flat and start sawing and chopping. I expected him to quit on the spot, but he said he'd head on down. When Kevin did return to the canyon, he took along his handicapped buddy, mostly carrying him down on his back. Meanwhile Bill and I drove south to take Dick home to Monterey and collect supplies.

While we were away, our next two new crewmembers arrived in the canyon: Steve and Susie Hughes. I barely knew them even though they were also based in Big Sur. They'd been managing a small lodge called Deetjin's. Bill had worked with Steve on the trail-building project at the beautiful McWay Cove. He'd talked Steve into joining the mining crew after he watched Steve deftly learning to run a jackhammer properly.

Bill thought Steve would be a hard-working miner. Steve thought so, too. He'd talked Susie into coming along, so they'd packed up their things, including their baby girl, Delisa. They came north to the High Sierras like hippie gypsies laden with gear, marijuana seeds, and high hopes. Steve proved his worth at the start, at least to Kevin, when he helped carry Ivan back up the hill.

Bill and I set out a week later from Big Sur to join them. At last, we were beginning an organized, all-out effort. This was the Going-For-Gold project of 1966!

Big Pool with the dredging raft (center) and the small raft (right). The drums at left support the suction hose.

CHAPTER 22

Bare Ass Bar

Summer 1966

"This ain't bad once you get used to it."

—On a gravestone in Berry Creek cemetery

Bill and I got back to Brush Creek in early June. We stayed at the Morgenroths' to make Zap Juice packets. Starting with 100 pounds of raw cane sugar, we sorted it into easy-to-use portions, two tablespoons at a time, plus a pinch of salt. We sealed the plastic bags with Mrs. Morgenroth's iron. The mix would go into water or juice, often with added vitamin C tablets or other flavorings. Basically a rehydration mix, Zap Juice was a good tasting, revitalizing drink. Bill and I knew personally about the summer heat, and this year was bound to be as bad or worse. Keeping people hydrated was one of my jobs.

We left most of the Zap Juice packets in Hesperus and loaded ourselves with a portion of the other supplies we'd bought. We carried down wholesale amounts of spaghetti noodles, brown rice, wheat flour, oatmeal, dried milk, beans, peanut butter, jam, honey, and tins of tuna. I carried a bucket full of tomato plant starts, balancing trays of eggs on my head.

Bill and I reckoned we could get fish and maybe deer in the canyon. We still had some venison in the Morgenroth freezer. I hoped we would seldom have to go out for supplies. Alas, that was a false hope. I hadn't yet fully appreciated the human animal's need to socialize and get changes of scene.

We arrived on the flat late in the morning. Kevin was gone. He left a note: "I've always wanted to visit Ireland where my people have roots. In short, I am off in search of my muse."

I sighed. So much for that crewmember. I cheered up a little reading Kevin's P.S.: "A nice guy came down named Hans. He told me he was a VW mechanic and a diver too. He said a guy named Walter Fischer contacted him. Hans will be back in a week or so to see if you'll take him on as part of the team."

If we could replace Kevin with a real mechanic and diver, whoopee! Since Kevin had gone to seek his muse, I took a closer look at his buddy Steve. Would he be a stayer? Steve had a stocky physique, wore raggedy clothes and hair, and smoked pot. He looked and acted like a hippie but was energetic and strong. Strong-willed as well. He didn't seem to know whether to be a responsible citizen or zoned-out pleasure seeker and exhibited both traits.

His wife, Susie, seemed softer and more stable. They had produced Delisa, a delightful, healthy infant who quickly became a treasured mascot. Susie was lean and lithe, with long blond hair. She was pleasant to be around, talked incessantly, and had a wide range of interests.

Susie took a huge load off me. She helped in the garden, washed dishes, pots, and pans, and tried to keep the lamps full. Best of all, she and I shared cooking duties. Susie and Steve had their nest downslope from camp. Steve built a platform into an oak tree and brought down a mattress. He rigged a fishnet around the bed. The mesh kept infant Delisa from falling into the river or onto the rocks below.

Susie and Delisa in their nest overlooking the river

We were set up for a season of dredging for gold, but Gridley decided we should wait for Hans. While we waited, he and Steve went up top to do odd jobs for cash to pay our bills at the Brush Creek and Berry Creek stores. Susie and I were left carless and careless. Since the crew was not yet going full tilt at our windmill in the river, I had precious time to write and doze in my Mexican golden hammock. Susie and I gabbed. We played with the camp lizards and the ever-entertaining ringtails.

Days were baking hot, so Susie and I got used to going around mostly naked or wearing sopping wet shirts. I began to feel less awkward, glad to be getting rid of some of my puritanical "modesty." Susie seemed comfortable with nudity. I wondered how hippies so casually cast off the shackles that bound my generation.

Summer solstice came and went. Bill and Steve tinkered with the equipment and the three of us did some diving. We all went around in various stages of undress. Not only was it hot but dressing and undressing to put on a wetsuit was tiresome. We put a big umbrella on the raft to provide shade.

The vegetables and flowers in my garden thrived and attracted pollinators. Bees and paper wasps kept me alert. Two-tailed swallowtails and pipevine butterflies floated around like phrases escaped from a poem. I noticed the absence of ladybird beetles. The blue sail butterflies had sailed on, too. Where did they go? The season was moving on.

Finally, in late June, Hans arrived. He was a handsome hunk of a man, muscled and beaming. In his arms and on his back, he carried a big load of equipment and personal stuff. He told us he wanted to bring in a friend, another German mechanic, named Georg. We felt as though we'd been given the promise of a summer's supply of free ice cream. At last, we would be a proper team.

Hans quickly settled in and got familiar with the setup. Usually after breakfast, the three men went to the raft. For most of the morning they took turns handling the dredge and tending to equipment. A week went by with a relatively relaxed attempt at dredging. Diversions and difficulties meant the men were usually back at camp for lunch. To keep them on the job longer, I developed a routine. I made breakfast before the sun peeked over the canyon's rim then banged on a pan to get people up. After everyone ate, Susie and I cleaned up, fixed lunches, watered and weeded. Either or both of us would take out lunch midday.

Susie would bring lunch when I went early to take a turn diving. If there was no raft at shore, she packed the food into a Navy Seal bag and tied baby Delisa to her breast. Climbing aboard a huge old inner tube, she floated out to us. Though there wasn't much danger, we feared she might get carried on downstream into rapids so rushed to catch her as she bobbed towards us. We had a good communal laugh of relief each time.

Despite efforts to facilitate dredging, all too often hours would pass with the engines idling or quiet while the men fussed with the equipment. Steve, stark naked, might be straightening the air hoses. Gridley, half-out of his wetsuit, could be checking over the compressor, while Hans, stripped down to undershorts, worked on the engines. I sometimes took a moment to admire these men's physiques, especially Hans's fine-looking body. Bill's wiry sturdiness was not unattractive in comparison. And Bill remained the one in my bed and heart, not Hans.

Early one midsummer day, I crept out of bed at dawn. Fumbling around inside the dark cabin for a frying pan, I got a shock. A shiny black widow spider had attached her web to the rim, hiding her egg sac in the pan. Bill once told me how he got a black widow spider bite and woke up two days later, struggling through

Black Widow spider with egg-case

fevered dreams. I was very respectful of the lady spider and apologized as I put the sac in a jar. A cabin full of spiderlings would be as welcome as invaders blasting us with buckshot.

Sunshine spilled down the great stone cliffs above as I started a fire and prepared coffee. I put out stacks of plates, cutlery, and cups. After making fake maple syrup, I put the cleaned-out spider's frying pan on the flames and poured in some oil, got eggs from the burlap-bagged cooler, scrambled them, and sliced bread. I stood ready to dip slices in the egg goo and waited for customers.

Steve came and forked a pile of French toast onto his plate, sweat already gleaming on his bare chest. Bill came next in torn shorts, shirtless, wiping his brow. Susie and I started assembling lunch. Still no Hans. Gridley and Steve wandered down to the Big Pool. A soft whistle alerted me. I looked around for Hans, but he didn't show. The whistle came again. Already on the flat, a man in the shadows was approaching. I glanced around for clothes because I was clad only in my cut-off jeans, chest bare, my breasts bobbing about. I grabbed a partly dry shirt off the line, and Susie quickly wrapped her sarong more firmly around her.

A pleasant voice came from the trees, "No need to dress up, ladies, I'm an old nudist myself." And thus, our nature-spirit, Walter Fischer, arrived. He walked briskly into camp with his knapsack on his back. We were glad to see him. This time he'd brought a bag of home-grown tomatoes ranging from green through white, pink, and luscious red.

While I served Walter, Hans finally appeared. The two men chatted away in a mix of German and English, then went down to the beach. Dumping their clothes on the shore they swam out to the big raft to join Gridley and Steve. A while later, Susie and I paddled out on the little raft with a tub of potato salad and freshly-baked bread.

CHAPTER 22: BARE ASS BAR

We all sat on wetsuits or bare boards as we feasted on salad, bread, carrots from our garden, peaches, and Walter's tomatoes. Gridley stood up, knocking the big jug of Zap Juice over, splashing us with sugary water. We laughed and rinsed ourselves in the pool. Feeling jolly, we decided that we were having an impromptu celebration of the dredging season. We raised cups of the Zap Juice and cheered.

Mr. Fischer held out his cup for a refill. Wriggling his bottom, he said, "Got to be careful of all those raft splinters on my bare ass." Bill, also naked, looked at Walter and said in his commandant's voice, "Hear ye, hear ye. I now bestow upon Evans Bar a new and more appropriate name—Bare Ass Bar."

We all laughed uproariously and pounded on our bums like drums. Walter and I ignored the others to talk over our plan to hike to Feather Falls. We'd decided to test our clambering skills before seriously thinking of a trip through Bald Rock Canyon. I told him I'd phone him in the next few days when I went out to get supplies. "See you soon!" he called as he jumped off the raft and swam to shore against the current. I admired his 70-year-old agility and strength. I sincerely hoped we'd take on the challenging canyon trek together.

A few days passed while the men worked hard. Then they started drifting from the routine. At dawn one early morning, I started breakfast, watered the corn patch, and straightened the crooked bench at the buckeye table. I sat on the bench and waited for the crew. It was full daylight and as hot as my cast iron skillet when Bill arrived. He filled a cup with coffee and meandered off to the Meditation Chamber. I fried eggs and sausages and yelled, "BREAKFAST!" No one responded, so I ate by myself.

I'd had enough waiting around, so left for my sanctuary by the river. I sat on a rock and tried to write about the river project. I grew curious about what was hap-

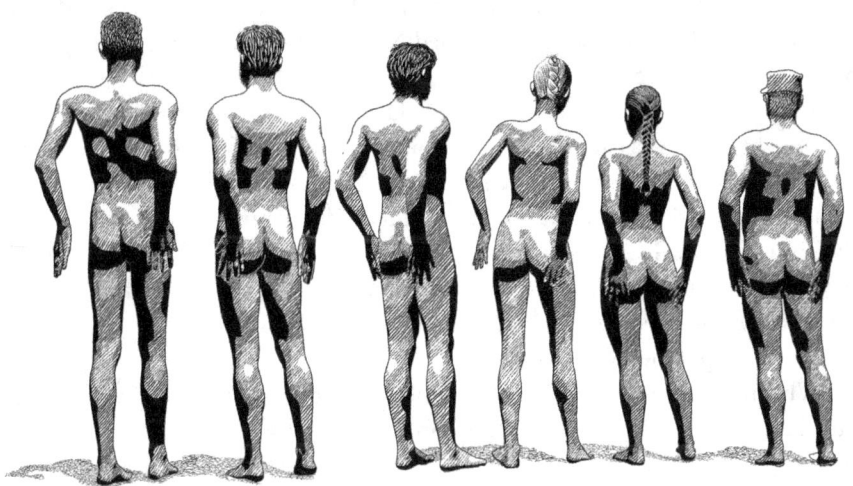

"We all laughed uproariously and pounded on our bums like drums."

pening because of the quiet so dog-paddled downstream. The three men were on a sandbar stooped over something. I laughed when I saw what they were inspecting—about 20 cannabis plants. Steve's plantation. One leafy stalk had given up the struggle, but the others looked fine.

Dredging problems grew along with the pot plants. One day Hans tried to start the engines. Not enough gas. Steve went to get fuel. He put the gas down the pipeline; I guided it into the drums. Bill primed the pumps; Hans started the engines. Kaplooey! went the fitting for the foot valve. Bill fixed it, then started the engines again. They roared to life. I was relieved because I'd noted the brief irritation on Hans's face each time something went wrong.

We were still learning how to work as a team. Tolerance of daily disasters and a sense of humor helped a lot. Working well together included teasing each other about our mistakes, irritations, even the wounds and bruises on our butts. Teasing helped ease tensions. But sometimes tension boiled beneath the surface, erupting in nastiness. For example, one evening we were sitting around, talking about nicknames. We named the baby Deliriously Delightful Delisa. Susie said being called Silly Suze was OK with her. Hans got the name Hero because he came to rescue us from failure. We decided to give Steve the name Toro because he could work like a bull. Bill already had the nickname Gridley, and we laughingly gave him the added name Grizzly because he growled a lot. He took the tease with a grimace and did an exaggerated growl for us.

Then Bill looked at me, and I thought he'd propose some funny name. Instead, he pointed to me and intoned in a deep broadcaster's voice, "Here we have Nero." Next, he lifted his chin and eyebrows, and pointed to Hans. He said sarcastically, "And we have Hero." Then he gave Steve a look that could have skewered a squirrel, saying, "And here is Zero."

We laughed, what else could we do? Was Bill just trying to make a rhyme? Somehow, I didn't think so. Being named Nero implied I was lazy, fiddling while others worked, or bossy and ineffective, like Nero in Roman times. None of the implications was positive. As for Hero, Gridley's sarcastic pronunciation implied he thought of Hans as anything but heroic. But the Zero for Steve was a flat-out insult. All three of us were offended.

I was glad Gridley decided to duck out for a day, letting tempers cool. By the time he returned, Georg still hadn't arrived. The men continued their struggle with the machinery and each other. I needed a break from the tension and went out to get mail and supplies, call and Walter about our Feather Falls trek. I asked Susie to take over camp duties for a day.

Whistling and humming my way uphill, I dropped cares behind like stale breadcrumbs. A beautiful sight stopped me in my tracks: a single doe poised like a statue on a ridge with the backdrop of U-I-No's bald granite head gleaming in the sun. The stunning beauty of Bald Rock Canyon sometimes overwhelmed me.

Reaching the top, I got into my hot box of a car and drove to the small spring by

CHAPTER 22: BARE ASS BAR

Encounter with a deer

the track. I dipped myself and my sweaty shirt in the water, leaving me damp and cool. I found Alonzo there, sitting in the mud. Alonzo, my favorite and one true example of the Maidu Indians, was drunk. He waved feebly and called "Hallo thar Miner. Got any gol' yet?"

"Not yet," I replied. "But we're working on it."

Seeing Alonzo looking wrinkled and crumpled saddened me. He struggled to his feet and told me he'd just come back from Reno. He pulled a fist full of keno cards from his pocket. I didn't even know what keno cards were. Alonzo told me they were like poker chips, but now, worthless. I splashed myself, filled canteens, and offered him a lift home even though it was in the opposite direction from my errands.

After the detour to Alonzo's, it was late morning when I reached Manuel's at Brush Creek. I bought gas and waited as Manuel pumped up a soft tire on my car. I took a look at the beer sign. There, on the bank of the idyllic mountain lake, stood a camel and a palm tree. The scene struck me as so inappropriate that I started laughing uncontrollably. My sides hurt, and I was gasping for air as Manuel patted my shoulder. He smiled at my glee and said, "I appreciate your appreciation of my art. Thank you for your excellent imitation of the laughing lady at the circus show."

Feeling more lighthearted, I cruised down the hill and impulsively stopped at the Berry Creek cemetery. I strolled around the shady, weedy plots, reading headstones. Suddenly the howl of a chainsaw spooked me. I fled straight to the Berry Creek Store. Just as I arrived, Andy pulled up in the Merrimac stage, his face deep red and bristly, his beaky nose like a gravestone on his face. He sighed a worn-out moan and said, "Goddamn, it's hot." Indeed, it was. I looked at the bare blue sky and asked after Hedy. "Not so hot," he said. "She's gone off to see her cousin and left me with all the chores."

I didn't know what to say, merely waving goodbye as he left. As I parked next to Tex's store, I realized how seldom we saw Hedy and Andy. I'd ask Gridley later.

Tex greeted me with a huge smile and a wave. "Howdy, Sprout," he said. "You're barefoot again. Ho hum.. But stickers and stones are out there. Are your feet so tough they don't hurt?"

"Sometimes they hurt," I admitted, "but shoes hurt more." I looked at my dirty feet and asked them how they felt. They just stood there, sulking.

"The usual?"

"Yep, please!" I puttered around for groceries, the melting ice cream dribbling on my hands. Tex kindly pumped up the tire again, while telling me another of his lame stories.

"A fellow named Jim used to live here. He was a real con artist. He tricked, hoodwinked, conned, and finagled. Ho-hum. That Jim bought and sold chickens, eggs, furniture, and most any ol' piece of equipment. He traded washing machines, rifles, chainsaws, pumps. He even got a car for $40! The guy gave him the pink slip on trust. After a month of wheedling and begging, the guy gave up and left. Ho-hum. That was Jim."

I had to laugh at the way Tex could rattle on about anyone and any event. His stories usually had no moral, and many went nowhere. Even so, they amused me. Laughing certainly was a tension reliever.

My next stop was the Morgenroths' to get my dose of current affairs. They caught me up on the national news. I listened in a distracted way while they told me about President Johnson's views on racism. They seemed more concerned about the Vietnam conflict. I felt a glimmer of interest as they described the protests in Berkeley, the widespread use of LSD, and the popularity of a music group called the Beatles. The Morganroths found the mid-1960s fascinating. I couldn't summon much concern about the decade or the world outside our tiny social bubble in the canyon.

From the Morgenroths', I phoned Walter to arrange a date for our trek to Feather Falls. On my way back to the trailhead, I stopped to pick wild blackberries on an abandoned farm. I felt much better after a day away from my crewmates, especially Grumpy Gridley. Setting off downhill with my load of supplies, I sang happy songs.

Deep shadows lay over the flat by the time I reached the bottom. I found four disgruntled crewmembers at the table. Bill, Steve, Susie, and Hans sat there silently, but Bill stood as I approached. He didn't even acknowledge me as he strode off into the dark.

Bill Hargis, sketched from life by Jeannette

The crew, late 1966, L to R: Jeannette, Georg, Hargis, Suzy & baby Delisa, Hans, Steve

CHAPTER 23

Dredging Up

Summer 1966

Soon golden leaves will festoon the ground,
And dainty toadstools sprout all around.
Rains will come and gloom, and more,
To dredge up doom where hope went before.

—Genetta, "Dredging for Gold"

I sat down at the table with Hans, Steve, and Susie as Bill stomped off. Hans immediately started enumerating disappointments. "The engines broke down today. Again. We needed spare parts that aren't here. I can keep the engines running by using bits from my car, but then I'll find there's no fuel or oil."

Steve took his turn to complain. "We aren't moving many boulders, and when we do, more just fall into the hole we've made. Our tailing pile needs moving again, guy wires need repairing, we need to weld the tube again, and we need to agree on where we dredge. Bill simply won't listen to or tackle the problems. We have to run every little thing by him, or he gets huffy."

Susie summed up the situation, saying meekly, "The reality is, we aren't getting any gold."

She got up and started putting away the groceries I'd brought down. The group broke up in a cloud of silence as hot and humid as the weather. Tempers were fraying like those cables on the raft, ready to break. I went down for a swim before bed and found Bristly Bill sitting on a rock fidgeting. He couldn't be appeased and grumbled about unappreciative, incompetent people, and frustrations with the operation. He was irritated by how Hans and Steve couldn't keep the operation going without his constant double-checking. He complained about their slipshod use of tools, how they both ignored requests and disappeared when needed.

I tried to cut short his tirade by remembering to ask about Andy and Hedy. He brusquely told me, "I'm staying away because whenever I go there, they're arguing. I get caught up when they want me to take sides. I can't do it. I reckon they might even break up."

A few days later, on a hot evening, I heard a hoot. I looked up and saw a light flickering through the trees above camp. Behind the flashlight came a surprise, my friend Dave from Big Sur. He brought down cherries, chocolate, and cheer. Gridley and I rafted Dave through the Big Pool in the moonlight and went skinny-dipping off the sand bar. Bill stood proudly, pointing out features on the raft, the cliffs, and shimmering pool. He turned to Dave, patted my bottom as he would a pony, and said, "We've renamed this place Bare Ass Bar."

Embarrassed, I looked at Dave, who just grinned. He stood naked as a Greek god. I turned to look at Bill and I caught him glancing at Dave's body then at me, a frown on his face. What was he thinking?

Dave asked to stay overnight to go to Feather Falls with Walter Fischer and me. He and I sat together at the camp table talking and watching the stars until Bill came to interrupt us. In a voice like the slap of a riding whip he said, "I'm off to bed now." Friend Dave took his sleeping bag to the spare cot we were reserving for Georg. I stayed up for a while with the ringtails. I hoped Bill would be asleep by the time I joined him. He was, and I sighed with relief.

In the morning, I got breakfast going early and went into the cabin to get cooking oil. I was shocked to see little spiderlings, as delicate as dandelion fluff, everywhere. The jar with the egg sac lay lid-less on the floor. It had been overturned by a skunk, ringtail, raccoon, or a careless person. Getting a wet cloth, I quickly gathered all the baby spiders I could.

Worry about the remaining spiders was eclipsed when I heard Walter's whistle. Down the hill, he came, laden with goodies: sandwiches, tomatoes, apple strudel, and a melon. Walter, Dave, and I set out. Bill grumbled at our suggestion that he come along, saying, "Someone has to stay and do some work."

Not feeling a wisp of guilt, we three trotted, swam, hopped, and climbed. A flat rock in the middle of a pool invited us to sit and eat. Rested, we scrambled up Fall Creek to the base of Feather Falls that pounded us with noise and spray. Cascades of yellow monkeyflowers hung from rocky cliffs, and the tang of sweet sage and minty herbs surrounded us as we stood under the rainbows from the waterfall breathing in friendship.

Swimming back through the Big Pool, we found Bill, Steve, and Hans hard at work. Grumpy Gridley barely spoke to me during and after dinner. I knew he was angry, jealous, and probably just tired, too. He woke when I came late to bed, grumbled at me for being away all day, accusing me of not supporting him and the project. Enraged, I accused him of being irrational and undermining morale. In retaliation he got out of bed, picked up the mattress, and dumped me out on the ground. I retreated to my Mexican hammock.

CHAPTER 23: DREDGING UP

The next morning, Susie and I made two huge pans of frittata without seeing any baby black widow spiders. She and I planned meals she could cook because I wanted to go out with Dave and Walter. Dave was leaving, and Walter and I wanted to do some exploring. I was glad to leave Bill and the canyon for the day. At the roadhead, Walter and I said goodbye to Dave and drove to a spot near the canyon rim.

We aimed to get to the top of Bald Rock Dome for a view of the canyon bottom, a spot we'd have to pass if we pursued our adventure. Feeling intrepid, we crawled under a barbed-wire fence with a big NO TRESPASSING sign. When we got to the top of the dome, we realized we couldn't see the river at all. We were pleased with our exploration even though we got caught by the owner.

On the way back to the trailhead, Walter wanted to do a side trip to buy eggs at a little farm. A withered woman with dull eyes and dusty, gray hair came out. The porch stairs wobbled and squeaked as she came down to greet us. She put the eggs in bags and noticed me admiring the flashy peacocks strutting among the hens and ducks. Peacocks were an odd bird to find in the mountains but certainly added local color to this dreary farmyard. "Amazing to see peacocks here," I said, adding "My mother raised them. They remind me of her."

"Wait here," she told me firmly. She went into her house and brought out a bouquet of radiant peacock feathers. Thrusting them into my hands, she told me, "Always keep something beautiful nearby to cheer you up." The image of her stern face and advice has stuck with me through life.

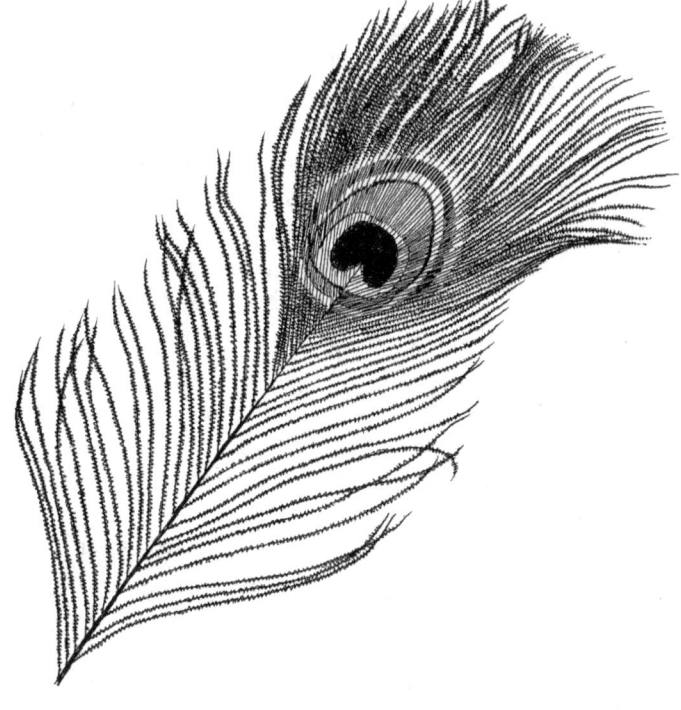

I started down the trail as dusk fingered its way into the canyon, pulling in handfuls of dark clouds and gloom. I'd had a good afternoon out, so I tried my best to pass on some cheer to Gridley by recounting details of my outing. He interrupted me and launched into how I spent too much time out. "You're not supportive when I need you. Like today, why did you have to go up with Dave and Mr. Fischer?"

I didn't want to have to justify my excursions so didn't argue with him. Instead, I took his hand and led him to our outdoor bough bed, hoping that the cacomistles would appear. They were usually good at distracting Bill from further verbal and physical intercourse. I wasn't in the mood for either. Luckily Shatze, his favorite, appeared. She jumped onto his thigh, waiting for a treat. Bill went off to get something for the ringtails, and I gratefully slipped into sleep.

Bill had already left when I woke in the morning. He'd tucked a note to me under the coffee pot on the table: "I need to make a quick trip south to get spare parts." I knew he was going partly to dodge the disgruntled crew and me, too. Hans somehow got the engines running. We dredged on.

Then we had an emergency. Baby Delisa got sick. Susie brought her to me. I felt the child's hot skin and knew she had a dangerously high temperature. Had a spider bit her? A tick? Stung by a wasp? We discussed if we needed to take her out and try to find a doctor. Susie and I conferred. We figured the heat had caused the little one to dehydrate. We would first try cooling the baby and wait until dark when a trek up top would be more bearable.

She and I spent hours in the shade patting water on Delisa, dipping her in a water bath, and making her sip watered down Zap Juice. By evening the baby had cooled down. We were all enormously relieved, especially the doting father, Steve. Even so, Susie and I decided to go up the hill at daybreak and check with a doctor in Oroville. We found a doctor in town who assured us we'd done the right thing shading, cooling, and giving the baby rehydration drink. He talked with Susie about vaccinations; she made an appointment.

We shopped for special baby foods and fruits in town, returning by way of Tex's store where we bought supplies and ate ice cream cones. I called our sponsor, Dick, with a report of developments. He told me he'd deposited another $500. Next, I called Bill at his mother's place with the good news. He hardly acknowledged it, only saying he'd return in a few days.

On the way down the hill carrying most of the supplies, I stubbed my big toe badly. All night I tossed and turned. At first light, a trumpet sound splatted the dawn like a giant's fart. My heart raced as I bolted into shorts and a shirt. Hobbling up the path to camp, I saw no one.

The trumpet sounded again. Was the military, a posse, or a church group arriving? I looked up the slope to see one man coming down the trail laden with objects. He looked like a tramp out of an old movie, bent over, carrying everything he owned. The man waved his trumpet in greeting, saying, "Hello, I'm Georg!"

CHAPTER 23: DREDGING UP

Georg arrives

"Hello, and welcome," I called back. I gestured to the communal table; he unpacked his gear. I watched in awe as he laid out his baggage: the trumpet, a guitar in its case, a movie camera, a slide camera, tripod, binoculars, camp stool, fishing spear, a canvas bag, and a huge backpack. Georg was still bright-eyed and not even breathing hard after his 12-hour drive through the night from Los Angeles. I was in awe of his strength and fortitude, as well as his good humor.

With a smile, Georg told me he'd gone out of his way to see Oroville Dam. "Very impressive, so huge. Higher than the Aswan Dam in Egypt. Hard to find your trailhead up here in the mountains. Took me a long time on those back roads. Finally, I spotted Hans's VW."

I gave Georg food and Zap Juice to drink. Susie came into camp with baby Delisa. Georg stood up immediately to take the infant in his hands. He raised her high, the baby bubbling with giggles and Susie smiling broadly. He won their hearts and mine, too. Georg gave the baby back, then said, "Now, please show me where you are dredging."

When Bill finally returned with gear and replacement parts, he welcomed Georg enthusiastically. With all crew on hand, we tried our best to dredge. Tried is the operative word. The men mostly wrestled with the dredge, dove, fished, and chopped wood. In addition to diving, I had supplies to gather, meals to prepare, and the garden to look after. Susie had kitchen and camp work and the baby, too.

Jeannette, Hans and Georg

Evening meals were a time to relax. Having Georg with us was a new and welcome treat. He sat strumming his guitar while we cooked, cleaned up, sang, and played cards. Hans and Georg usually carried on a lively banter and did silly things. For example, Hans amused himself and some of us by tying strings to yellow jacket wasps. He then let them fly around tethered to twigs. He also showed Georg how to catch flies by slapping hands together midair.

Some things were more than silly. Hans dared Georg to dive from the rocks where the wooden crane hung over the steep cliff. Georg took the dare and dove, a scary plunge followed by a huge splash. We held our breaths, waiting for him to emerge. His head finally came up a long way downriver. We clapped, and I glanced at Hans's smug, almost arrogant expression.

Georg sometimes retaliated. One early morning when we were all finished with breakfast except for Hans, Georg went to their camp and trumpeted a reveille. The sound echoed around the canyon. Hans hustled in shortly afterward, and we all chuckled at his grumpy face. On a day when Georg was doing laundry, he hung his and Hans's sheets on our sagging clothesline between two pines. Candide scented the flapping sheets in passing. I thought Georg would re-wash them. He washed his own and kindly made Hans's bed with the skunk-tainted ones. He winked at me when Hans told us about his bed's skunky smell.

The crew worked well together most of the time. There were little spats such as when Georg came to the table, furious that one of us had taken his shoes and hidden them. We looked at one another's innocent faces and then looked for the shoes. We found them not far off in a little gulley. We recited the list of usual suspects: fox, porcupine, cacomistle, skunk, bobcat, mountain lion. The amusement on various faces didn't reassure me that none of us had done the deed.

Georg joining the crew made me realize the impact of an individual in a small group. His music and even temper helped moderate all our relationships. He also seemed to figure out when and how to help, without shoving his ego into the operation. I especially appreciated how he played with baby Delisa, freeing Susie to help with cooking and cleaning.

Georg showed me how to run the VW engines so I could stay on the raft and he in the water. I'd been spending long periods in the murky underwater, and my ears hurt and itched. Being on the raft let me dry out. I could also tend to little chores, such as checking guy lines, sanding down the wooden deck, and regluing seams on wetsuits. When things were slow, I whittled away at hard manzanita wood. It glowed a deep reddish-brown and became a tangible symbol of what I loved in the natural world of California. Carving it joined my practical with my spiritual side as I tried to make useful hair clips and animal figures from branches and twigs.

One sluggish afternoon, I was whittling while Georg and Hans were dredging. Georg came out of the water and went to camp, leaving Hans and me on the raft. Hans shut the engines down. He told me about living in Germany during the war. As a youth he was terrified when people ran screaming into reservoirs to escape phosphorus bombs. He described burning pools where dead people floated with crisped black heads and soft, intact bodies.

I was horrified. His grim stories made me realize how little I knew about World War II. I'd been born during the early years of the war, too young to understand what was going on. My clearest memory of that time was how upset my mother became when our kindly Japanese neighbor and sometimes housekeeper was abruptly taken away. Years passed before I began to fathom just how monstrous the war had been, devouring lives and places over so much of the world.

Hans and Georg went out on a hot day to get some engine parts. They came back loping down the hill early the next morning, having driven all night. Before they began repairs, they decided they wanted to set up their camp in a more permanent and private spot. They asked for my advice. We searched for a good campsite. They finally chose what Bill and I considered our "guest room," a nearly level spot in a semi-circle of sheltering boulders. Dirt flew, leaves rustled, stones were carried and thrown aside. Soon, the little nook was as neat and tidy as could be.

Midday Bill came down the Skid Trail enveloped by a cloud of dust and a dark mood. He'd gone out to see about a job offer at the Oroville Dam site. He also bought a new compressor waiting to be brought down. While we put away supplies, I brought him up to date. He was less than thrilled by my giving away what he considered our private space. He growled that I'd allowed Hans and Georg to make a "German concentration camp."

His wording unsettled me. I wondered if he had a grudge against Germans. Bill had a German car, used German engines for the project, and had German mechanics on the team. Walter Fischer was a German friend. Did his huffiness have to do with the war years? Was he jealous of Hans's and Georg's "German" skill and efficiency? I left the questions escape, unanswerable.

We went to the cliffs to see what the crew was doing. Steve, Georg and Hans stood around on the raft talking. Gridley pointed to them and said, "Why aren't they dredging?" He turned to look at me as though I had failed to whip the crew into action. Gridley started heckling me, making negative statements about how we were all inept, unappreciative, undisciplined, and inconsiderate. His unfairness made me angry. Gritting my teeth I told him, "Calm down and find a better perspective. Meanwhile, I'm going up the hill to check with Tex about our orders and bills."

Hans had offered me the use of his neat and reliable VW. Driving his car certainly made my expedition more enjoyable. When I whirled by Brush Creek, the power had gone off. Tex's store was also dark, but he filled my order while telling me a tortured story about a woman trying to get him to marry her. Pixie brought me the mandatory melting ice cream cone for free because they didn't know when the freezer would work again. I returned to the trailhead with my pack heavy, but with a lighter heart.

I'd bought a bottle of wine for Grumpy Gridley, hoping it would make him more mellow. And it did. We had a conversation about expectations. Bill didn't even argue much when I suggested he spend his worry and energy on the equipment rather than punishing or pushing the others and me. Things improved for a while, but the hard work, fatigue, and the undercurrent of tension took its toll.

Then we had a series of small disasters that demoralized all of us. They started with a cascade of equipment problems. I arrived at the raft when Bill was taking a turn underwater. Suddenly the compressor quit, so up came Bill. Then the engines stopped. Hans muttered grimly, "Seems we're out of fuel."

Georg went to check the fuel drums. The gasoline that came down the pipes had water in it, so when the engines started up, they sputtered in protest and went silent. Hans and Bill tried to clean the fuel. Hans tilted the drum up so Bill could draw off the water. The drum rack broke. Hans looked at the wreck, his jaw set as hard as if he had lockjaw. Grizzly Gridley growled like a bear awakened in winter, jumped on the little raft, and went to get something from camp.

Steve and I re-erected the rack, then the drum, checked that the water was out, and hooked the lines together. Hans re-primed the engines. Georg went down for another half hour but came up again when the air hose got tangled. Meanwhile, the lift bag floated away. I swam as fast as I could to tow it to the side of the river. Then one of the engines died. Bill returned to see what we were doing. His face wore a mask of disgust—with us, the day, the season, the equipment, and the lack of gold.

Back at camp, we found Susie was trying to get rid of two arrogant fellows who'd entered the compound with their dogs. The dogs had chased and treed P.Q.,

Porcupine

our local porcupine. I was glad the mutts had received quills in their noses as souvenirs. I, too, was in a foul mood.

Then, a furry newcomer added stress, like a spray of kerosene on smoldering coals. Steve and Susie returned from one of their outings with the usual load of gear. Susie carried Delisa and Steve had an extra backpack. He placed it on the table. "Guess what I've brought?" The backpack moved. Steve grinned and took out a squirming cat saying, "This here is Dilly, our new mascot!"

Bill walked in and stared at Steve standing with the dangling cat. Steve dropped the creature to the ground and asked, "Any gold today?" Mutters and comments came from the crew then a yowl from the cat. It had gone into the cabin and presumably encountered a skunk, ringtail, porcupine, or raccoon. Steve ran to snatch up the "mascot."

Bill stood with his hands on his hips, frowning. He looked at Steve under his lowered eyebrows and said in a low, slow voice, "Why have you brought this domestic animal?" Without waiting for Steve's reply, he added, "That cat is bound to cause trouble. Take it out with you or send it up with someone. Soon."

Steve blithely retorted, "Why? We like this cat, it's a Dilly." He laughed and passed the cat to Susie. Delisa reached out to hug the animal. Steve added, "And the baby likes Dilly, too." Bill frowned and kept quiet, but I could tell he was fuming.

Next day, Bill, Hans, and Georg went out to get a new engine, bringing it down the hill on a sled-like arrangement. They positioned it on the raft and went through a successful trial run. Dredging started again. I took a turn diving and came back in the late afternoon to start dinner. Susie sat on a pine round feeding the baby—and the cat. I tried to say in a neutral voice, "It would be better if you don't bring the cat into the compound." She innocently asked why, and I pointed out that at that moment, the cat was stalking Tailless, my favorite lizard. She agreed to keep the cat away from the common area.

But on a day not long after, I found a dead lizard near the stove by the kitchen table. There were bite marks on it. I left the carcass on the table with a note, "Did anyone notice what killed this lizard?" I figured the cat chomped the lizard but didn't want to make an outright accusation. After a stint diving, I returned to camp and to find the dead lizard and my note gone.

That evening, Mike came down with his girlfriend, bringing a ham. I forgot about the lizard as I plopped the ham in the Dutch oven and spooned brown sugar dissolved in pineapple juice over it. A magical evening ensued with P.Q. stomping around in the black oak leaves, Candide a flicker in the firelight, and the ringtails cruising around the perimeter of the cabin while Georg played a tune for their dance. Guests and crew all seemed relaxed, even happy.

Then Steve's cat came to join us. The cacomistles, porcupine, and skunk disappeared. Everyone stopped what he or she was doing. The cat meowed. Bill glared at Steve and growled, "We just might have to come to a humane solution about your cat." Pause. "Keep it away or get rid of it."

Steve picked the cat up with barely controlled fury and shuffled off to his and Susie's treehouse bedroom. The rest of us looked at one another with perturbed expressions. The tension was suddenly relieved when baby Delisa vomited all over the table, and we scurried to clean up.

Cat with lizard prey

Dredging in the Big Pool. Main raft in center, small raft lower right. The lift bag is visible to the left of the line of floating drums.

CHAPTER 24

Winding Down
Autumn 1966

> In a Canyon, in the mountains,
> dredging waters deep for gold,
> we sixty-sixers are ardent fixers,
> we live naked, lean, and bold.
>
> —Genetta, "In a Canyon"

Another series of threats to our equilibrium started on a sultry September morning. Our benefactor, Dick Thorup, came for a visit. He arrived puffing, looking hot and sweaty. Most of the crew had left for dredging, but Steve was still sitting at the table. He was complaining to me about how Bill treated him like a nincompoop. I was glad to have the distraction of welcoming Dick. I gave him coffee, then Steve and I took Dick out to the baby raft. We lugged along my lunch basket full of tomatoes and lettuce from my garden, smoked salmon, fresh bread, and avocadoes. And, of course, Zap Juice.

Hans, Georg, and Bill were there in a cloud of noise and fumes. The engines sputtered to a stop just as we pulled alongside the mother raft. Hans stood frowning, clenching his fists, coldly furious. Georg gritted his teeth. Neither said a word but looked at Gridley, who swam over to the cliffs to check our storage drums. He returned to say, "Empty. No fuel."

Grumpy Gridley knew it was his responsibility to ensure enough fuel on hand. With a glance at the perturbed-looking Dick, Bill glared at the rest of us, saying, "After lunch, I'll head to Oroville and get six drums of gasoline. When I get back, it'll be dark. Be ready to get all that fuel down the hill and into the barrels on the cliffs and beach."

I laid out the food on the big raft and hung up the wetsuits. The men settled to eat, the tension tangible. All of us were wearing clothes in deference to Dick, who looked extremely uncomfortable in his trousers and a long-sleeved shirt. I playfully flicked some water on him to cool him down and felt pleased that he smiled.

After eating, Dick and I returned to camp to wait at the buckeye table for Bill. Dick told me, "I'm not too pleased by the fuel shortage and general grumbling. But I'm invested in this project, and after my penny comes a pound. Yes, I bring good news. I've persuaded a friend to support the project, too. I'll put some more in your account."

I was delighted but also worried. How were we ever to get enough gold to pay back our investors, let alone earn something for the crew? Bill ushered Dick up the steep hill in the afternoon heat. Steve and Susie decided to go to Oroville as well. They intended to come back in the evening to help with the fuel delivery.

While Georg followed the long uphill pipeline to make sure it was intact, Hans and I decided to do some dredging. Sniffing a smell like woodsmoke, I scanned around. There seemed to be a hazy glow over the canyon. "Hans, that has to be smoke from a distant fire," I said with just a bit of alarm.

"Not to worry then, if it's distant" said Hans as he started the compressor. I went underwater to use the lift bag on a large rock. Surfacing, I looked up into a sky fogged with smoke. Hans now looked worried, saying, "That fire might not be so far away."

I knew that forest fires in the dry season were often formidable and dangerous. Lots of dry trees and leaves gave the flames plenty to eat, and the terrain was daunting. Having no contact with the outside world, we fretted. By evening, the sky was dense with billowing smoke. We hoped Bill would come back with news, as well as the fuel.

Hans, Georg, and I were waiting at the empty drums at 8 p.m. A trickle of fuel started coming down the pipes right on time. By 10 p.m., we were cleaning up, but the smoke was choking us. Not knowing where the fire was, we tried to be calm.

Bill appeared, waving his flashlight back and forth, a deep frown on his forehead. Not a happy Hargis. He'd borrowed the Morgenroths' old pickup truck to carry the fuel barrels. Grumbling, he told us, "Fixing the gears wasn't an option. I had to use second or low gear all the way to Oroville and back. Definition of frustrating tedium."

We weren't overly sympathetic, being desperate to know more about the fire than his labors. We prodded Bill for news. He fed us a few facts. "The fire is at Kanaka Bar and already burned up 5,000 acres. There's another fire close to Canyon Creek. People are concerned that the two fires will join up." He looked at our attentive faces and asked mockingly, "Were you worried?"

Were we worried? Filled with fear was more like it. Trapped in a dark, deep canyon filled with smoke? We were terrified! We slept poorly, if at all, in what remained of the night. At dawn, we discussed going up to get the cars out. But first, we had to secure camp. The men went around gathering equipment and isolating the newly filled drums of fuel. I used our slow-flowing garden hose and buckets

CHAPTER 24: WINDING DOWN

Throwing water on the cabin roof

of water from the river to soak anything accessible and burnable in camp—wood pile, benches, tables, and the cabin roof.

Midday, Susie and Steve came down. They told us they'd tried to return in the night, but the roads were closed. They ran a roadblock set by the police only to meet the forest fire head-on near our roadhead. Frightened, they detoured to spend the night in Alonzo's front yard, sleeping in the car. Driving through the charred landscape in the morning, they didn't see any flames. They thought the fire had moved on and maybe was under control.

I certainly hoped the fire was controlled. But fire or no fire, I realized I had to hustle up the hill. I wanted to keep my appointment with journalist Bill Talbitzer. He'd published many articles about mining, pioneers, Oroville Dam, Bald Rock Canyon, and threats to the Feather River. Our meeting had taken weeks to arrange. I had no way of canceling or postponing it.

Hans offered me the use of his VW. I ran uphill and drove like a rally driver to Lake Madrone. I arrived barefoot and unkempt, heart pounding, my braided hair grimy and wet. Mr. Talbitzer waved me over to his table. We immediately started talking about the fire. "Worst fire here in 20 years," he told me. "Men were called in from all over. Finally, it's under control."

I was so relieved, I gasped. But he alarmed me anew with news about another, more insidious threat to the Middle Fork. A company had proposed a hydroelectric project that would build a dam upriver. Mr. T. told me, "It's more worrisome than most of us thought. It would ruin the Bald Rock Canyon's wild river. Dams have already messed with the North and South Forks of the Feather. The Middle Fork is the only one left free."

We discussed details that only worried me more. I begged to be kept informed. He assured me he would. Turning the conversation to a more pleasant subject, I asked him about the use of the name Feather River. He said it was possibly because some explorers in the 1830s came upon a stretch of river covered in feathers and named the place El Rio de las Plumas. Talbitzer's personal interpretation, however, was that the word applied to the feathery appearance of the splashing water. I liked his idea.

He asked me questions about our mining project. I gave him a summary, extolling the canyon's beauties as well as the dredging effort. As I prepared to leave, he said, "I'll be in your area soon to take photos of climbers on Bald Rock Dome for the newspaper. Afterward, I'd like to come to see your place, OK?"

"Yes, we'd be delighted," I replied with genuine enthusiasm.

I was making mental plans for Mr. Talbitzer's visit as I drove to Tex's store to get supplies. He, too, was relieved the fire was nearly out, his house and shop undamaged. While I chatted with Tex, we saw 14 truckloads of men wearing filthy prison clothes go by. They waved at us on their way to mop up the fire. Three more trucks full of local firefighters stopped outside the store. They staggered into the shop and came out with handfuls of candy bars, ice creams, and cookies. A wave of sympathy flooded me for these exhausted men so covered with ashes that they looked like ghosts.

Leaving the store without an ice cream (all sold out), I drove along a side road through the burned region. Stumps still smoldered. Pillars of smoke rose like escaping devils that disappeared into a brown cloud, dimming the sun. I saw Alonzo shuffling along through the ashes looking dejected, so gave him a ride home, returning to the trailhead at dark. I walked down in dappled moonlight, surrounded by the stink of charred wood. Susie had done the dishes and left me a covered plate of food. Grateful, I ate and fell into bed beside Bill. "Fire's out," I told him. "Not mine," he said. I closed my eyes and endured.

A few days later, Bill Talbitzer descended our trail adorned with cameras. He was already sweating and panting. We headed upriver to get good photos of Bald Rock. Mr. T was as graceful as an elephant. Sliding down a rock face on his rump, he dropped his glasses. I retrieved them and had an instant flashback to Mexico, picking up the Scandinavian man's hat. What a difference in scenery between the Bald Rock canyon and the ball court of Chichén Itzá!

Mr. T. was red-faced and worn out by the time we got back to camp. I gave him some Zap Juice and a sandwich, hoping he'd revive. After he recovered a bit, he staggered after me to the Big Pool to look over the operation. "Impressive," he wheezed. Returning to camp, he sat on the bench under the buckeye table, breathing deeply while mopping his brow with a bandana. Eventually, he stood and said, "Thanks for a most enjoyable day. I hope the photos come out. Drop by my office in Oroville next time you come in. I'll let you know about what's happening with that hydroelectric project."

I fell asleep in my hammock right after Mr. T. left and didn't wake until well after dark. A tired Bill was already asleep in our bed. Leaving him to slumber, I crept away on the little trail to the quiet kitchen area. Steve's cat was there stalking something. I cursed the creature and threw stones at it. It retreated towards Steve and Susie's treehouse.

Hans was also up, writing letters at the camp table. We chatted in soft voices, and I looked at his calm, handsome face. He was far more attractive than my beloved Bill, but I knew I'd better restrain myself and not flirt with him, or worse. I went to bed and put my arm around Gridley's steel hard back, seeking the love I felt for him. Was our bond strong enough to survive the bickering, stress, and poor sex? I slept poorly, unsatisfied physically and mentally.

We worked steadily for several more days. My lift bag was in constant use. Once I was underwater attaching the bag to a boulder and the guys pulled the raft too close. That caused the bag to rise. As the rock lifted to the surface, it tilted, and the cables slipped, dropping it back down. The boom as it hit the bottom of the pool hurt my infected ears. The lift bag continued to rise and tipped the whole raft sideways. Georg, Hans, and Steve fell like dominoes into the water. I looked up to the surface to see them splashing about and came up to enjoy a tremendous restorative laugh.

I decided to go back to camp and let my ears dry out. Sitting at the buckeye table, I carved designs on my manzanita stick. Nearby, Susie sat naked on a towel draped over a pine round. The afternoon sun shone through her blonde hair.

"Georg, Hans, and Steve fell like dominoes into the water."

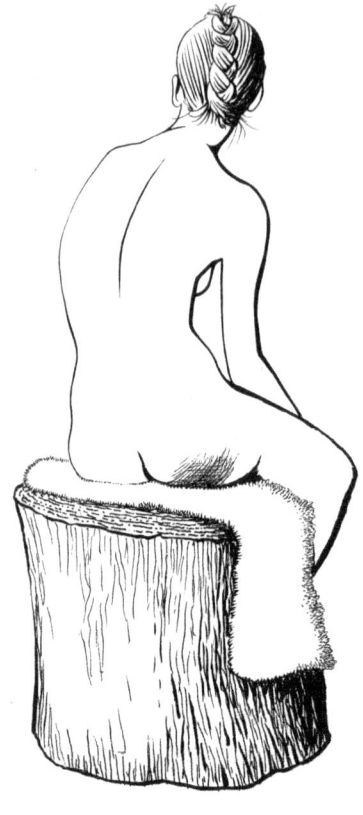

She was a beautiful statue, a golden girl. Her fawn-colored flesh was as smooth as chamois. The black soot on her bare bottom looked like a tattoo of a feather and made me chuckle.

While I whittled, Susie told me a story about a customer at a department store. "This guy entered one of those revolving doors and didn't know how to get out. He went around and around with people laughing, not helping. Finally, a panel on the door slapped him, and he tumbled out on the floor, like in a Charlie Chaplin movie."

I knew what the man must have felt, trying to get out of that revolving door. It reminded me of my emotional whirlpool: with Bill, the gold mining project, leaving Big Sur, and getting myself to graduate school. I was even stressed thinking about Walter Fischer and our plans for our heroic river trip. I worried that Bill would be a problem. I didn't want him to go along, but feared his response to being excluded. My zeal to make the trip alone or with Walter had become a fierce resolve.

Walter and I both wanted to test our endurance, so we arranged to do a long hot hike. My associate, Mr. Work Ethic, chastised me for escaping duties as I scurried up the trail one early morning. I drove to Walter's house, feeling truant. We loaded our lunches in his VW van and set out, going south to where the three forks of the Feather River merged. Crossing the newish Bidwell Bridge, we took the road to the top of Feather Falls.

By the time we parked at the trailhead to the Falls, the heat was hellish. The nine-mile trek to and from the falls was sweaty and long. We stopped often in shady spots to admire California sister butterflies and late-blooming flowers. Angelic breezes and waterfall spray blessed us when we finally reached the top of the falls. Trudging back to the car was purgatory.

Despite the heat, Walter and I thoroughly enjoyed the hike. It affirmed our growing conviction that we could get through the canyon. On our way back, Walter proposed we check out the grinding holes on U-I-No's top. It was a place I'd wanted to see ever since Hargis mentioned it.

Walter and I searched around until we came to an enormous rock with 15 well-worn holes in it. "The acorn-grinding rock!" I enthused.

Walter stood with a slight frown and said, "Yes, but odd."

"Why, what puzzles you?" I asked.

CHAPTER 24: WINDING DOWN

View from Bald Rock Dome

He cocked his head and said, "Why here? Why so many grinding holes in this rock in this spot? It's out in the open, no shade. But there aren't any oak trees for acorns, no level place for shelters, no water nearby. It's as if the place was just for the vista. Why would the Indians care about the view?"

With absolute assurance, I said, "Surely, they would value beauty, all humans do. It's probably related to proximity to shelter, water, and food. But I'm positive views of the surroundings mattered to them too." I told him about the tin cans full of scarlet geraniums and other flowers nailed to shacks in Mexico to beautify them. After many years of living and traveling abroad, I can confirm that humans everywhere will go out of their way to find beauty.

Back at Bare Ass Bar on the next day, I tried to prepare a special dinner. In addition to fried trout, I put together what I called Gridley's Garden Pot: squashes, eggplants, onions, and sweet peppers sliced and sautéed then layered between breadcrumbs, bits of butter, and mixed herbs in our big cast iron pot. I added slices of tomatoes and grated cheese on top and let it all blend. The meal helped us blend, too.

After dinner, I allowed myself to soak in the ambiance. The canyon's evening orchestra tuned up: chuckles and groans from the chess players, the crunch of Susie eating candied popcorn, baby Delisa gurgling, and the mellow sound of Georg strumming his guitar. The river sang a background score enlivened by the clicks of bats and bright notes of crickets. Leaning back, I looked up at the wedge of sky above, a sheer blue-black scarf, flecked with sequins. The stars almost chirped from the heavens. I smiled at myself for being a romantic.

Although the river purred along at its lowest level, we noticed the water growing colder each day. Daylight hours were shorter, too. We all knew we didn't have much dredging time left. One late afternoon Steve and Georg were on the raft checking the engines when I rose from the frigid pool and flopped down on the boards. Steve immediately plopped into the pool, not to take over dredging, but to chase salmon! He swam with all his might, catching one by the tail before it wriggled away upriver. I couldn't help but think that chasing slippery salmon was very much like chasing gold at the bottom of the pool.

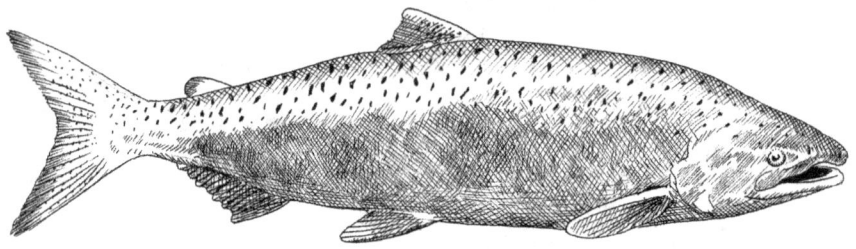

Chinook salmon

That was about the last day we had a bit of fun dredging. Soon after, I saw Steve's cat with a bird in its mouth. I threw sticks at the cat, venting my frustration, loathing it, wishing it would vanish. It had become a symbol of human mistakes. Why did we bring domestic animals into a wild canyon to add to the mess we humans made? I wished I could put my arms around our precious planet and protect it from dams, mines, deforestation, overfishing, the scars of wars. And cats. Deeply disturbed, I put my head on the table and sobbed. Bill found me there, weeping.

"What's wrong?" he asked in rare gentle tones. "Humans," I said through sniffles. "And the cat."

Not long after, I heard the shot. No more cat. The next day a folded note addressed to Bill, lay on the table under a rock. It was from Steve.

"To avoid what would be a nasty incident, I choose a note to convey my feelings. You're a pompous bastard. Yes, the cat is dead, and you have affirmed your manhood. If I had thought you were serious about your fucking 'humane solution,' I'd have smashed your fat head but quick. No talk. It's over and done. And don't remind me of it. I'm liable to unbottle myself."

The shooting of the cat turned the whole enterprise around. We all tried to ignore the antagonism between Bill, who felt he was in the right, and Steve, who felt he was wronged. The crew began to find excuses to do other things. It was clear the season was over.

We shared out what black sand held gold flecks, tiny amounts to each. Hans and Georg were the first to leave. They said they'd come back for another season. Steve and Susie hung on for a few days. I was grateful for their presence, giving us some time to reconcile a bit. Despite all the season's setbacks and traumas, they too said they'd return next season.

When we were alone, Bill brought up his proposal of marriage again. He kept

CHAPTER 24: WINDING DOWN

pressuring me, telling me we were such an incredible pair; we worked well together, had great potential, needed each other. He insisted we needed a commitment to cement our bond before I left for graduate school. He persisted until I finally agreed to go with him to Oroville to get the license.

Bill and I cleared up camp as best we could. We left the river in two cars, he in the crumpled Hesperus and me in the VW I'd bought from Hans. We returned to Big Sur, where we stayed for a short while before I set out for graduate school in Oregon. We promised to write and phone often and also meet up for a ski holiday at Mt. Shasta in Northern California.

Bill left Big Sur to start his new job in Oroville. I said goodbye to pregnant Claire, smiling Eric, and others. I stopped in Oroville to see Bill. Glad to see me, he bragged about building a boat and his new job as a work captain. He oversaw crew tasked with clearing vegetation in the lakebed behind the Oroville Dam. He was proud to be earning good money.

Bill and I talked about our winter rendezvous. He promised to have special skis prepared for me with his very own patented ski bindings. He was going to teach me to ski. Me ski? That was something I, a sunny southern California gal, had never wanted to learn. Even so, the trip would be a point in time we could look forward to. We hugged goodbye. I headed to Oregon, eager to explore, to have the solitude to think, keen for the coming adventure.

CHAPTER 25

Hurt Hawks

Winter 1966-67 to Summer 1967

Falling into the river,
The hawk struggles, grows tired.
Her feathers are soaked and heavy,
No more can they lift her from the water.
She floats, flaps her wings in desperation.
Her mind flies away, circling and circling,
High above the canyon, seeking freedom.

—Genetta, "Freedom Hawk"

Driving Hans's VW was a pleasure. The blue-green car had a shiny piston for a shift knob and a solid walnut steering wheel. It worked, and it was clean and reliable. It even had a radio! It was certainly no Hesperus. I'd almost died too many times in Bill's old car, feeling like the Hesperus captain's daughter, tied to the mast, about to sink with the ship. My old Renault had also sunk, sold for a few dollars in Monterey.

I gave my new car a name, Calypso: in Greek myth, she was a sea-nymph, and the car was the color of the open ocean. Calypso was also the name of a class of ships the Navy used, so the name honored Bill in a way. Best of all, calypso was a jolly type of music that I liked, reminding me of Nepenthe. Sometimes I found calypso tunes on the radio and listened to other music to entertain my itchy inner ears on the long drive to Oregon.

I drove by way of the mountains around Lassen Peak in northern California. Eastern Oregon beckoned, a new place to explore. Glorious, fiery fall forests greeted me with multihued mushrooms on mossy logs, crystal creeks, and frothy, graceful waterfalls. I visited lava caves, ice caves, and wind caves. I discovered a lost forest and shifting dunes in juniper tree country. The Oregon desert was a surprise, full of life. A herd of pronghorns running wild and free, with raised heads and white bustles filled me with pure pleasure.

My future stretched ahead like the open highway. My experiences in Big Sur, on the Feather River, and my time in Mexico had bolstered my self-confidence. I felt excited, mature, ready for almost anything. While my thoughts went forward, Bill receded behind me. I loved him profoundly but not passionately. Does such love make a marriage? Would he join me, or would I follow him?

In Eugene, I rented a small apartment. My peacock feathers, a twisted carved manzanita branch, and bay leaf sprigs went into a jar. I needed to keep beauty and memories in view. I called Bill and gave him my address. He wrote back immediately. As usual, his letters contained pages soaked with longing for me.

One of Bill's early letters made me laugh and shake my head. He wrote in pencil on a blood-stained paper towel. He decorated the page with bright orange and black flicker feathers stuck all along the margins. I read his words, stuffed full of puns: "Dearest Feezer, Enclosed is a print called Appendix by Antlered Buck (Pearl's eldest son). He's dead now, but while alive, he was a quite the hoofer and a horny bastard. He's soup stock now, skinned by Mike the Knife who meated out the punishment in a game played for high steaks. Now it's time to de-liver and pre-pare a gutsy gland bleckfast."

When I checked into the University, I learned that the ethologist, my intended Ph.D. supervisor, was still in Britain. He wouldn't come until the following semester. That was a blow; it meant I'd have to muddle along without a mentor. I brushed up my best social smile and went to classes feeling like a wild animal captured and caged. Socially, I was again a misfit, feeling shy and awkward, an outsider. I yearned to join my classmates when they gathered to watch Star Trek or protest the war but didn't feel bold enough to participate without being invited.

I didn't have much time to feel sorry for myself. My courses laid out a rich buffet of intellectual dishes. I fell to eating up anthropology, genetics, perception, and developmental psychology. In addition, I had a job as a teaching assistant for an introductory psychology course. I was busy.

Although the golden returns had not yet materialized, I hoped next summer might be more lucrative. With a smile to myself, I thought, it just might "pan out"! Even if we didn't strike it rich with gold, a summer on the river was something to look forward to. I was especially glad that I wouldn't have to organize the crew. Hans had agreed to take on the task and Gridley had stepped aside from commander-in-chief to oversee equipment only. Steve, Susie, Georg and another fellow were coming back. I'd be there too, not only for the golden possibilities but for the canyon trek with Walter Fischer.

Then there was Bill. I'd revealed to my family that we had a marriage license. My sister Betsy wanted to give me an engagement party at her house in Southern California. I acquiesced with deep discomfort, asking myself over and over whether this was a good idea. I made a flying visit to see my family at Thanksgiving time.

At my sister's party, relatives and friends gave me gifts and good wishes. One gift was an important and negative one. My aunt June pulled me aside and said,

"*Do not* marry this man. I married your uncle when I fell for his style and devotion to me. He's 20 years older than I am and I learned the lesson. You are too young. You will hurt him, and yourself, trying to be what he wants."

She looked at me long and hard, my wizened sour-looking aunt. I loved her and my uncle. I'd not taken any notice of their age difference. Aunt June's admonition made me think about my situation. Marrying Bill, a strong-minded, older, wilful man, might require more devotion and self-effacement than I could muster. I left the gathering with gifts and misgivings.

While I was in Southern California, my buddy Dave came to visit me. He took me to see his special friend, Buckminster Fuller, known to Dave and friends as Bucky. At the time, the only thing I knew about the famous man was that he'd developed the geodesic dome.

Dave and Bucky chatted about the shape of galaxies and designs for buildings. They ignored me, so I surveyed the room's globes, models, and maps. Bucky's wife stood at the edge of the room ironing his shirts. The domestic scene and listening to the men talk was as intimidating as it was illuminating. The occasion taught me another valuable social lesson. I didn't have the intelligence or ambition to be a star in society. Nor could I bask in the reflected glory of others. I'd have to be content with muddling along.

Buckminster Fuller and his geodesic dome

In late December, Bill and I met at Mt. Shasta for the ski break. I disliked the snow, cold, skiing, and ski lifts. Also, we were an emotional disaster. We spent too much time arguing and making up, leaving one another frustrated and tormented. Back in graduate school, academic work overwhelmed me. I barely kept in touch with Bill, friends, or family. Claire wrote she'd given birth to a baby girl named Heather. Bill wrote about his many projects. He seemed to keep so busy he couldn't get up to Oregon. However, Hans came to visit me. My friend Nathan stayed with me and my brother, too. But not Bill.

Reading between the lines of Bill's letters, I could see how much he still wanted me to see him in a shining light. He bragged about his foremanship, clearing the brush behind the soon-to-be-finished Oroville Dam (status and pay for real work). He congratulated himself on hiring my brother to wield a chainsaw ("tough boss" and "kindness to your relative") and how he'd reinstated his pilot's license by merely doing the physical exam ("great physique"). Bill boasted about his designs for his test boat ("quite the engineer"). He was especially proud of how he'd done a day-long ditch cleaning exercise with a local crew at Lake Madrone, besting the young bunch in every way ("endurance and skill in the bush").

Some chest-beating was OK, but many of Bill's letters were upsetting. He mostly wrote when he was exhausted, drinking, taking a break, or falling asleep on what he called the road treadmill. Reading his rambling discourses disturbed me. Phone calls were not much better. During one of our phone exchanges, Gridley warned me, "Sadly, Feezer, I won't be at Evans Bar to welcome you. Work demands."

I blurted out, "Don't apologize. I'll be glad to have some time to settle in and organize myself."

He snapped, "Organized? You? Ha, I've already organized everything for you. I'm working on getting money for the next season and our future. I've got the garden going. I've brought in supplies. I've kept up with the ringtails for you. What more do you want?" The call ended with me in tears.

While in Oregon, I kept trying to research the status of the Middle Fork of the Feather River. I read everything I could about the proposed hydroelectric dam. I wanted to do anything I could to prevent the last wild part of the Feather becoming what one author called "a whispering ghost river." Bill Talbitzer, the journalist, and Walter Fischer, my local informant, kept me updated.

Walter and I conferred. We wrote letters to local politicians and bureaucrats. We wrote to Secretary of the Interior Udall and Senator Bobby Kennedy, trying to make it clear that the proposed project was not just for electricity but an insidious attempt to get cheap irrigation water for rice farming. A dam for any reason would destroy the inherent beauty, fishing, history, the whole mystique of the river. Walter added a personal invitation to take Secretary Udall to see the area.

Kennedy's office and other politicians sent standard replies thanking us for our "thoughtfulness." Most of the others didn't deign to reply at all. Udall responded to Walter, saying, "I'm aware of the problem and appreciate your offer to take me into the Middle Fork canyon area." He ended with, "There are many who agree with you in opposing any disturbance of the Middle Fork Canyon...you may be assured of our continued interest in scenic river values...."

We were heartened about legislation in Congress to establish a nationwide system of scenic rivers. The Middle Fork of the Feather River had a good chance of being included in the federal wild river system. If the Wild and Scenic Rivers Act passed, it would protect a forty-five-mile portion from Sloat in Plumas County to the Oroville Reservoir in Butte County, including the portion we wanted to traverse.

I left Oregon in late June 1967. Feeling bold, I drove south via the eastern High Sierras, following the old pioneer roads. The word *grok* came to mind when I thought about wanting to see how the land tucked itself up. I tried to grok the landscape that channeled so much water into the mighty Feather River. My last night on the road I slept in a meadow near Quincy, a small town in Maidu territory.

The road from Quincy to Buck's Lake was severely rutted. Buck's Lake to Brush Creek was worse. Brush Creek Store extended its welcome with a stack of letters from Gridley. He warned me about the extremely high level of the river. He and the others had concluded that conditions weren't right for dredging. I felt relieved not to be mining that summer. I'd have quiet time to enjoy the place, read my many textbooks, and study wildlife. Maybe Bill and I could even work out our future together.

Bill's letters brought me up to date: "Kerosene and other stuff in the stove for its protection. Ringtails come and go. Marauding raccoons and sneaky squirrels are messing up supplies in the cabin. The raccoons can unscrew lids from jam jars and knock things off shelves. The squirrels eat my carefully planted vegetables, but melons and zucchini are coming along. If you need money, there's some coin cash in a can on my house's top-shelf at Morgenroths."

Bill's most recent letter said he had to return to Oroville for his job. "But I'll be up to see you soon!" He ended the letter with a surprise, "Oh yes, your buddy Dave showed up again as I reached the trailhead. I directed him and his friend into the canyon. There's enough food in the cabin for them and you, too."

Delighted with the news, I downed my beer and rushed out without even checking the beer sign. When I reached the trailhead, I saw a car. I left Calypso under a ponderosa pine, stuffed my pack, and started down the Skid Trail, eager to see Dave. Two men sat at the buckeye table, looking wilted. Dave stood and hugged me then introduced me to his friend, Lee. They explained how the heat had spoiled some food and poisoned their stomachs. Even so, they insisted they were recovering. I gave them Zap Juice with Vitamin C fizz tablets, which they drank gratefully.

We chatted, but I soon excused myself to run to the river. As I stood in the shallows, I was amazed to see the water level higher than I'd expected. The river frothed and foamed as it roared its way through the Big Pool. Luckily all the equipment was high and dry. The rafts sat on top ledges. Tarps covered the engines squatting on a high spot, and the floatation drums were safely corralled among the rocks. Gridley had guarded the place well.

After dinner, Dave, Lee, and I sat by the fire. The ringtails kept to the periphery, and I noticed there were babies around. Both men oohed and aahed at the graceful creatures. The next day we three loafed and swam at the beach. Lee went fishing upstream after lunch. Dave took pictures of the setting. We sat together by the river watching the roiling water, listening to the canyon wrens singing and watching the water ouzels catch insects.

Dave took my hand, looked at me affectionately, and said, "I've known you for a good while now. We've done some delightful things together." I squeezed his hand and said, "Yes, I appreciate all the times we've shared. You are one of my most precious friends."

He smiled, saying, "I hope you think of me as more than a friend. I love you. Will you marry me?"

I sat speechless. My mind swirled in confusion. Here was a kind, gentle, intelligent man; a responsible, good looking one who would make an ideal husband. But not for me. I didn't love him that way. My heart was a mess, tortured by an agonized love for Bill; there wasn't any juice left to squeeze out for Dave. I looked at him with what must have been a sorrowful and conflicted expression because he took both my hands in his and said, "I do truly love you and want you as my wife."

I shook my head and said, "I'm so sorry, but no, I can't marry you. I'm engaged to Bill." Dave dropped my hands, lifted his eyebrows, and leaned back, "Really? I thought you were just working companions."

I struggled to find something to say but couldn't. They left in the afternoon. Dave stopped at the first switchback and slowly waved goodbye. I felt both sad and glad to see him go. Thoughts of marriage proposals and relationships twisted my emotions into knots. To escape the stress, I spent the next days sleeping, dozing in my golden hammock, or flopped like a half-dead fish on a rock by the river.

Finally, I re-emerged into reality and started to do what I'd come for: read, observe, and learn. Focusing on the world around me kept my inner demons quiet. I listed the different butterflies and the flowers they preferred. I peered into the mouths of monkeyflowers, fireweed, and fringed clarkia. I watched night-blooming primroses and did experiments with their pollinators, the hummingbird sphinx moths.

Marking lizards with small blobs of paint gave me the chance to know them as individuals. I became interested in daddy longlegs or harvestmen. The fragile, thread-legged creatures bounced in tangles under the camp table and moist shady spots. They looked like spiders, but I found they were more related to scorpions and not venomous.

While taking notes and reading textbooks, I drank teas made from mountain coyote mint (*Monardella odoratissima*), and yerba buena (*Satureja douglasii*). Slowly, I was able to enjoy the canyon more fully. I wrote to my friend Nathan: "Lying on warm rocks after dunking myself in the cold river water is purely sensual. I'm

White-lined sphinx moth

CHAPTER 25: HURT HAWKS

Monardella odoratissima - Mountain Monardella

reviving. This afternoon I simply sat still under the pines and let their shadows rest on my lap. Now, the moonlit cliffs glow like a stage set as I watch meteor streaks and starshine on U-I-No's face. I'm opening to the wide world again."

I was sunbathing on a river rock one afternoon when something in the water caught my eye. A large hawk flopped around mid-river. I dove in and swam to the rescue, brought it to shore, and wrapped it in a towel. I put the miserable-looking creature in a box lined with towels and soft grasses. I named my patient Draggle.

Draggle wouldn't eat; its health did not improve. I wondered if it was simply an old bird, fallen from the sky. Or was he chased by other birds, poisoned, or injured? Draggle made me think about death, impermanence, and the shortness of life.

Gridley came down, bringing supplies and strife. He dropped his load on the table and turned to look at me with disdain as though I'd smeared some nasty repellent on myself. I offered him coffee. He smirked as he asked, "Have you been enjoying yourself? Did you have a good time with your friend Dave?" I winced and said with deliberation, "They only stayed overnight."

Bill stared at me. I stared back. He said sarcastically, "I'm sure you enjoyed the company." I kept quiet, unable to respond to his snide remark. Luckily, he switched the subject. "Well, I'm glad you made it OK. Have the cacomistles been around to greet you?" I told him about the young ringtails, the marked lizards, and showed him Draggle. "Probably a juvenile red-tailed hawk," he said.

Bill took me in his arms and held me tight, saying nothing, his body tense. He sat on the bench to drink the coffee and launched into an account of what he'd been doing. He ended by saying he had to go back up right away. I sighed with relief. Two days later, he returned saying, "Tonight, I can stay overnight."

I tried to smile but felt no joy at the idea of sleeping together. The wine in his glass disappeared as we bickered about keeping in touch with one another over the past months. Luckily the ringtails came to distract him when I began to droop. I wanted to go to bed but was afraid to suggest we sleep separately. Smiling his special sweet 'n' sour smile, Bill put his arms around me and said, "I know you aren't feeling sexy, but let me hold you awhile. I need to be next to you, smell you, feel you near me." I sighed and gave in to his lovemaking, too tired to protest.

I woke in the morning feeling ashamed. Finding a balance between love and sex in our relationship was not working. Somewhere deep in my psyche, I knew I was partly using unsatisfactory sex to justify us drifting apart. I felt that sexual shame and frustration were my problems, not his. I hadn't tried hard to work sex out with Bill. His jealousy and bad temper did not inspire me to try. I felt stuck in a sexual swamp.

Over the next days, we got along reasonably well. Then Bill left again, promising to return soon. I got to grips with observing and reading, my way to avoid the pain of introspection. Thinking about the Bald Rock Canyon adventure with Walter lifted my spirits. Walter duly arrived, bringing gifts of garden vegetables, including a first watermelon. Bill came down the hill while we were happily spitting seeds.

Walter and I had decided to take a day to check out a trail to Dome Falls, a waterfall along Brush Creek in preparation for our river trek. Bill invited himself along. The hike was a sweaty slog mixed with delightful dips in the creek. On the climb back up to where Walter's VW van was parked, Bill strode ahead while Walter and I followed slowly, wilting in the heat. I wished Bill would stop. His habit of pushing on ahead irritated me. He'd pause to turn and look back at us with a stance and tilt of his head as though pitying his feeble followers.

Reaching the car, I made the mistake of mentioning this. He was miffed. That started a fight about leading and following, sharing, and sensitivity. Walter listened to us quarreling and got fed up, saying, "I'm not coming to see you two anymore if you are so unhappy in my presence." That shut us up. Bill and I returned to the canyon laden with mutual irritations. After more petty arguments, he told me he needed a break and went back to Oroville.

Walter appeared a couple of days later, smack into my glower and gloom. He ignored my mood and turned my mind to our intended trip down Bald Rock Canyon. I tried to explain how I wanted the two of us to go together, without Grumpy Gridley. Walter told me, "I wouldn't mind so much having Bill come along. He's a reliable sort who could help us out in a pinch."

Walter's statement perturbed me. I desperately wanted to do the hike without him. I wanted to make the trip with just Walter Fischer. My vision was "Old Man" and "Young Woman," facing challenges together without any help from "Strong Man." I didn't want William Hawley Hargis to steal our thunder or help us out. The testing myself meant a great deal to me.

CHAPTER 25: HURT HAWKS

Sultry August slipped into autumnal garb. Days were still hot, but sunburned hours shorter. Nights got cooler. I fretted about getting through the canyon before my determination withered or storms broke over the mountains.

The buckeye leaves went brown and spider-webbed, falling at the slightest breath. Stray cattle got in, broke down the fence, and ruined the garden. Candide, the skunk, sprayed the cabin so we couldn't use it. Bill shot a deer. Draggle died. I was not deterred; I would be going through Bald Rock Canyon with Walter.

Draggle the hawk

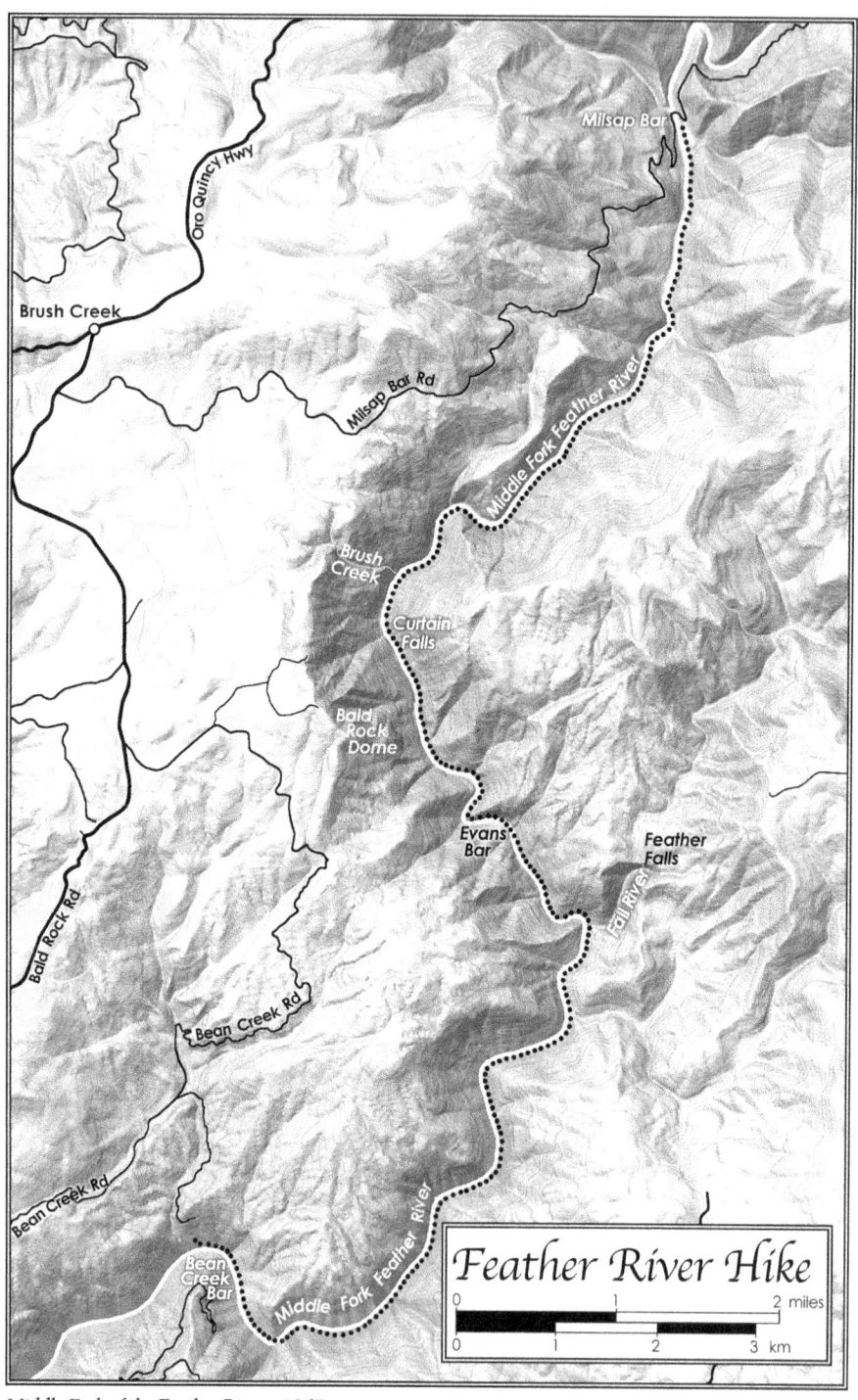

Middle Fork of the Feather River - 1967
The route of our hike, from northeast to southwest, is shown by the black dotted line.
Since then; Lake Oroville has flooded the Middle Fork as far upstream as the Falls River.

CHAPTER 26

Bald Rock Adventure

Summer 1967

Worldly treasure is but a trifle
Adventure, I find, is more worthwhile.
Searching for gold can be so bleak,
Experiences are the nuggets to seek

—Genetta, "Treasure"

Walter Fischer and Jeannette Hanby embarked on their adventure through Bald Rock Canyon—accompanied for part of the way by William Hargis. Yes, we'd compromised. Bill would be with us at the start, leaving Walter and me to traverse the central "impassable" part of the canyon by ourselves.

The sun kissed the head of Bald Rock Dome while I built a fire and got the coffee perking. Bill and I ate a hearty breakfast, then headed up the shadowed hill. Already the air was hot, the sky clear with hardly a breeze. U-I-No's bald top shone brightly as the sun stroked it.

Sweat stuck my backpack to my shirt. I was pushing, worried we'd be late for our meeting with Walter at Brush Creek Store. Bill wasn't worried at all and teased me about my impatience. I looked at Manuel's clock when we stepped into the store; we were fifteen minutes early. Bill snorted, pointed at the clock, and gave me his I-told-you-so look. I ignored him, turning my head to check out the beer sign. It wasn't lit up, so Manuel turned it on for me. An upside-down canoe floated in the water at the base of the waterfall, with a head and oars bobbing about. We had a good laugh at the scene; I reminded myself I didn't believe in omens.

Walter arrived; we conferred. That day was to be a prelim. We aimed to follow Brush Creek to the canyon's bottom and search for a route around the spot where the creek entered the Feather River. The following day, Walter and I would set out—without Bill—for our trek through the exciting and most challenging part of Bald Rock Canyon.

From Brush Creek, we drove in Walter's VW van along a dirt road, twisting and turning through the red dust. At a patch of tall conifers, Walter pulled onto a logging road and parked. The mighty sun glared through the trees, getting ready to scorch us and the landscape. We loaded our packs, then stalled as Bill gave us a lecture on the difference between red and white firs. White fir trunks look white at the top, and its needles are flat, in a horizontal plane. Red fir needles come out all around the twig. Now you know.

I trotted down the hill in my new tennis shoes, but within a half-mile, my feet protested. I took the shoes off, but hot footing over burning stones made me put them on again. Down we went, the trail zigging and zagging. Coming down a wooded canyon, we rounded the ridge and headed into the more open oaks and manzanita with an occasional pine. The glare and heat made us grimace, despite hats and wetted bandannas. We dripped with sweat.

Crossing dried-up streambeds, we entered a shadier side canyon choked with azaleas and ferns. Amid this lush vegetation, Brush Creek roared along, frothing and plunging. The water charged off the cliff towards its rendezvous with the Feather River. I flopped into a pool with relief.

Walter and Bill sat in the shade talking, then stood. I reluctantly got out of the water, put on the dreaded shoes, and followed. We continued through a glade with an abandoned cast iron stove (miners of yore?), boulders spotted with orange blobs (someone marking a trail?), and across a slippery rock face. Around and down we went, almost to the river at last. And lordy! It was hot.

Bill strode on, but Walter sat down with an oomph a couple of switchbacks from the end of the trail. I sat next to him, watching heroic Bill standing on a rock in the river waving at us to come on. I waved back, hoping Walter would catch his breath. He needed to get down the trail into the cold water. Instead, he passed out.

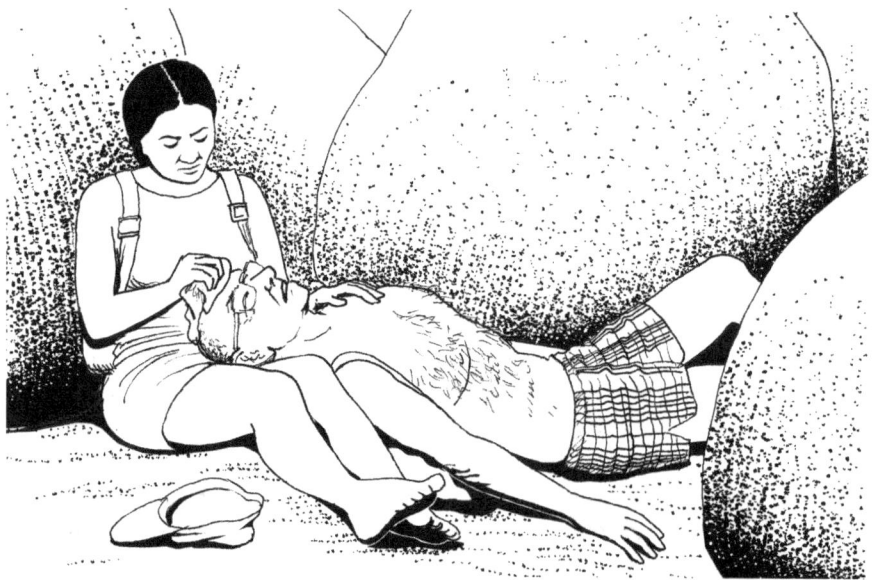

CHAPTER 26: BALD ROCK ADVENTURE

Walter slid past me and fell backward, unconscious. I grabbed him and pulled his head onto my lap. His fall could have been much worse if his head had hit a rock. I held him until he came to, blinking at me. While he rested, I felt his temple and forehead. Hot, sweaty, but not bleeding. I poured some water on him from my canteen.

Walter opened his eyes wide, sat up and leaned against my shoulder. We rested for a while until he thought he could move. I mentally girded myself to getting him up and out to a doctor. No way could we continue our hike down the canyon the next day.

Bill came back up the trail to see what we were doing. I explained; he looked worried. Walter said, "I need to get into the water." Bill and I put our arms around Walter's waist, carefully descending the trail. Walter quickly shed his clothes at the edge of the river and sat in a swirling pool. I joined him. We stretched out in the water for a long while cooling off. Finally, we collected ourselves and our clothes. I looked back up the sun-struck trail, then at Walter. He looked at me full face, tried to smile, and said, "I'm OK now. Let's go downriver before going back up."

Still, both Bill and I worried. We were fully prepared to abandon this day's trek as well as the Bald Rock Canyon attempt. But Walter insisted we go a bit further. "I need to test myself and drink more water," he said firmly. We worked our way downriver towards some waterfalls. We came to a you-can-go-down-but-maybe-not-come-back-up place. We found ropes, showing that other people had tried to pass this spot. Working our way along the cliffs, we eventually dropped down a smooth inclined rock leading to the foot of Brush Creek Falls.

We found a nice spot to eat lunch, fish, and worry about Walter. Walter got out his store-bought rubber worms to put on hooks while Bill looked for a bay branch for a pole. Bill caught three big trout while Walter and I alternately wandered and sat in pools. Bill and I left Walter resting and climbed boulders to get to the old Davis mining camp. It was a total mess. A stout limb had fallen from a black oak and smashed a flimsy shelter. There were cans, bottles, plastics, mounds of debris, broken dishes, and glass littering the site. Bill commented with a smile, "Yes, miners aren't known for neatness." Indeed. I also noted that the supposedly full drums of gasoline were not among the remains. I wondered who'd taken them out and how. U-I-No might know.

As we hurried back to Walter, long shadows crept towards us. The sun was letting its weight and heat fall to the west. Finally, feeling cooled enough, we three started the uphill slog back to camp. Walter and I went very slowly with Bill zooming ahead. He was looking at a frayed rope when we caught up with him at a tricky place. We looked around at the huge boulders we needed to negotiate. Would we need ropes? Crawling around, I discovered a natural tunnel that cut beneath some apartment building-sized boulders. No need for a rope.

The red and white fir trees spread a carpet of patterned shade by the time we got back to the car. We filled our bellies with Zap Juice and drove on to find a camp spot near Milsap Bar. Relaxing, we inhaled the cooler air of twilight and campfire smoke. Then came the delectable smells of grilling fish. Over supper, we talked about how we'd negotiate the river the next day but were too tired to make any sensible plans.

Dawn seemed tired too, sunlight creeping slowly through the dust. Our camp was still cool and shady, the river nearby rumbling along. I looked at Walter sitting by his van drinking coffee and eating the remains of the fish. I sat down next to him, shoulders touching, and said as softly as I could, "Please be honest about how you feel now. You'll need strength and will for this venture. There's no real chance of help or rescue once we get to those boulders and waterfalls."

Walter nodded and patted my hand. "I know. But I'm fine now. It was the heat yesterday. I didn't drink enough. I will take more care today." He stood up and said firmly, "Let's go."

Bill watched us, drinking the last of his coffee. Walter and I put on our hats with their tethers and looked at Gridley. He flipped his bushy eyebrows up and down as though sending a telepathic message to a pair of horses to get going. Off he went, without a word, taking my tennis shoes with him. Despite my inner apprehension, I turned to Walter with a buoyant feeling of freedom. He smiled back.

We shook hands, two adventurers, two intrepid idiots with a thirst for risk and challenge. Did we secretly doubt we'd make a successful trek through the famously impassable Bald Rock Canyon? Well, yes. But we were determined to try. Taking our time, we followed along the noisy river, alternately walking among the rocks or swimming. The small backpacks strapped tightly to our shoulders and waists hardly made a difference to our movement through the water.

Before long, we encountered larger and larger rocks as the canyon narrowed. We climbed slowly and carefully over and through them. The bloated sun rose higher, radiating such heat from the rock surfaces I could barely walk on them. We took any chance to slide into the water and float or swim through pools. Various passages and tunnels between the rocks appeared whenever we needed them.

We stopped to appreciate the deep green crevice where Brush Creek came tumbling down. It was a beautiful sight, the water flowing over terraces, then forming a broad waterfall. A giant boulder protruded from the middle of the falls, and to the left, a towering rock stood high, sculpted by the creek. The great stone deflected the water to the side, where it shot down the vertical canyon side into the pool. Neither of us wanted to shoot down those falls.

We sat contemplating the scene in the shade, pleased to have made it that far. I was still secretly concerned about Walter's collapse the day before and watched him closely. We looked up to the rock shelf to the right of the waterfall. We had to find a way around the steep granite wall rising to about ten times my height. We decided to climb back up the cliff, then come down on the shelf and walk along it before confronting the boulders again.

Back on the edge of the galloping river, we stared at the boulders. They were huge, several stories high, blocking our way. We took the time to greet them before

CHAPTER 26: BALD ROCK ADVENTURE

Walter Fischer among huge rocks

deciding how to pass. I wanted to get some photos with the camera I'd packed, wrapped in plastic bags, in hopes I could document the trip. Climbing the canyon wall opposite where Brush Creek came in, I tried to capture the scene. But no pho-

"Let's watch the water for a while and decide which spot is safest…"

to could depict the burning heat from the rocks and cliffs, the cool spray from falls and rapids, the roar and rumbles of the river, the roiling water, and hot pine-scented air. So much to absorb!

Taking one last look at our chosen route, Walter and I clambered up then slid down the massive blockers. Reaching a stretch of open water, we flopped into the nearest eddy. Ah, so refreshing. Next came small rapids and more pools. We floated and swam downriver.

The passage seemed relatively easy until we got to a place in the canyon where the water fell across the river's whole breadth. Cliffs on either side of the canyon were like pursed lips with the tongue of the falls hanging down. We only had two real choices, jump into the falls or clamber around the cliffs. The third option, to turn back, was out of the question.

The rocks were egg-frying hot, too hot for my bare feet. We found a bit of shade and contemplated what to do. We didn't want to climb up the sheer cliffs in the heat yet were frightened by the idea of jumping off a waterfall. What about rocks under the water?

"Let's watch the water for a while and decide which spot is safest," said my doughty companion. We sat; we watched. It got hotter and hotter. One spot where the roiling water was consistently calmer attracted us. We looked at each other. Finally, we walked into the flow and stood still to throw our hats—with rocks in them—into the water below. We watched the hats sink then emerge. Walter took my hand and squeezed.

We jumped. And almost drowned. The falling water pressed us down and down. We bumped against rocks. Gasping for air, we both came up simultaneously, hearts pumping, relieved to be alive. Our hats, of course, had gone on without us. We floated along together, trying to relax.

Pulling ourselves out, we sprawled in the shade of a cliff and looked at the rocks and rapids awaiting us. The high water of the river that season was both a boon and a threat. The river pushed us along without much effort on our part, but there were hidden boulders and frightening whirlpools.

Getting caught between boulders was our greatest worry. Avoiding such traps occupied our full attention as we worked our way downriver. We'd thought that jumping off the falls was the most dangerous thing we'd done. However, when we were spun round and round in a whirlpool, we were taught another lesson in danger. After emerging, we took our time to stop and rest, humbled by the river. We floated and swam some more, finally coming under the dome. Looking up at Bald Rock, we bowed respectfully and took deep breaths. We smiled at each other. We were alive. U-I-No was watching over us with what we projected was a benign expression.

More slick rocks, boulder clumps, and rapids awaited us. Each plunge in the river made us colder and more tired. We spent increasing time outs walking alongside the water, working our way through the rocks. The sun exited the canyon with an almost audible snap as we reached the rapids leading into the Big Pool below Evans Bar. We'd made it! No broken bones, not too many bruises and scrapes.

We stood smiling in stupid wonder at the river's edge, euphoric, sunburned, and weary. Walter and I hugged and congratulated each other. We laughed and chuckled in relief as we wobbled toward the cabin. Bill stood waiting with a meal of grilled fish and vegetables for us. I was happy to see him in a good mood, not making any remarks about leaving him out of the trek.

The next morning, Walter and I entered the Big Pool to complete our expedition through Bald Rock Canyon. This was a section we knew well. We swam, floated, boulder-hopped, and swam some more. We dog-paddled through pools and rapids, finally reaching the spot where the Feather Falls River joined up with the Middle Fork of the Feather. Leaving the water, we climbed the cliffs to get a view and take a break.

We got a surprise. Two fellows were sitting on the rocks resting. They'd come down the river from much further up, using rafts to carry supplies. They were amazed that we'd made it through the canyon on foot. Bill suddenly joined us. He'd driven Walter's van to Fall River junction and hiked down to meet us. The five of us hiked and swam a little further down the Middle Fork. Then Bill wanted to climb up a ridge to get back to the car. He told us there was an old water ditch he knew would be a good trail, "just around the next point." The trail led out of the canyon to Bean Creek bar where he'd meet us.

I should have known. Walter, the two rafters, and I had a terrible scratchy, sliding, scrambling crawl around several "next points." We failed to see a ditch trail, so we went back down to the river. One fellow and I swam and boulder-hopped through pools and riffles while the other man and Walter took to the cliffs and shores. Eventually, we saw the promised ditch and ascended.

The ditch trail became a visible narrow trail, then a jeep trail, then a wide bulldozer road. We reached Bean Creek Bar breathless and stopped, partly because we were tired and partly because it was such a lovely spot, near a burbling creek. Bill came striding down the hill to join us. Our fellow travelers decided to camp there. They would return to the river and finish their trip the next day. We bid them a good journey then drove back to Brush Creek as the daylight disappeared, along with our energy.

Walter and I were jubilant, happily weary. We had accomplished what we'd planned and survived intact. Bill was silent most of the way back to where we'd parked next to the wreck of the Hesperus and gave over Walter's van. Walter said he was too tired to drive home, so Bill and I decided to camp next to his van. I desired nothing more than to sleep off my exhaustion, flopping on a blanket thrown over fir needles.

Morning sap smells and feathery strobes of light through breeze-tossed needles woke me. We three watched the sunrise, nibbling bread and devouring a melon. I hugged Walter and said farewell. My deep love and admiration followed him in the dust trail of his van.

A small piece appeared in the Oroville newspaper. The main article told the story of the pair of fellows who'd rafted through the canyon. The two men were incredibly proud of having made it through the three-mile stretch of Bald Rock Canyon, which the article described as "virtually impassable."

Our bit in the article was brief: "They were met by two other hikers who began their walk at Milsap Bar…Jeannette Hanby, 26, of Big Sur hiked the canyon with

River explorers

Walter Fischer, 70, of Oroville. Miss Hanby, who made the hike barefoot, said they caught up with Laursen and Braddon-Walker after they passed Bald Rock Canyon on Tuesday. Fischer and Hanby left the canyon at Bean Creek while the other two continued the hike to the dam."

I was gratified that Walter and I got a note of recognition for having traversed that same "virtually impassable" stretch. It was a three-plus milestone in the river of our lives. Other good news was that a significant part of the Middle Fork and all of Bald Rock Canyon had a realistic chance of being protected by the Wild and Scenic Rivers Act. Yes, that important act had been passed.

Capital Pair Finishes Hike In Butte Canyon

OROVILLE — Richard Laursen of 5143 Teichert Ave. and Brad Braddon-Walker of 5605 Moddison Ave., both in Sacramento, completed a hike through the canyon of the Middle Fork of the Feather River late yesterday, 12 days after they started the trek at Sloat, Plumas County.

They were met by members of their families at the Oroville Dam observation point shortly after 3 p.m. yesterday. The hike took them through some of the most rugged country in the United States, including a 3-mile stretch of Bald Rock Canyon which has been considered virtually impassable.

Laursen said it was necessary to swim much of the way, including in the Bald Rock area where the river churns into fierce rapids. Laursen and his companion were in excellent condition when they emerged from the canyon and said they had enjoyed the experience.

They were met in Bald Rock Canyon by two other hikers who began their walk at Milsap Bar 2 miles upstream from Bald Rock on Monday.

Jeannette Hanby, 26, of Big Sur, Monterey County, hiked through the canyon with Walter Fischer, 70, of Oroville. Miss Hanby, who made the hike barefoot, said they caught up with Laursen and Braddon-Walker after they passed Bald Rock on Tuesday. Fischer and Miss Hanby left the canyon at Bean Creek on Tuesday while the other two continued the hike.

"I sat in the sand and wrapped seaweed fronds over my shoulders…"

CHAPTER 27

Bows and Flows
Summer 1967

With feathered shadows in my ears
My eyes hear a song of time.
I bid farewell to all my fears
And try to leave all I love behind.

Genetta — "Farewells"

The time came to leave that wild and scenic Feather River. And wild Bill, too. He told me he'd see me in Big Sur before I headed north to Oregon for my second year in graduate school. In the meantime, as usual, he had jobs to do. On my way down the wiggly mountain road, I stopped at the Berry Creek Store to say goodbye to Tex. He grabbed me and whirled me around then went to get me the usual ice cream cone.

While I was slurping, he gave me a parting gift—one of his stories.

"I was caught driving drunk. They were going to give me a year in jail but let me out to go to Texas. Ho hum.. Yes, Tex in Texas. Ho hum. Well, I went but came back here and got soused again. The state took my driver's license away. Social worker told me to write them powers-that-be that they were depriving me of making a living. I did. I got a reply. License reinstated. Ho hum.. Whaddaya say?"

I laughed while my ice cream dribbled on the floor. My laughter turned into tears. "I'd better get going," I said trying to stop crying.

Tex looked at me sadly. "Peanuts, we'll miss you. I think of you as the petite one who walked out of the canyon barefooted, feeling so good you jumped up and down like a frisky filly let out of the barn in springtime. Ho hum. I hope you'll keep on hopping up there in that concentration camp at the University."

Driving down the winding road towards Oroville, I wondered when I'd come back to the high country. I knew I was done with gold mining. I would not be a member of the crew again. Next summer, I'd be working at the Oregon Primate Center, collecting data for my Ph.D. dissertation. I was going to study a troop of Japanese monkeys there. My research would center on how sexual behaviors are used in social groups for bonding. Spending time with the monkeys, plus taking and teaching courses, would tie me down 'til completion of my degree. After that, the winds of fate would blow me along. And I now knew something about the direction I was going.

Bill and I would not be traveling side by side into the future. We would continue to write letters but inevitably drift further apart. We'd been unable to agree on how we could maintain a close tie without living together. Living apart, I saw no way we could work out our problems. He couldn't fully accept a relationship without sexual intimacy. I couldn't provide genuine responses without facing up to my hang-ups and what I felt was his fragile self-image as a lover.

We discussed the impasse. I'd given up completely any idea of marriage. Sadly, our partnership was to be like one of those songs that irritated Bill—at the ending, our melody together would slowly fade away.

I returned to Big Sur for a last farewell.

Awkwardly, I said goodbye to people and places I loved. I went to stay with Claire on Rancho Rico. Her baby daughter, Heather, was a joy to behold. Claire treated me with exceptional kindness, somehow intuiting that leaving was very difficult for me. She left me alone to listen to my inner voices. I took lingering solitary walks along the oak-studded ridges, in the sun and moonlight. Stopping among the trees and chaparral, I crushed bay leaves and sage, rubbing them on my face and arms. Smells of dust and sea smoke enveloped me, the shadows of hawks and seagulls in my ears.

It hurt to know I was leaving Big Sur and the Feather River behind—willingly. I'd keep in touch with people like Claire and Eric and even Bill. But from now on, I would only be a transient visitor in the places that meant so much to me. I had no pretense of living in Big Sur or the Sierra Nevada mountains. I wanted no little cabin on the cliffs, on hills, or in the woods. There would be no Bill or boat or gypsy-like traveling. A great feeling of loss made me numb.

I sat in the sand and wrapped seaweed fronds over my shoulders, smiling at the slimy, salty, prickly feel. I watched the surf spank the sand and run back in gleeful curls to join Mother Ocean. I lay on the mossy rocks and watched the continents of clouds drifting by, listening to their comments on the planet.

I let myself drift and blend and harmonize, knowing that my feelings were ephemeral. A tide was going out, yet wavelets of freedom were coming in. I felt the kind of freedom that comes from being committed to a goal, not having to decide between heartrending options.

A mere four years had passed since I set out from Southern California, wanting an adventure. And I'd had plenty: Big Sur, people, jobs, wildlife, hot springs, Mexico, mining, the Feather River trek, and the swirling whirlpool of love. Lessons galore. That did not make me content; I wanted more. And I was positive there would be more.

CHAPTER 27: BOWS AND FLOWS

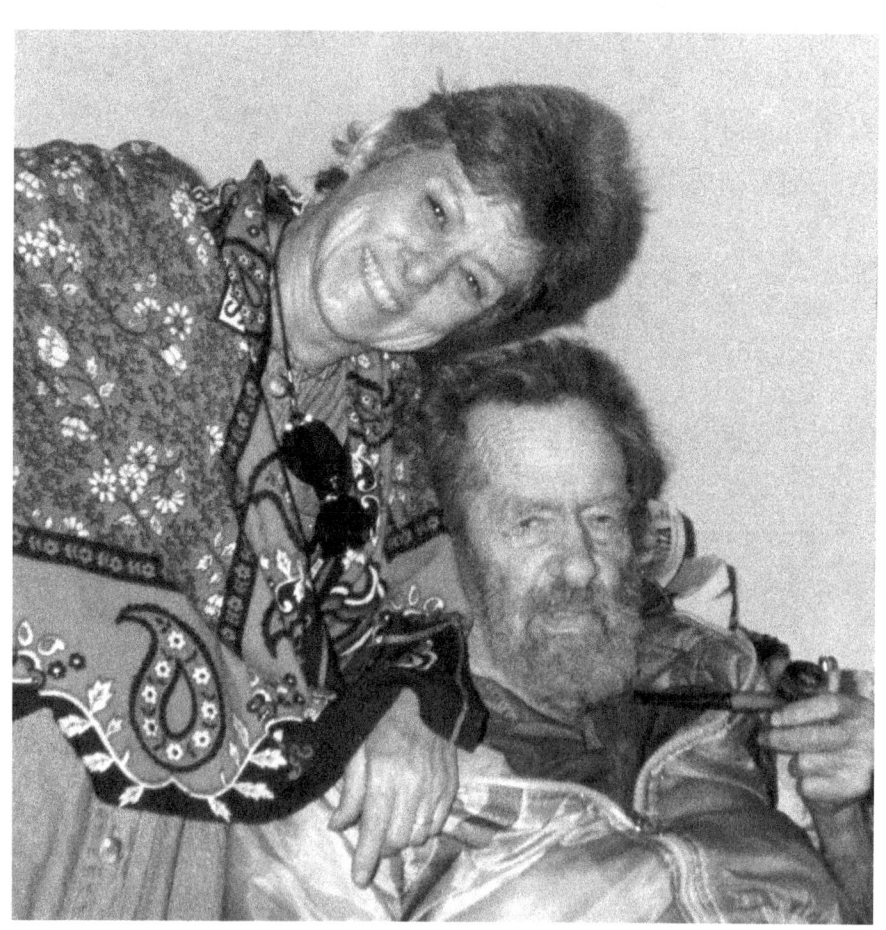
Jeannette with Bill Hargis, Nov 2001

Epilogue

California was my oyster,
I, a speck of sand.
A flawed pearl slowly formed,
California made me what I am.

—Genetta, "Ex Speck"

I still have the Chinese silk quilt from Mildred Hargis, the mother of the man who needed to straighten his eyebrows. The comforter stayed with Bill until he finished dying his long death after a series of strokes. For years he lay in a sleeping bag in his squalid house in the oak canyon near his childhood home ranch in Salinas Valley. He'd returned there, using it as his base after his mother died.

In the remaining years of the 1960s, Bill continued with his job on the Oroville Dam project. He spent a couple more summers as part of the Feather River placer mining team. His main source of funds continued to come from what he could earn from his usual assortment of work.

I made a special effort to see Bill on one of my visits to California from Africa in the 1970s. He drove his mother's car, full of trash, including empty wine bottles, to Point Lobos. From there, he let me take him in my clean rental vehicle to the fascinating but crowded Monterey Bay Aquarium. Outside, he reminisced about his time with John Steinbeck while we watched waves wash back and forth in the tidal pools.

Bill turned his deeply lined, bristly face away from me as he coughed, trying to hide the fact he'd taken up smoking again. I felt a soul-wringing flood of love that poured out in tears. The emotion brought back memories of struggling to come out of my post-war cocoon and find my path in life. I realized that Bill had no way of knowing back then how to help me other than love me in his own way. I felt overwhelmingly grateful that, in the end, he let me fly free, unburdened with blame, remorse, anger, or a wedding ring.

On another visit in 2001, I brought my husband, David Bygott, to meet Bill. By then he was trapped, virtually immobile in his house. Even so, he was still full of mischief, complaining about how friends had mistreated some cacomistles because they didn't understand those "marvelous creatures." He was especially angry that his friends cleaned up his house without his approval while he was away getting treatments. Grumpy Gridley had become a curmudgeon.

I think of Bill often. I continue to be puzzled by the depth and endurance of my love for him. It's a bedrock love embracing all he stood for: wilderness, concern for nature, a willingness to try new things, an enduring curiosity—an ironic, eccentric, skeptical slapper at life's dealings. I've written this book because he inspired me, one of my unsung heroes needing recognition. He treated me to a series of adventures that carved some character into this middle-class girl.

Bill Hargis is gone. Most of the mining crewmembers are dead, or I've lost touch with them. Susie and Delisa remain, with lots of photos and memories of the gold mining days. Tex died; Pixie moved away. Walter Fischer and Alonzo Johnson died long ago. Bean Creek, Brush Creek, and Lake Madrone are all still there, or were, until disastrous forest fires. And indeed, the Oroville Dam and the lake changed everything. When the lake is full, boats swarm the waters like water spiders right up to where Feather Falls stream enters the Middle Fork.

Upriver from that point, the Middle Fork of the Feather River stays wild, protected by the Wild and Scenic Rivers Act. Bill Talbitzer wrote about that conservation victory using a photo of me he took with Bald Rock in the background. The canyon remains a wild, challenging place for the few who dare to experience it. Search for Evans Bar or go on a rafting trip. Appreciate the Canyon's ruggedness and bold beauty. Listen for the glissading notes of the canyon wren singing and smell the Ponderosa pines. If you go there, greet U-I-No for me.

Big Sur is still breathtaking, if not pristine. Words aren't enough to portray its "divinely superfluous beauty." If you can't go yourself, look for the classic Sierra Club book on Big Sur with its photos of the brilliant blue ocean splashing onto cliffs of tortured rock. No photograph can give you the calls of sandpipers and gulls, the swish of the waves on the shore or the smells of sage and kelp. Go and see Big Sur in person. Enter the feathered canyons graced with redwoods. Wander through the twisted groves of shore pines to follow the lazy little rivers winding through huge driftwood piles. Open your senses, smile.

I am grateful to the local people who fight to keep Big Sur as unsullied as possible. Unfortunately, the area has attracted too many short-term visitors and part-time owners; it's a very different social scene these days. My friend Claire died many years ago. I miss her still. Rancho Rico lives on, and Claire's daughter, Heather, has kept Hill o' the Hawk as a roost. Heather, her family, and others are doing what they can to add energy and love to the Big Sur community. Mike and Mary Trotter remain, their roots deep into the historical soil of Big Sur.

Nepenthe, the Big Sur Inn, and the fancy new Post resort are there. Alas, most of the California coast has the disease of creeping commercialism. Big Sur has some defense because of its single two-lane road along steep slopes. Occasionally the road slips away, leaving Big Sur isolated. It's all as intimidating, and glorious as ever, a place like no other on earth.

And gold? Did modern miners on Evans Bar get any gold? Well, it's a mystery. I've never heard about any bonanzas. I didn't get any creditable amount of gold; Bill didn't, Susie didn't. Hans and Georg never mentioned getting much. And from the others, no news. Some property was bought, and some rumors circulated, but I suspect no one got enough to brag about. The real treasures were experiences: living in natural surroundings, the self-confidence that comes from coping with unusual challenges, and the lessons we learned about relationships.

And my adopted-out daughter? She has her own story, an interesting one, as a mathematician and actress. The years have brought us together.

What about the young woman learning about life in the tumultuous mid-1960s in California? Well, after I discerned my path in life, I moved on. Following graduate school, I went to Cambridge, England, to study monkeys and tutor students. There I met a fellow primate, David Bygott, working on a Ph.D. He had just returned from his own life-changing wilderness experience studying chimps with Jane Goodall's research team in the Gombe National Park in Tanzania.

We married, and the two of us went to Serengeti National Park to study lions. After years of poorly paid or unpaid academic and conservation work, we started our artwork and writing business. During that time, we chose to move to a remote area of Tanzania. We spent a couple of decades trying to understand a fascinating mix of cultures in a rugged part of Africa's Great Rift Valley. Two illustrated books tell of those years: *Spirited Oasis* and *Beyond the Oasis*.

For much of life I've been searching for wisdom or "enlightenment." Thich Nhat Hanh's words sum up what it means to me now: "Enlightenment is when the wave realizes it is the ocean." I'm part of the waving ocean, still moving, still learning, having adventures, wending my way through life like the Feather River finding its way to the Pacific.

Ishi, last lonely member of his tribe, said in farewell, "You stay, I go."

I'm still going.

Acknowledgments

I salute the memorable spirit of Bill Hargis. He and plucky survivors in the Sierras, like Ishi and Alonzo, as well as several unnamed friends are my significant personal heroes. David Bygott is my main life hero, making me laugh and enjoy life, teaching me new things in nature and illustrating our books. I acknowledge and admire truth seekers, scientists in general, biologists, artists, writers, and musicians. They sing praise to the planet in different ways, giving me gifts of understanding, happiness, wellbeing, and life.

We are grateful to family and friends who have nourished and supported us for years: the Mushik, Horal, McDowell, Olson, McCarron and Cooper families, John Hanby, Chris and Nani Schmeling, Aadje Geertsema, Mary Strauss, Ruth Matiyas.

We wish to give individual thanks to those who have encouraged us, read, or commented on earlier versions of this memoir, listed here alphabetically: David Belden, Kristine Bentz, Wynne Brown, Donna Branch-Gilby, Heather Chappellet-Lanier, Marinda Cox, E.T. Ellison, Jill Frey, Susie Hollenbeck, Julie Johnson, Sheryl Joy, Holly Lovejoy, Susan Lovejoy, Delisa Mannix, the Milagro community, Jenny Saar, Peter and Katy Stock, Mike and Mary Trotter.

References

Anderson, Walter Truett. 1983. *The Upstart Spring: Esalen and the American awakening*. Boston: Addison-Wesley.

Anderson, R.A. 1906. *Fighting the Mill Creeks: Being a personal account of campaigns against Indians of the Northern Sierras*. Ithaca: Cornell University Digital Collections.
Horrifying stories of murdering the Native Americans in the Sierras, giving a clear picture of attitudes of the times.

Barker, Eric. (1905-1973) Among his books of poetry: *The Planetary Heart* (1942), *Directions in the Sun* (1956), *A Ring in the Willows* (1961), and *Looking for Water* (1964). He was awarded the Shelley Memorial Award of the Poetry Society of America in 1963. Eric gave me copies of most of his books. I've used some of his poems to grace chapters.

Brautigan, Richard. 1964. *A Confederate General from Big Sur*. Boston:Mariner Books.
When Richard Brautigan was 28 years old, the intellectual landscape was changing. While the beat generation of the 1950s celebrated freedom and spontaneity in postwar America, the counterculture movement in the 1960s focused on the rejection of social norms and the nation's involvement with Vietnam. Brautigan bridges the two movements' themes and highlights the romantic beauty of the Big Sur region.

Charlesworth, Kira. 2013. *Big Sur: a history and guide*. San Luis Obispo: Central Coast Press.
This book gives a history of the region, stories about Big Sur, and descriptions of some of the special places and hikes you should look for. Lots of photographs of the coast, hills and forests to entice you to visit Big Sur.

REFERENCES

Hensen Paul, Donald Usner and Valerie Kells. 1996. *The Natural History of Big Sur.* Berkeley: University of California Press.
Presented in two sections. The first covers geology, climate, flora, fauna, and human history. The second section describes particular sites, scenic trails, and other Big Sur features.

Jeffers, Robinson. 1965. *The Selected Poetry of Robinson Jeffers.* New York: Vintage Books

Jeffers, Robinson. 1953. *Roan Stallion, Tamar and other poems*, New York: Random House.
The poems, some of them stories in prose, are part of Big Sur history. Jeffers was not only a poet, he had a big effect on his culture of the '50s and '60s. He died in 1962 but as part of the environmental movement he left behind an impetus to protect the Big Sur and Monterey coast. He worked with photographers, showcasing that "superfluous beauty" of Big Sur, particularly in the book: Jeffers, Robinson (Author) and Brower, David Ross (Editor), 1986 *Not Man Apart: Photographs of the Big Sur Coast*, New York, Arrowood Press

Kerouac, Jack. 1962. *Big Sur.* New York: Farrar, Straus and Cudahy.
Written years after his other books, *Big Sur* recounts his traumatic lifestyle, swinging from paranoia and debauchery in San Francisco to Big Sur with friends to find solace in nature. Not an easy read but provides insights into Kerouac and some interesting depictions of life at that time in Big Sur.

Kroeber, Theodora. 1961. *Ishi in Two Worlds.* Oakland: University of California Press
A genuine and fascinating account of Ishi, the last of the Yahi tribe of northern California. Written by the wife of the anthropologist Alfred Kroeber who found the starving Native American near Oroville. Ishi lived at the Museum of Anthropology in San Francisco until he died in 1916.

Kroeber, Karl and Clifton Kroeber. 2003. *Ishi in Three Centuries.* Lincoln: University of Nebraska Press
A book composed of perspectives by various authors, including Native Americans, that contributes to our understanding of Ishi and his legacy.
Note: read Theodora Kroeber's book first.

Lussier, Tommie Kay. 1979. *Big Sur – A Complete History and Guide.* Big Sur Publications.
A basic enduring handbook about Big Sur and one I still refer to.

Miller, Henry. 1957. *Big Sur and the Oranges of Hieronymus Bosch*. New York: New Directions.
A memoir about his life in Big Sur where he resided for 18 years. The first two main parts of the book are portraits of Big Sur, with descriptions of its inhabitants, plus reflections on events from Miller's past. The third is a complex story of his relationship with a French astrologer.

Reinhardt, Richard. 1966. "Shadows on the Feather." *Cry California* 1: 4.
An article that covers the threats to the Middle Fork that worried us until it was designated part of the wild rivers system.

Smith, Jordan Fisher. 2006. *Nature Noir: A Park Ranger's Patrol in the Sierra*. Boston: Mariner Books
This is a fascinating book about the American River, not too far from the Feather. I include it because it is so well written, striking, compelling, and important for understanding what life is like for guardians of our wild lands.

Steele, Romney. 2009. *My Nepenthe: Bohemian Tales of Food, Family and Big Sur*. Kansas City: Andrew McMeels
Excellent book with stories, history, recipes, and lovely photographs of family and Big Sur.

Talbitzer, Bill. 1963. *Lost Beneath the Feather*. Oroville: Bill Talbitzer Publisher.
Talbitzer describes what the building of the Oroville Dam did and would do to that part of California, including the Feather River system.

Wall, Rosalind Sharpe. 1993. *A Wild Coast and Lonely: Big Sur Pioneers*. San Carlos CA: Wide World Publishing/Tetra.
A compact booklet about early settlers in Big Sur. It gives a glimpse of life in the early days and is full of photos.

Appendix: Life Lessons

As I adventured my way through the mid 1960s, I was exposed to many life lessons. Some I learned, others I'm still learning. New lessons appear into my eighth decade. In this appendix, I've listed a few of the life lessons chapter by chapter.

I offer these insights for those readers who also ponder enlightenment or wisdom. Some of the examples might resonate with your own life or be a point of discussion with others. What lessons do you think are important in your own life?

Prologue
Accept that both world and personal events will change your life's trajectory.

Chapter 1. LOS ANGELES - March 1964
Make plans; be prepared for the unexpected.
Explore your social environment; avoid stereotypes and labels.
Be aware that your short-term decisions might have long term consequences. Think ahead.

Chapter 2. ON THE ROAD - Spring 1964
Take breaks on long road trips; stop to refresh and reorient yourself.
Having friends is important, they require work to maintain over time and distance.
Learn about both your natural and social worlds, absorb lessons in humility.

Chapter 3. BIG SUR - Spring & summer 1964
Be aware of the difference in your three smiles: a "fear grin" (a smile full of teeth), a phony smile (no spark in the eyes) and a genuine smile. A real smile will earn a smile.
Music, singing, and dance generate good feelings.

Chapter 4. NEPENTHE - Summer 1964
Being a peripheral participant in a social scene can lessen stress while giving a sense of belonging.
Residents of a community are worth more of your time and esteem than transients.

Chapter 5. HOT SPRINGS, SEX and SEEKERS - Summer 1964
Having a stable companion helps alleviate sexual distractions and emotional swings.
When you say no to someone, mean it.

Chapter 6. HARGIS - Summer 1964
Be willing to share time and experiences while building a friendship.
Find a mentor, if you can, to guide you in learning about nature.
Be aware of difficult situations, extricate yourself as best you can.

Chapter 7. MOVING ALONG - Summer 1964
When agreeing on a date, meeting, or arrangement, ensure there is a plan B.
(This lesson repeats itself endlessly in my life).
Self-examination may be depressing but necessary to maturation.

Chapter 8. FRIENDSHIPS - Autumn 1964
Finding friends requires openness, reciprocation and being vulnerable. It's worth the work.
When your faults stare at you, try to deal with them rather than put them aside.

Chapter 9. MERRIMAC STAGE - Late autumn 1964
Satisfying curiosity often leads to challenges that will strengthen you.
Let new people introduce themselves to you.
Listen to silence and smile.

Chapter 10. BALD ROCK CANYON - Late autumn 1964
On backroads, flatten the hump!
Be grateful for answers to questions, absorb what you can.
Pay attention! Ground yourself in a place, look around.
Learn the history, as well as the present condition, of a place.

Chapter 11. RINGTAILS - Late autumn 1964
Wallow in any new experience that pleases and enlightens you.
Take chances, test yourself; let others test you.

Chapter 12. BIG POOL and OLD MINERS - Late autumn 1964
Observe carefully; ask questions to understand what you need answered.
Let people talk before pestering them with more questions!

Chapter 13. TRANSITIONS - Winter 1964-1965
Be patient with yourself, time will answer many of your questions.
Accept new opportunities with caution as well as enthusiasm.

Chapter 14. PROPOSALS – Winter 1965
Humor helps a lot in stressful situations.
New experiences teach you something whether you enjoy the lessons or not.
Postpone crucial decisions until you are sure of your choices and feelings.

Chapter 15. MEXICO - Spring 1965
Be prepared for the worst and it's bound to be better.
Try new things, accept diversity, amazement, and wonder.
In unfamiliar situations accept help and suggestions from local people.
Don't try to do too much, especially at night and when tired. Save your energy.

Chapter 16. HAWKS AND HAPPINESS - Spring 1965
Reconnect with supportive people after an absence.
When you can, ruminate on your experiences, digest, appreciate.

Chapter 17. FEATHERED CANYONS Spring - 1965
Resolve past hurts or traumas as best you can, don't bury them inside.
Restlessness means you need to get outside, explore, give your churning mind a break.

Chapter 18. GARDENERS OF EDEN Spring - 1965
Face disappointments and loss with plans for recovery and rebuilding.
Gardening and befriending wildlife are sure ways to promote happiness.
Never underestimate the power of nature.

Chapter 19. IN A CANYON - Summer - 1965
Persevere when you have committed to a project, despite problems, but know when to quit.
Shift your attention or change environments when bogged down emotionally or physically.

Chapter 20. TURNING POINT - Winter 1965-1966
Read widely, learn new things, let yourself be surprised.
Committing to a clear goal can be very liberating.
When someone is focused on a task, don't hover, comment or offer advice.

Chapter 21. GOING FOR GOLD – Spring to Summer 1966
Stop often to appreciate and feel gratitude for all that makes you happy.
Don't prejudge people, let them reveal themselves.

Chapter 22. BARE ASS BAR - Summer 1966
Do your best to see humor in situations. Laugh yourself to tears whenever you can.
Teasing others can help relieve tension but also can be negative. Take care.

Chapter 23. DREDGING UP - Summer 1966
Have little adventures to distract and delight yourself.
Appreciate beauty wherever and in whomever you find it.

Chapter 24. WINDING DOWN - Autumn 1966
Test your endurance before attempting something strenuous.
Enjoy good times with others, relax into situations of simple joy.

Chapter 25. HURT HAWKS - Winter to summer, 1967-8
Don't try to bask in the reflected glory of others; avoid name dropping.
Become an activist about something you care about.
You cannot heal all hurt creatures, yourself included. Get used to fragility and death.

Chapter 26. BALD ROCK ADVENTURE - Summer 1967
Celebrate a success or reaching a goal. Recognize that as a milestone in your life.
Learn to understand "wedging", i.e. creating false situations or exaggerating real ones to rationalize your behavior.

Chapter 27. BOWS AND FLOWS - Summer 1967
Express your gratitude, to yourself, as well as to others.
Take time to say farewell to people and places you love, it helps relieve sadness as well as embed memories.

Epilogue
Keep track of people who've influenced your life, they always have something to teach you.
Be as adventurous as possible, especially in your youth.
Share your story in the hopes of inspiring or entertaining others.
Let your journey unfold. Let life reveal itself. Embrace the unknown.

APPENDIX: LIFE LESSONS

What's in YOUR fortune cookie?

Author and Artist

Jeannette Hanby grew up in Southern California as the citrus groves were uprooted and replaced by tract houses and shopping malls. Always aware of the threats of Progress she wanted to see more of the world before it was destroyed. Her education included adventures outside the academic world, many recounted in this book. Eventually she earned a PhD in animal behavior, and moved to Cambridge University in England for research on primates. There she met like-minded people, including David Bygott. They married, studied lions in Serengeti National Park in Tanzania, lectured their way across USA and published their first joint book, *Lions Share*.

Jeannette returned to Tanzania to establish a conservation education program and David to teach. Frustrated by bureaucracy and lack of support, they moved on to start a free-lance art and publishing business, called Kibuyu - the Swahili word for a gourd, a symbol of sharing. They produced guidebooks, children's books, conservation education material, maps, as well as original artwork, at their base in a remote Tanzanian village. Stories from their years living and learning in that wild setting are told in two books: *Spirited Oasis* and *Beyond the Oasis*.

David Bygott, British-born naturalist and artist, has always liked pen drawing, the main medium used in this book. He also works in pencils, watercolor, acrylics, oils and digital media. He has illustrated 27 books, as well as articles in various magazines, including National Geographic. He enjoys cartooning and much of his work has a humorous twist.

David studied zoology at Oxford, and earned his Ph.D. for research on wild chimpanzees in the Gombe National Park in Tanzania. While writing up his work at Cambridge University, he met Jeannette Hanby. They have shared the same path through life ever since, returning to the USA in 2003, where they live in an intentional community.

www.ingramcontent.com/pod-product-compliance
Lightning Source LLC
Chambersburg PA
CBHW050208130526
44590CB00043B/3091